IMAGES
of America

PITTSFORD

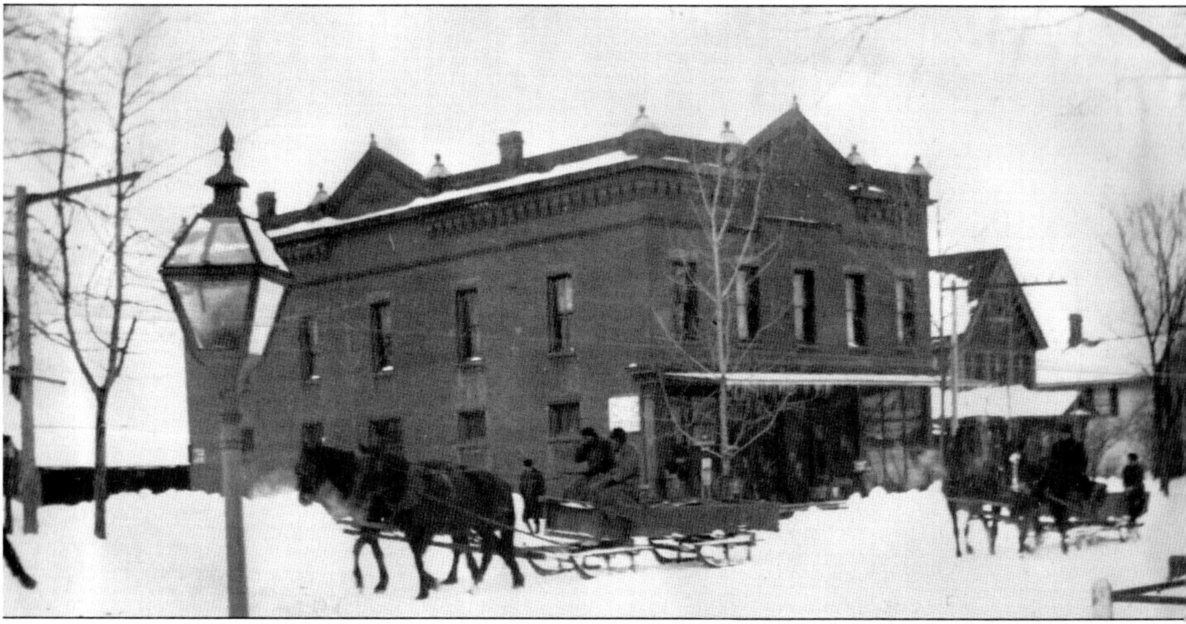

On July 5, 1886, fire destroyed four buildings owned by Seymour Boughton, S.G. Crump, and Hannah Gillam. The Wiltsie & Crump store was one of those that burned to the ground. Within four months after the fire, this brick building was constructed to house the new Wiltsie & Crump store and still stands today, at the corner of Main Street and Monroe Avenue. (Courtesy of Paul M. Spiegel.)

On the Cover: William J. Agate and his business partner Maurice Phillips purchased this store from John Buckley Bacon in April 1905. Phillips & Agate ran the shop for nine years before selling to Zeitler & Berg in 1914. For many years, this building, located at 19 South Main Street, housed Burdett's Food Market. It is now home to Rocky Greco's salon and Breathe yoga. (Courtesy of Paul M. Spiegel.)

IMAGES
of America

PITTSFORD

Audrey Maxfield Johnson
and Vicki Masters Profitt

ARCADIA
PUBLISHING

ISBN 978-0-7385-9900-7

Published by Arcadia Publishing
Charleston, South Carolina

Printed in the United States of America

Library of Congress Control Number: 2012950738

For all general information, please contact Arcadia Publishing:
Telephone 843-853-2070
Fax 843-853-0044
E-mail sales@arcadiapublishing.com
For customer service and orders:
Toll-Free 1-888-313-2665

Visit us on the Internet at www.arcadiapublishing.com

This book is dedicated to all the people who love Pittsford and call it home.

Contents

FOREWORD

We feel that the town of Pittsford, as well as the village, presents a bright image to all who know it. Those who came before us carefully nurtured this image. We think now of the brave families from Vermont and Massachusetts who left their homes with all their belongings in an ox-drawn wagon. The roads were indescribably bad, and the trip took many days. When they finally arrived, they found a mountain of forbidding work. However, they were blessed with good soil, and other sturdy families also settled in the area.

The Erie Ditch and railroads were tremendous boosts, and Pittsford prospered from both. The neat, little village formed up quickly and has always added focus and identity to our community. Maybe the comings of the Model T and the trolley line are symbols of the coming of suburban development, such as Long Meadow. The town boards and the planning boards were alert to the changes, and we were blessed with conscientious and intelligent developers who have provided us with various types of attractive homes and neighborhoods.

This book gives us a splendid review of the fortuitous growth of the town and helps explain to us what we have here and why we are so proud and why we must continue to enhance. Many thanks go to Audrey Johnson and Vicki Profitt for this rewarding volume.

—Paul M. Spiegel

Acknowledgments

This book is truly a community effort, and we wish to express our appreciation to the people who shared their family photographs and stories with us. We are grateful for the opportunity to illuminate Pittsford's history in such a personal way.

We appreciate the support of Janet Harris and Rev. Jeff Hedin of St. Paul's Evangelical Lutheran Church, Bill Keeler of the Perinton Historical Society, David Crump, Bob Woodruff, and Al White. Mike Mederski of the National Motorcycle Museum in Anamosa, Iowa, researched the Thor motorcycle. Mark Greene answered multiple questions about agriculture and farming equipment. Kathy Urbanic, Dawn Gruba, and Sr. Mary Anne Turner of the Sisters of St. Joseph supplied photographs from their archives. Kathleen Emerson Britton, director of the Rochester Medical Museum & Archives (RMMA), allowed us access, and RMMA archivist Robert Dickson scanned photographs from the RMMA collection.

Our colleagues on the board of Historic Pittsford have been extremely supportive of our efforts. Former town supervisor and Pittsford history aficionado Paul Spiegel has been a wonderful source of information and inspiration. We would also like to express our gratitude to Pittsford Village mayor Bob Corby and former Pittsford Town supervisor Bill Carpenter for their support.

Rémy Thurston, Caitrin Cunningham, Erin Vosgien, and Erin Rocha at Arcadia Publishing were always available to answer questions and guide us through the publishing process.

A giant thank-you goes to our families who have endured meager meals, our long hours spent at the computer, and less time with them.

Thanks to the residents of Pittsford—past, present, and future—for your interest in the history of our beautiful community.

INTRODUCTION

The earliest history of our area shows it was part of the lands of the Seneca Indians, the westernmost tribe of the mighty Iroquois nation. Records reveal that the Marquis De Nonville, a French nobleman, crossed Lake Ontario from Montreal in 1687 with a force of 2,000 French and Indian warriors to make war on the Senecas. De Nonville landed at what is now known as Ellison Park on July 10 of that year and marched overland, following roughly the path of Irondequoit Creek. That army camped at the Big Spring, a favorite camping site of the Native Americans. De Nonville and his punitive forces were successful in the mission, but in so doing, he created a powerful ally of the English against the French. Whenever there was a conflict between those two nations, the Senecas sided with the British.

In 1788, Oliver Phelps and Nathaniel Gorham of Connecticut settled with the state of Massachusetts for a title to the lands in Western New York. On July 8, 1788, Phelps and Gorham met with the Seneca Indians and signed the Treaty of Buffalo Creek at Geneseo in Livingston County, in which the Native Americans gave up title to all of the land between the Genesee River on the west and Seneca Lake on the east, and from Lake Ontario to south of the Pennsylvania line. This comprised about two million acres.

Simon and Israel Stone, two cousins from Salem, Washington County, New York, had been officers in the Revolutionary War. They had seen this fertile land in Western New York State when they had been part of the Sullivan Expedition commissioned by Gen. George Washington to annihilate the Seneca Indians. When they were separated from the Army, they were able to purchase 13,298 acres from land developers Phelps and Gorham, paying about 36¢ an acre. The two men came to the area in 1789 and built log cabins. Israel established his house at the site of the Big Spring, which had been a favored site for the Native Americans to camp. Simon built his log cabin just a short distance to the south. After remaining here for a brief time, they left their cabins and went back to Salem to persuade friends and family to join them in this venture in Western New York and to make new homes for themselves and their families. They were successful in that endeavor and were able to recruit a number of farmers and patriots to venture into this virgin territory.

The town was officially organized by a contingency from Canandaigua, which at that time was the county seat of the county of Ontario. The year was 1796, and it was established as the town of Northfield. The officials elected were Silas Nye, as supervisor; Dr. John Ray, as town clerk; and others, as overseers of the poor and road commissioners. Records were kept, and all was very official. Northfield extended over a very large parcel of land and encompassed the area that was eventually divided into seven towns in southern Monroe County. When those towns were divided, the name was changed three times. It became Boyle in 1803. In 1808, it was divided again into Boyle and Penfield. Boyle became Smallwood in 1812, when Perinton was separated, and Pittsford in 1814, when Brighton was divided. Thus, in 25 years, the District of Northfield that comprised the eastern half of what has become Monroe County spawned the seven towns that survive to this day.

Industrious Simon Stone built a gristmill on Irondequoit Creek that same year and established a sawmill the following year. With that endeavor, logs could be made into wooden planks, and frame houses soon began to appear, giving the community a more permanent look. The early settlers were proud of this Northfield and wanted to be sure that it grew and developed into a thriving community. They wanted to ensure the children were educated, and by 1794, a log schoolhouse had been erected and a schoolmaster hired. This school was named District No. 1 and was the only school in the whole community.

The name of the town was chosen by Col. Caleb Hopkins, who had proven himself a hero defending the Port of Charlotte from the soldiers who were threatening to cross Lake Ontario and occupy this country during the second war with England, the War of 1812. Hopkins had been very involved with the politics of this new town, had been elected supervisor, and had served in the legislature. He chose the name Pittsford, which was also the name of his hometown in Vermont.

A great event in the life of Pittsford was the opening of the Erie Canal in 1822. The village soon became a busy shipping port, sending produce to the Eastern markets. The soil was so rich and fertile, the town soon became known as the "breadbasket of the country." Farming was the major occupation of the settlers, and soon, more and more people from New England arrived and land values rose rapidly. The village expanded and was incorporated as a separate municipality in 1827. Another important event that contributed to the growth was the coming of the Auburn & Rochester Railroad in 1842.

There are stories of runaway slaves prior to the Civil War being hidden in homes, cellars, and barns that were a part of the Underground Railroad. Aiding these fugitives was against the law, and if a family was involved, it was kept very quiet. There is documentation of only one man, storekeeper Samuel Crump, who would hide the runaways, make sure they were fed, and transport them in his wagon under the pretense of taking vegetables and produce to market in Charlotte. In Charlotte, the runaway slaves could get on a boat going to freedom—Canada.

Pittsford was built on a limestone dome, and according to geologists, the Genesee River had once been a very large underground river eons ago. The running water may have carved some tunnels and caverns under the surface of the town. There are rumored sightings of these tunnels; however, no one alive today is able to corroborate this as a fact.

Pittsford has changed from a predominately farming town to that of a residential community in which single-family homes abound. The school system is considered to be of the highest quality in the United States with two high schools, two middle schools, and five elementary schools, in addition to a religious school and three nursery schools. According to the 2010 census, there are about 25,000 residents, a median income of $75,000, and a medium value of homes at $165,000. The town is comprised of approximately 24 square miles, with 45 percent dedicated to residential and 26 percent to agriculture. It is located eight miles southeast of the metropolis of Rochester and is easily reached via fine roads and expressways where business, industry, sporting, and cultural activities abound. Twelve churches/religious establishments, six parks, five country clubs, and two colleges are located within town limits as well as a shopping plaza, business area, and many small shops in the village and on Schoen Place adjacent to the Erie Canal. It is 25 easy minutes to Rochester International Airport and 3.5 hours away from the metropolitan city of Toronto, Canada.

Pittsford is a fine residential area nestled in rolling topography, lofty trees, and vegetation of the beautiful Finger Lakes region of Western New York State.

One

Early Residents

Among the early families were people who became involved in the politics and the running of the new settlement. Silas Nye settled on a large farm a short way from the nucleus of the others. When the town was officially incorporated in 1796, as the town of Northfield, he was chosen as supervisor. In addition to being a doctor, John Ray, who arrived with his wife and sons, was elected town clerk, a position he held for over 14 years.

Many consider Stephen Lusk and his father, John, as the first settlers in the community. They established a large farm and house on a very prominent corner at the confluence of three roads and at the apex of the area where many neighbors lived. The Lusk family remained in that place until 1992, when the house and land were sold and divided by a land developer.

Caleb Hopkins, who had served as supervisor, was commissioned a colonel when the War of 1812 broke out. He was assigned the task of training men to defend the Port of Charlotte on the shore of Lake Ontario and to keep the British from arriving from Canada. Having fulfilled his duties, the war hero was given the honor of naming what was left of the area when the town of Brighton was divided in 1814. Hopkins named the community Pittsford, after his hometown of Pittsford, Vermont. He established a large farm on what is now Route 65, and his farm is still maintained and run by his descendants.

The central part of the town became a separate municipality known as Pittsford Village, incorporated in 1827. Businesses such as a flour mill, a malt house, a lumberyard, and several dry houses and taverns were established. Due to its flourishing as a vital community, wealthy Rochesterians began to establish large country estates. Several of those remain in the village as well as the town. Evidence of them can be seen on Mitchell Road, Jefferson Road, North and South Main Streets, and Monroe Avenue.

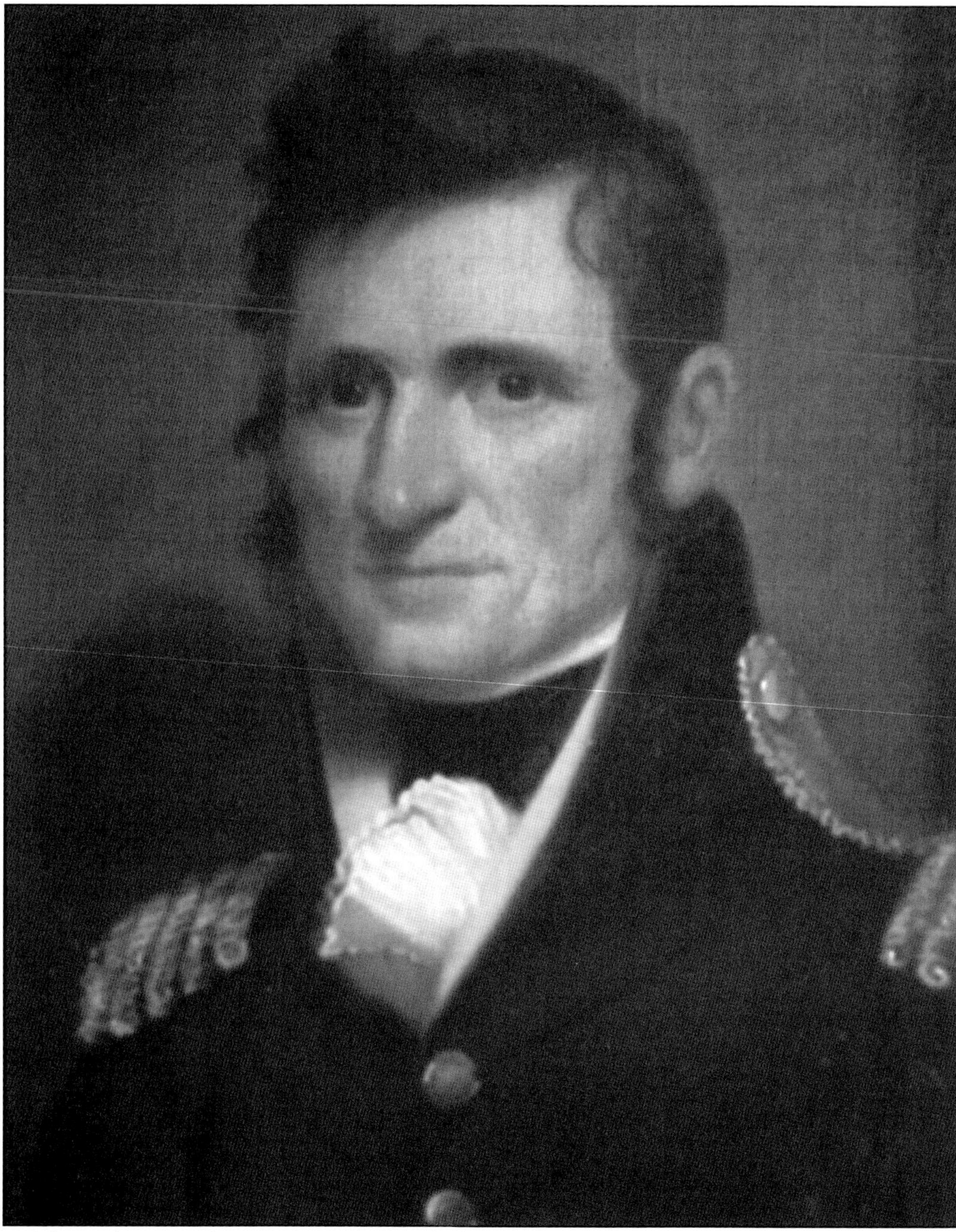

Caleb Hopkins was born in 1770 in Pittsford, Vermont. He left that state and settled in this region of New York at the age of 21. Caleb was very active in the growing community, serving as assessor, town supervisor, and customs collector. Tales of Caleb's War of 1812 exploits can be found elsewhere in this book. He established a 350-acre farm and homestead at 3151 Clover Street that is still in the family today. Caleb Hopkins died January 14, 1818, of typhoid fever, and was laid to rest at the Pioneer Burying Ground. He was survived by his wife, Dorothy Maybee Hopkins, and his sons James and Marvin. A daughter, Clarissa, predeceased him in 1813. (Courtesy of the Engert family.)

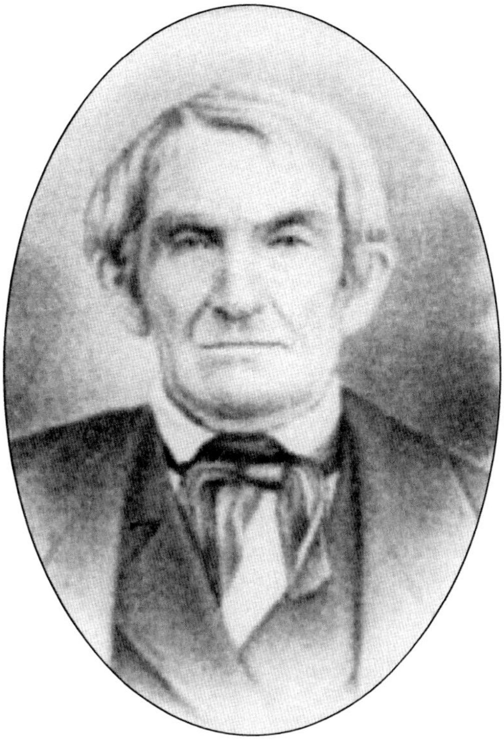
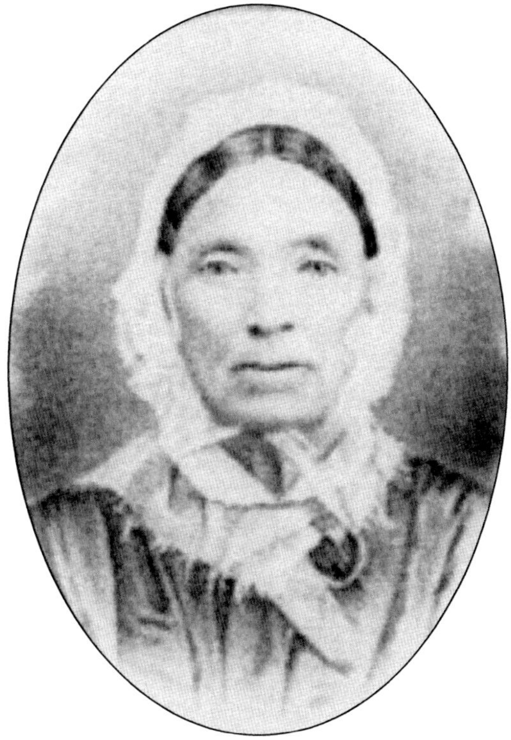

Stephen Lusk arrived in this area with his father in the late 1780s. They came from Berkshire County, Massachusetts, where Stephen was born in 1775 to John and Elizabeth Kellogg Lusk. John purchased over 1,000 acres of land in the area that became Monroe County. Stephen helped his father clear the land and also became a tanner. Stephen's first wife died in 1799. Two years later, he married widow Sarah Hincher Davis. Sarah Hincher was born in Massachusetts in 1777, the third child of William and Mehitable Moffat Hincher. The Hinchers moved to New York in the 1780s, ultimately arriving at the shores of Lake Ontario at the Genesee River. They were among the earliest settlers to this area. After William's death, Mehitable sold several acres of land to the US government. The Charlotte-Genesee Lighthouse was erected on that land in 1822. Sarah's marriage to Stephen Lusk lasted 55 years. They had six children together. Sarah Hincher Davis Lusk died in 1856 and Stephen in 1860. The Lusk family continued to farm the same land for nearly 200 years. (Both, courtesy of W.H. McIntosh.)

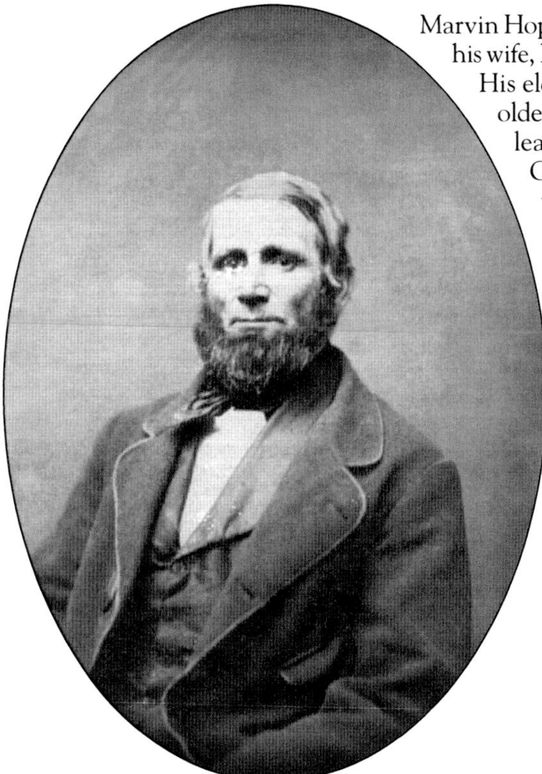

Marvin Hopkins, the youngest child of Caleb Hopkins and his wife, Dorothy Maybee, was born in New York in 1803. His elder sister Clarissa Hopkins died at age 18. An older brother, James drowned in Lake Erie in 1831, leaving a wife and three young children. After Caleb's death in 1818, youngest child Marvin ran the family homestead at 3151 Clover Street with his mother, Dorothy. He was elected supervisor of Pittsford five times. Marvin Hopkins died in 1867, aged 64. (Courtesy of Mark Greene and John Hopkins.)

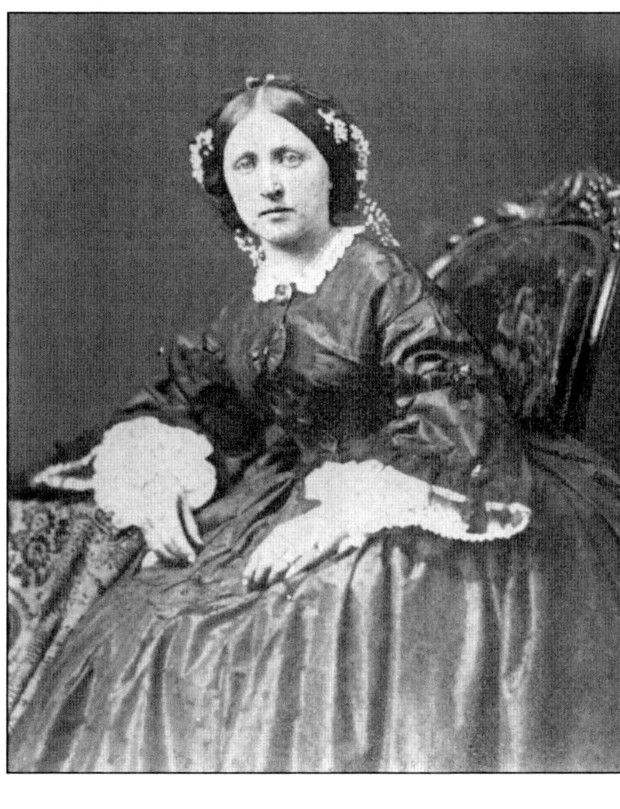

Jane Phelps became Marvin's wife in 1830, and the following eight children were born to them: James, Clarissa, Mary, Dorothy, Robert, George, Chauncey, and Jared. Jane Phelps Hopkins survived Marvin by 30 years. They are interred at the Pioneer Burying Ground. (Courtesy of the Engert family.)

Andrew Maxfield was born in Herkimer County, New York, in 1811 to Barnett and Hannah Ostrander Maxfield. At a young age, Andrew moved to Pittsford with his family. He married Sarah Powell on April 11, 1844, and they had four daughters and two sons. Andrew farmed 72 acres of land and died there on June 23, 1887. He was buried at Pittsford Cemetery. (Courtesy of W.H. McIntosh.)

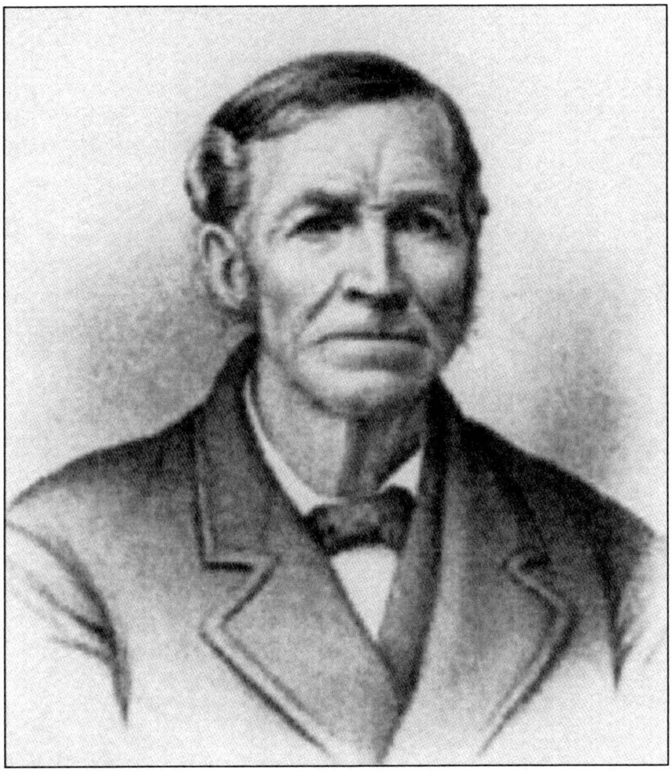

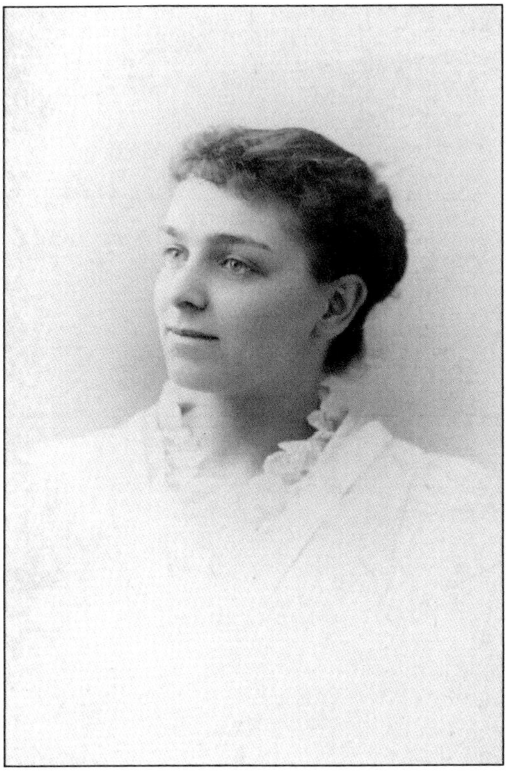

Carrie A. Thornell, born in 1875, was the daughter of Henry and Helen Hughes Thornell and the granddaughter of early Pittsford settlers William B. and Caroline Maxfield Thornell. Carrie married Frederick Gardner in 1899 but was widowed in 1910 and left with two sons, Frederick H. and Marvin Gardner, to support. (Courtesy of the Pittsford Town Historian.)

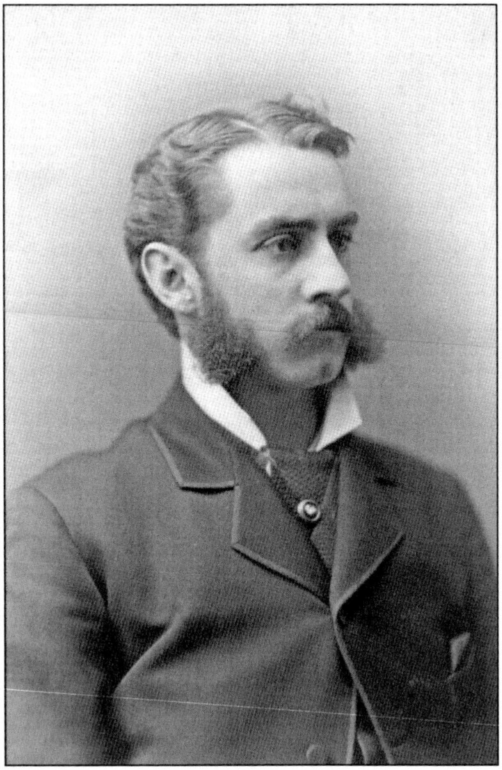

Lucius Seneca May was born in 1817. From 1854 to 1855, Lucius served in the New York State Assembly for Allegany County. After their marriage, Lucius and his wife, Jane, lived in Amity, New York, before returning to reside in Jane's hometown of Pittsford. Lucius S. May died in 1895, aged 77. His monument at Pittsford Cemetery is a distinctive large cross prone on the ground. (Courtesy of the John Bacon family.)

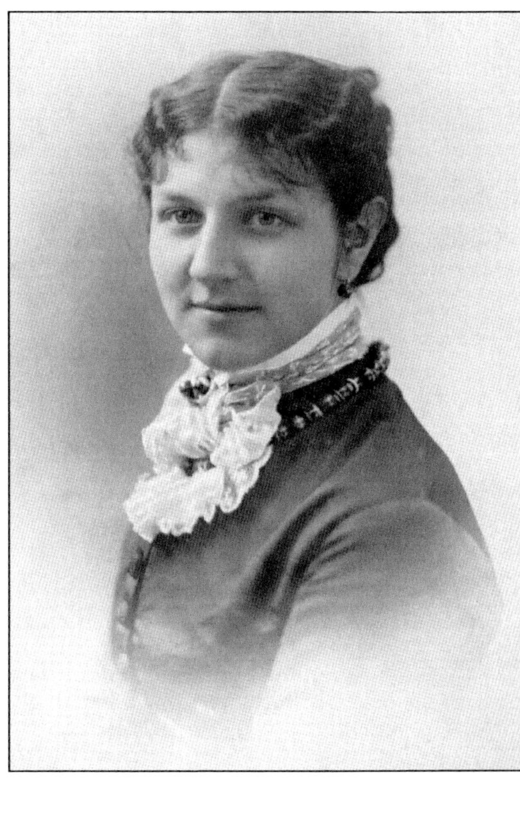

Jane Acer, the daughter of John and Hannah Whipple Acer, was born in Pittsford in 1819. John Acer owned the Phoenix Building, a fixture at the four corners of Pittsford for nearly 200 years. This charming photograph of Jane may have been taken on the occasion of her wedding to Lucius S. May in 1848. Jane Acer May died May 29, 1911, aged 91. (Courtesy of the John Bacon family.)

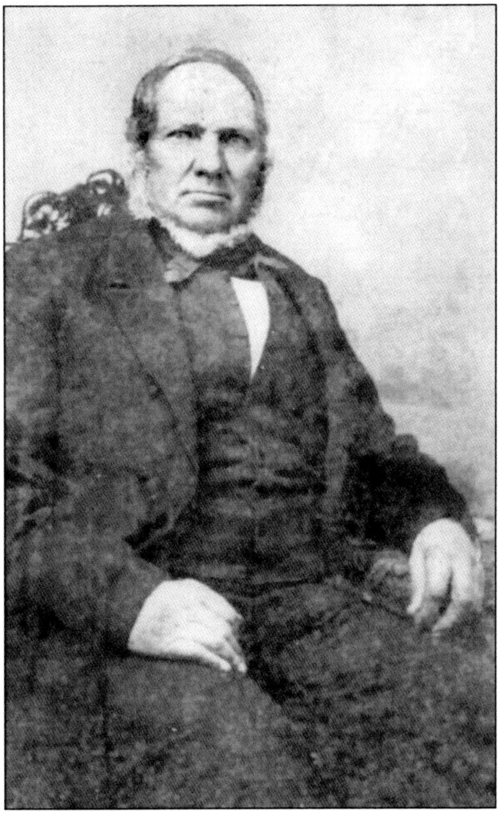

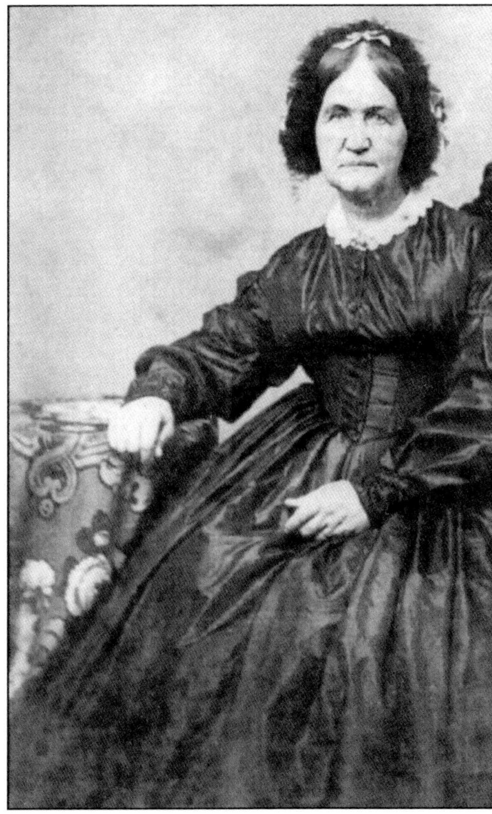

Alvin Foote was born in Massachusetts in 1798 to Beriah and Hannah Rossiter Foote. In 1824, he married Mary Ann Palmer. Although their oldest child, Charles, was born in Massachusetts, Catharine, George, and Emma were all born in New York State in the 1830s. By 1850, Alvin and his family lived in Pittsford where he farmed to support his family. Mary Ann Palmer Foote died in Pittsford in 1868, and Alvin died two years later. They are interred in a prominent location in Pittsford Cemetery. (Both, courtesy of Susie Carroll Summers.)

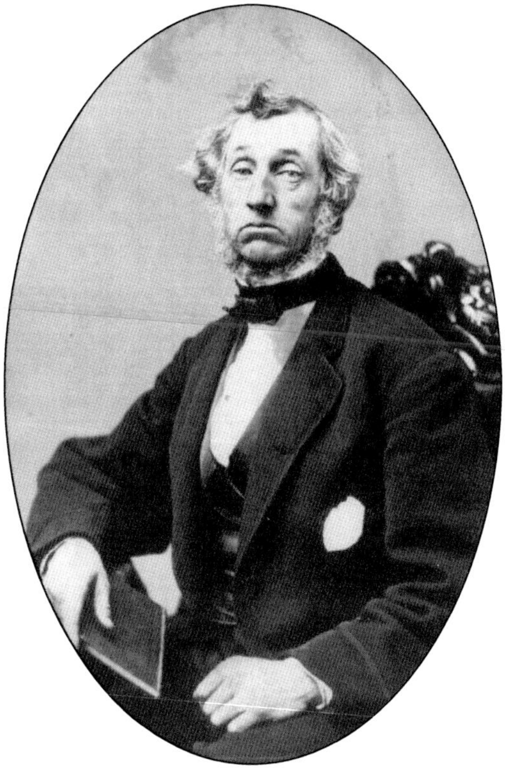 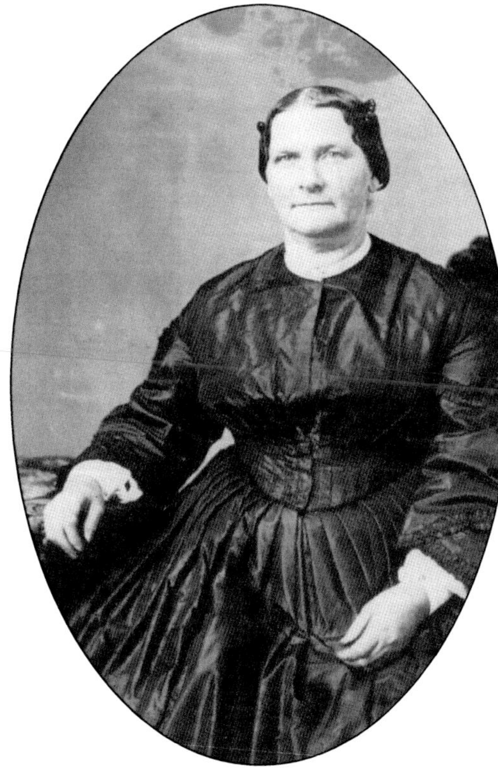

The child of David and Sylvia Martin Smith, David Wooster Smith was born in Clinton, New York, in 1811. After David's arrival in Pittsford in 1839, he worked as a carpenter before becoming an undertaker. In 1841, David married Hannah Paddock in Penfield. The Smiths had seven children. Their son Stephen also became an undertaker, assisting David with his thriving business in Pittsford before moving on to continue undertaking in Washington State. David's funeral parlor was based out of his home on Monroe Avenue, which was later razed to make way for the Atlantic gas station. In his later years, David was confined to a wheelchair due to his severe rheumatism. David W. Smith died in 1895 and was interred at Pittsford Cemetery. His wife, Hannah Paddock Smith, and four of their seven children are buried beside him. (Both, courtesy of Susie Carroll Summers.)

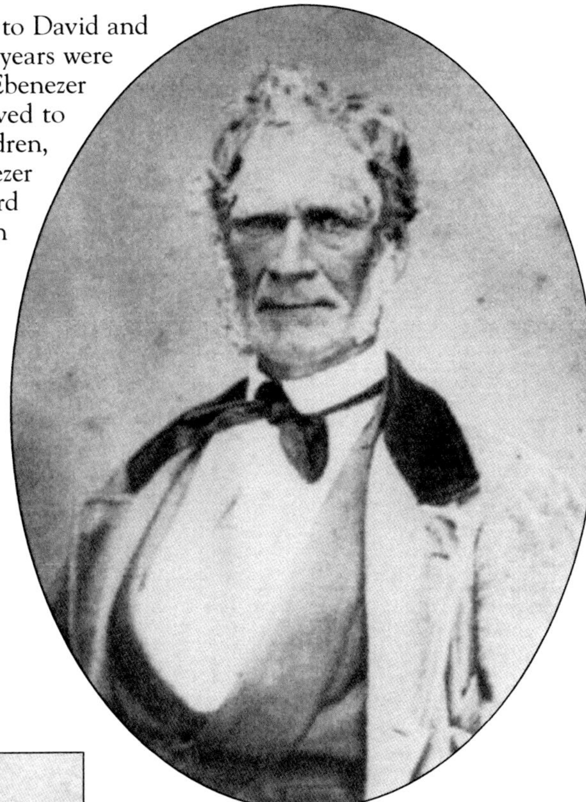

Ebenezer Sutherland was born in 1793 to David and Deborah Husted Sutherland. His early years were spent in Columbia County, New York. Ebenezer wed Gertrude Husted in 1819 and moved to Pittsford by 1824. They had seven children, five of whom were born in Pittsford. Ebenezer died in 1878 and was buried at Pittsford Cemetery in plot No. 1. Gertrude died in 1884. (Courtesy of Charles Lenhart.)

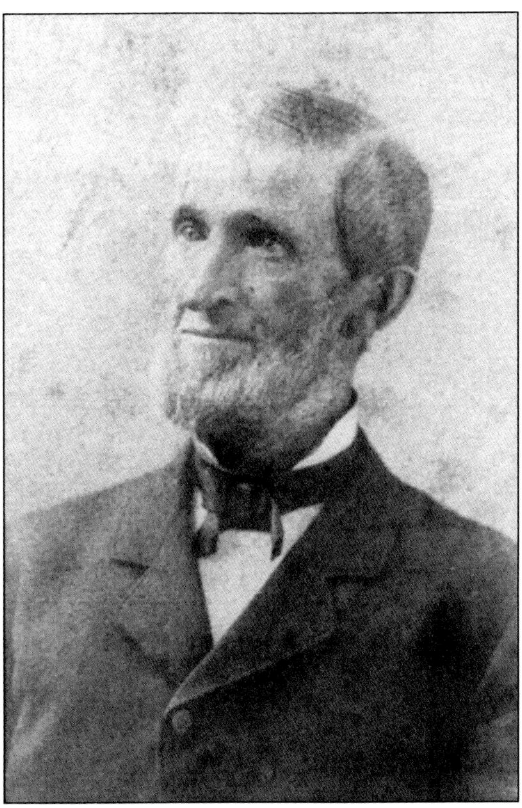

Isaac H. Sutherland, the second child of Ebenezer and Gertrude Husted Sutherland, was born in 1822. He moved to Pittsford as an infant, and it was there he met his wife, Gulielma Wilber. Their six daughters and sole son were raised at the family home located at 42 Monroe Avenue. Gulielma died in 1879, and Isaac followed in 1897. They are interred at Pittsford Cemetery. (Courtesy of Charles Lenhart.)

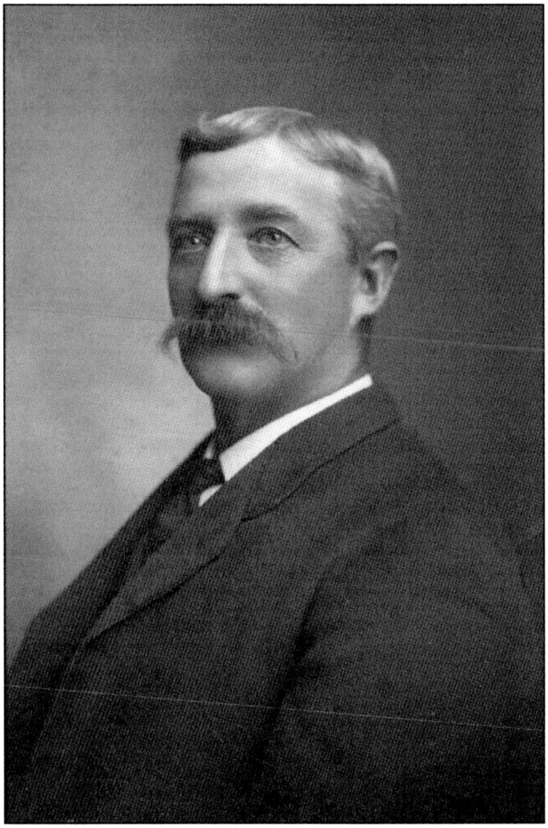

Charles W. Sutherland was the third child and only son of Isaac and Gulielma Wilber Sutherland. He was born in Pittsford in 1859. He wed Sarah Ardella Ladd in 1891, and they had four children, Norma, Gertrude, Irving, and Phyllis. By 1915, the family had moved to Greece, New York, where Charles was a farmer. Charles died in 1946, and Ardella passed away in 1963. (Courtesy of Charles Lenhart.)

Sisters Jane and Sarah Sutherland appear to be doing some household chores. Jane holds a basket, as if to gather some berries from the garden. Sarah is preparing to sweep the sidewalk of the family home at 42 Monroe Avenue. Jane, also called Jennie, was the fourth daughter of Isaac and Gulielma Wilber Sutherland. Sarah, or Sadie, was the youngest of the six daughters. (Courtesy of Charles Lenhart.)

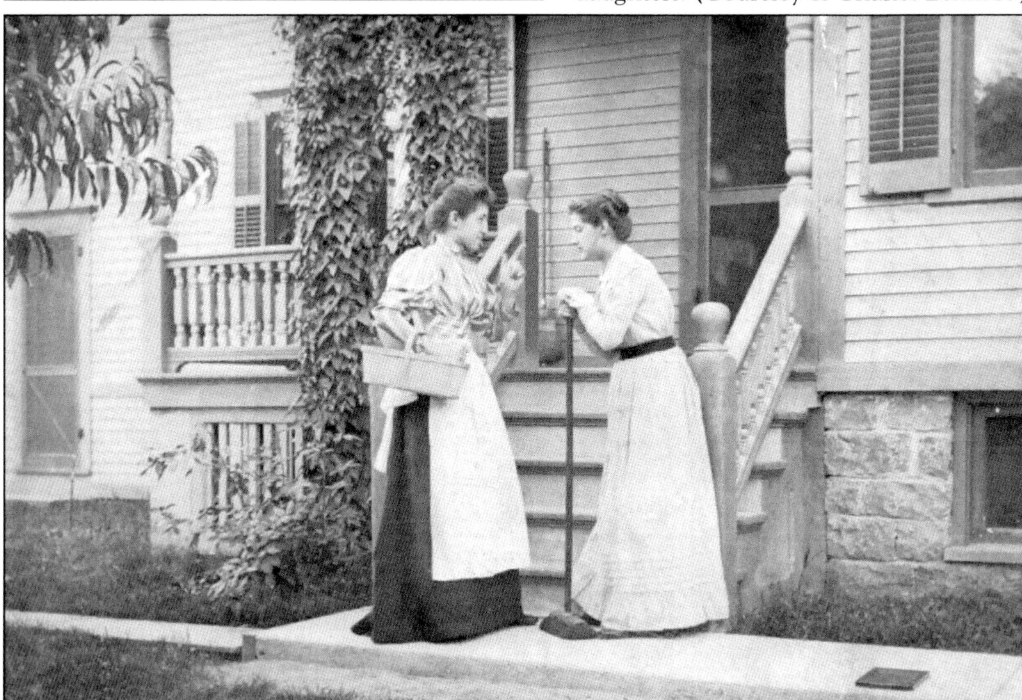

John Agate, the son of John and Emily Beers Agate, was born in 1838. He married Mary Jane Austin, and they had three children, Edith, Elroy, and John Herbert. The family lived at the brick home at 27 North Main Street, now the Canal Lamp Inn. He and his brother William were business partners, and they owned multiple buildings on the south side of the canal. John Agate died in 1928, aged 90. Mary Jane died in 1933 and was interred at Pittsford Cemetery beside John. (Courtesy of Connie Wilson, Ralph Parker Collection.)

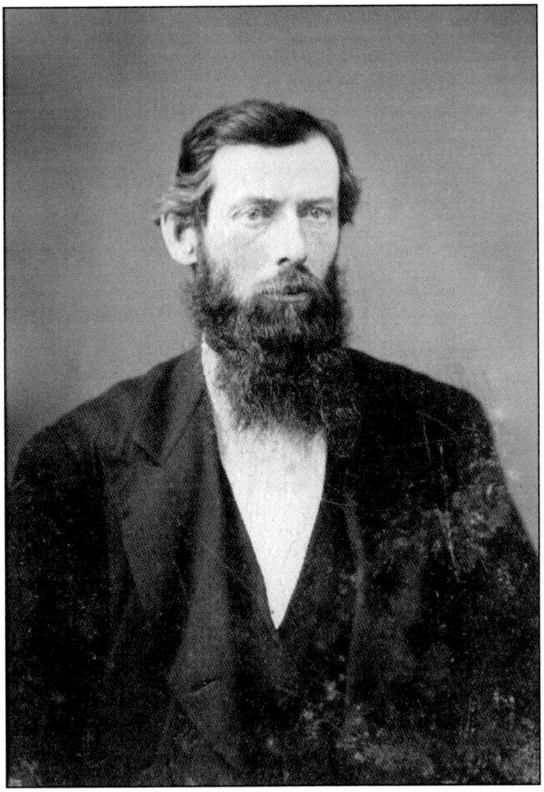

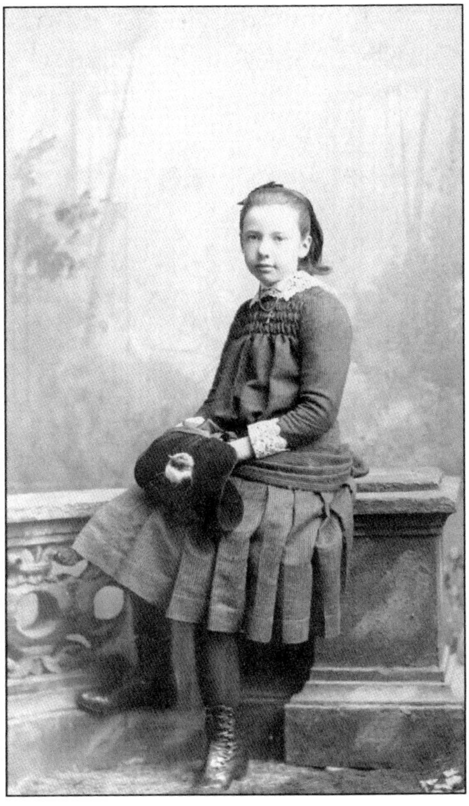

Rochester photographer J.H. Kent photographed Edith Agate, the daughter of John and Mary Jane Austin Agate, around 1881. Edith wed architect Gilbert Crump, son of Angelo Crump, in 1898. Following Gilbert's death in 1913 at age 43, Edith returned home to live with her parents. Edith Agate Crump died in 1961, aged 87, and was buried beside her husband at Pittsford Cemetery. (Courtesy of Connie Wilson, Ralph Parker Collection.)

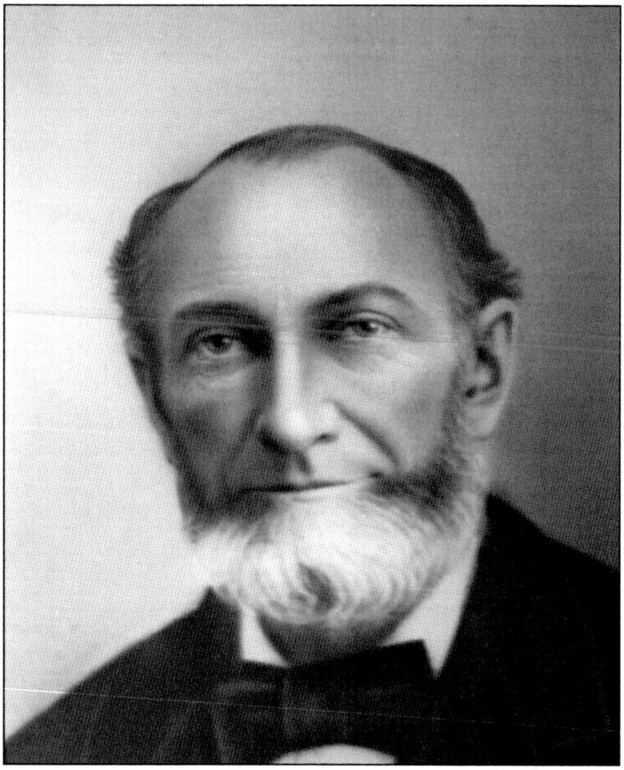

Alvin E. Nye, born in Pittsford in 1831, was the son of Silas and Sarah Stone Nye and the grandson of Revolutionary War veteran captain Silas Nye. He married Elizabeth Fowler, and they had six children. His farm, near the Clover Street and Calkins Road intersection, produced wheat, Indian corn, oats, and barley. Alvin died in 1908 and was interred at the Pioneer Burying Ground. (Courtesy of the Engert family.)

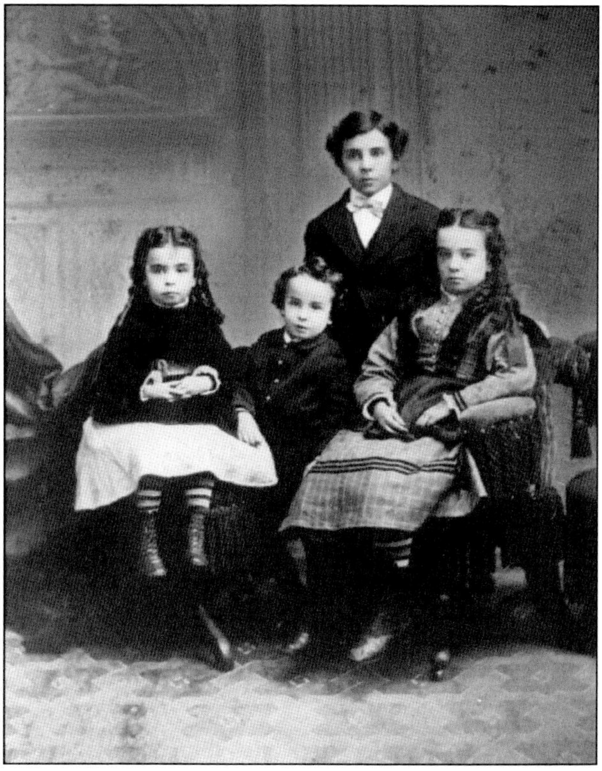

Four of Alvin E. and Elizabeth Fowler Nye's six children gathered for a photograph. Shown are, from left to right, Delora, Alvin F., Wales, and Lettie Maie. Hiram, the eldest Nye child, had died in 1864 at age six. The youngest child, Chauncey, is not shown. (Courtesy of the Engert family.)

Wales Nye was the second child of Alvin E. and Elizabeth Fowler Nye. He was born in Pittsford in 1862. In 1894, Wales wed Mame Frazer. He died in Pittsford in 1942, aged 80. Mame Nye died in 1951. They are interred at the Pioneer Burying Ground. (Courtesy of the Engert family.)

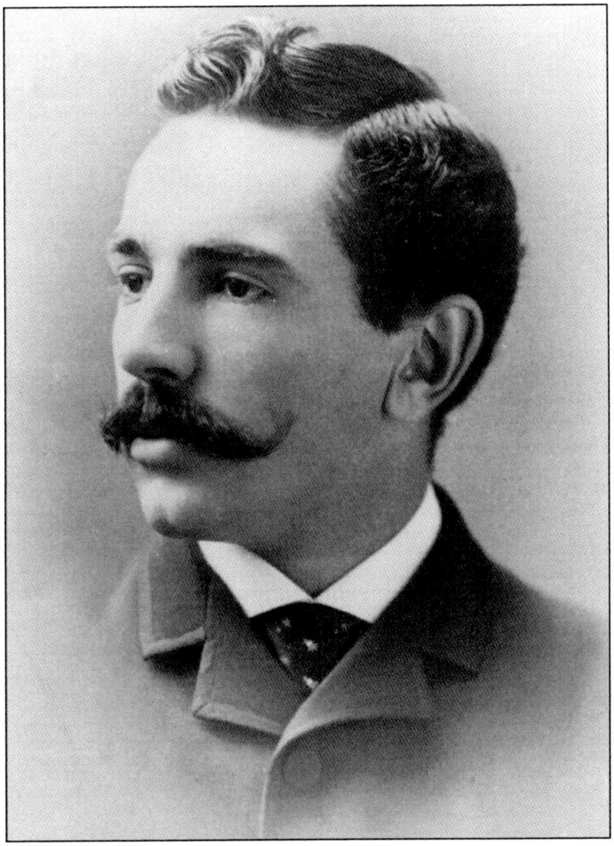

Members of the Nye, Parsons, and Hopkins family joined together for a photograph dated 1881. From left to right are Wales Nye, Clara Parsons, Lettie Maie Nye, and Jared Hopkins. Wales and his sister Lettie Maie were the children of Alvin E. and Elizabeth Fowler Nye. Wales married Mame Frazer. Clara Parsons, the daughter of Noyes and Clara Niles Parsons, went on to marry William J. Crump. She died at age 24. Lettie later married Jared Hopkins. (Courtesy of the Engert family.)

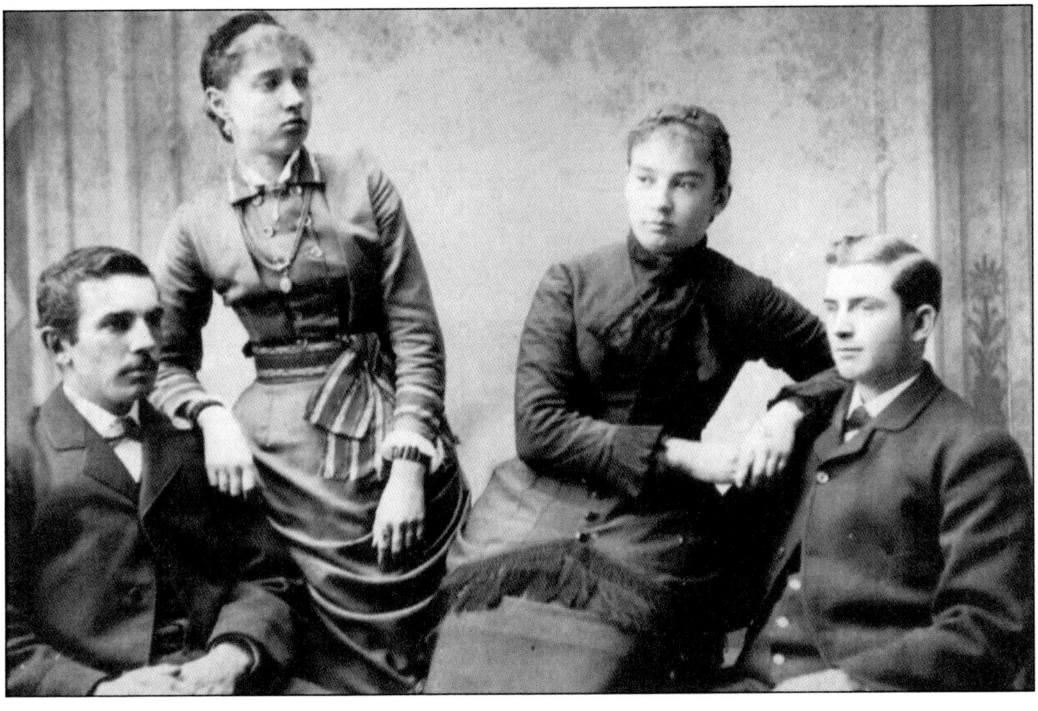

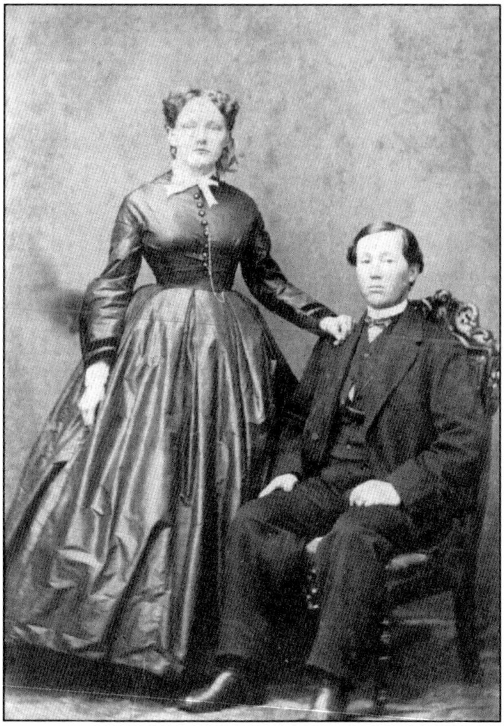

Evalena Ransom, the daughter of John H. and Margaret Ransom, was born in 1847 and arrived in Pittsford in the 1850s with her family. She married James, the son of George and Amanda Wolcott Knickerbocker, and they had two sons, George and Harry. Evalena and James are shown here, possibly on their wedding day. They died within days of each other in 1919 and are buried at Pittsford Cemetery. (Courtesy of Mary Knickerbocker Menzie.)

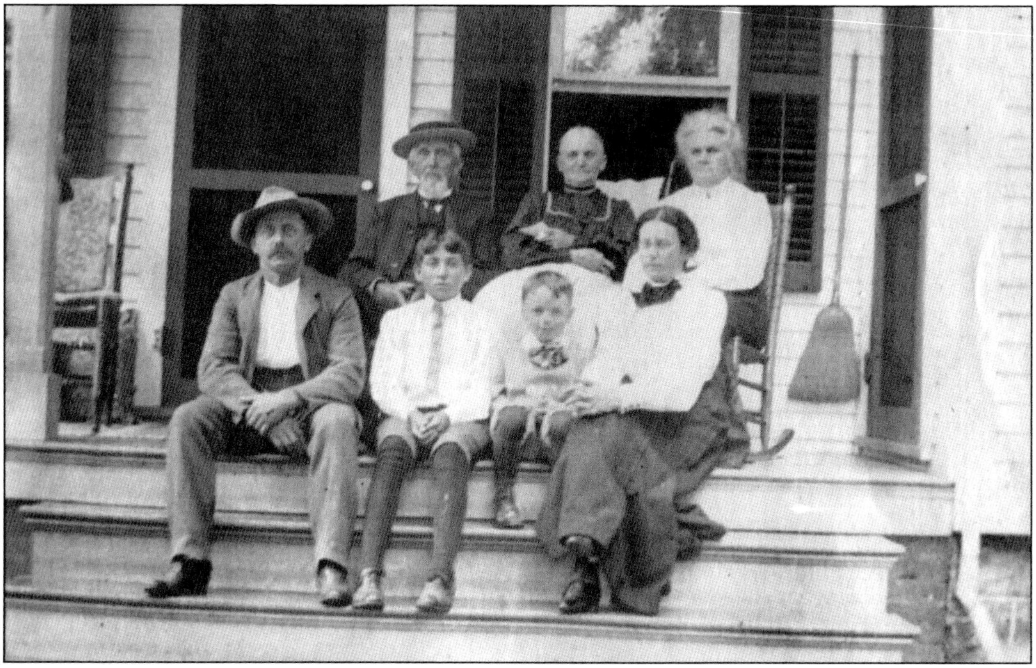

Sitting on the steps of the Barker porch around 1903 are, from left to right, (first row) Frank Barker, Albert B. Eckler, Harlan Knickerbocker, and Mary Barker Knickerbocker; (second row) James H. Eckler, Clarinda Eckler Barker, and Jane McWilliams Eckler. The Ecklers were a prominent family in Penfield. Albert was the grandson of James and Jane Eckler. (Courtesy of Mary Knickerbocker Menzie.)

A son of Joseph and Lucretia Buck True, Charles Henry True was born in 1853 in Pittsford. He served four terms as Pittsford's justice of the peace, was postmaster, and owned an insurance agency. Charles's father organized the first temperance society in Pittsford. Charles was a proponent of both temperance and rights for women and was a personal friend of Susan B. Anthony. He wed Mary Sutherland in 1881. Their only child, Harry Sutherland True, was born the following year. Charles True died in Pittsford on March 15, 1919, aged 65. (Courtesy of Charles Lenhart.)

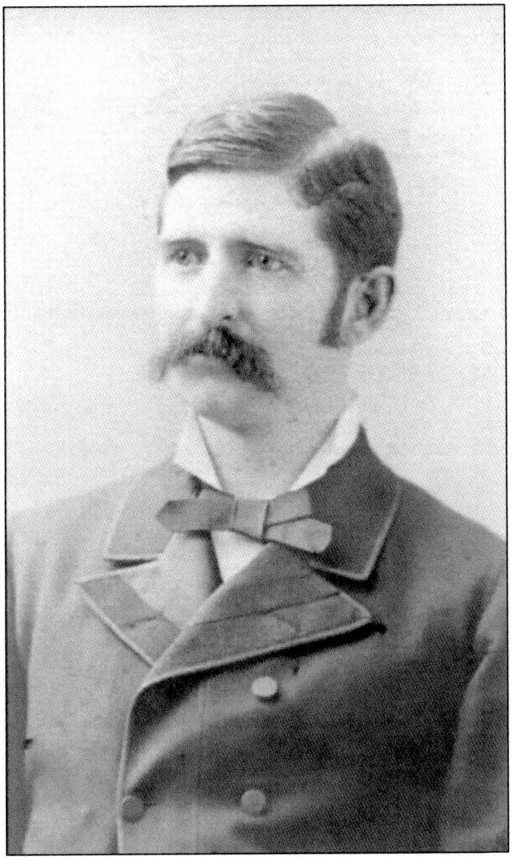

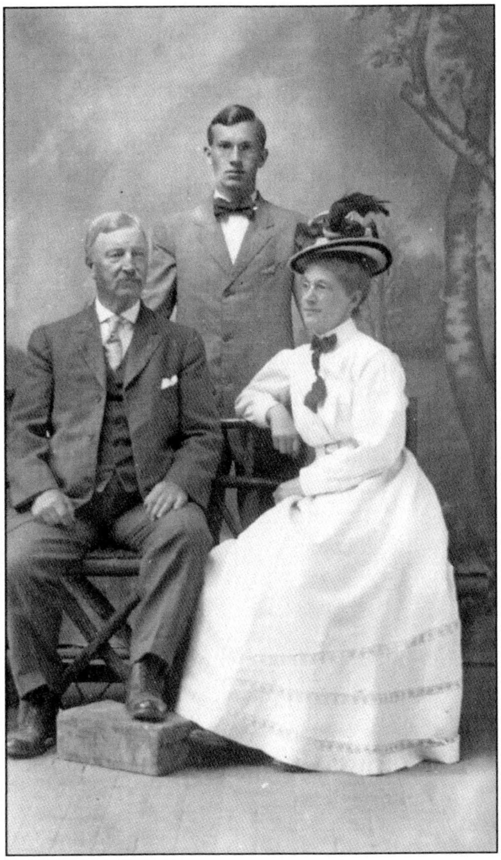

Seated in this studio portrait are John Buckley Bacon and his wife, Frederica Rogers Bacon. Their only child, Howard, stands behind them. John Bacon served as sergeant for the 4th Wisconsin Cavalry during the Civil War. He moved to Pittsford in the mid-1880s after purchasing the Armstrong store, located at 19 South Main Street, and was very active in the Grand Army of the Republic. (Courtesy of the John Bacon family.)

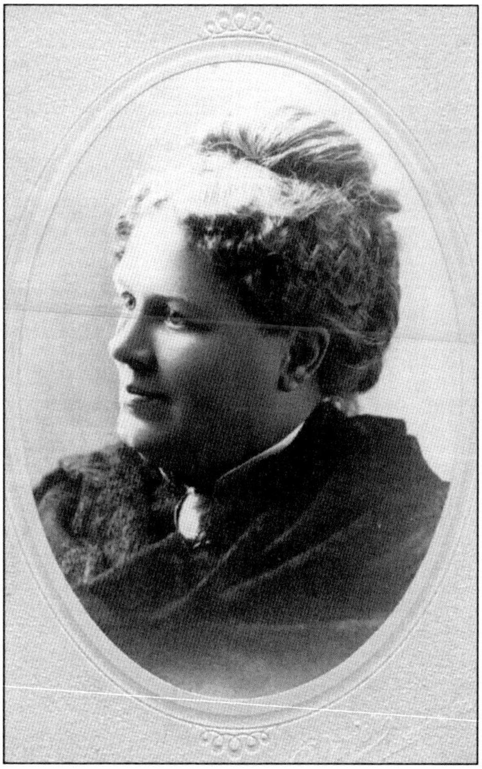

The eldest of James and Maria Devine Light's nine children, Harvey E. Light (below) was born in 1834. He grew to adulthood in Fairport and Pittsford, before moving to Michigan with his family. It was there that Harvey enlisted in the 10th Michigan Cavalry and rose to the rank of major. Harvey wed Mary Helen Shepard in Pittsford in 1861. They had five sons and one daughter. Mary Helen Shepard was born in Pittsford in 1833. Her parents, Sylvester and Matilda Palmer Shepard, were early Pittsford residents who were proponents of abolition and education for women. After living in Michigan and, for a short time, in Massachusetts, the family returned to Mary Helen's hometown of Pittsford. The Lights were very active in the community as members of the Grange, the Grand Army of the Republic, and the Presbyterian church. Mary Helen Shepard Light died in 1902 and was buried at Pittsford Cemetery beside her parents. Harvey Light died in 1921 and was laid to rest beside her on his 87th birthday. (Courtesy of Glenn Berggren.)

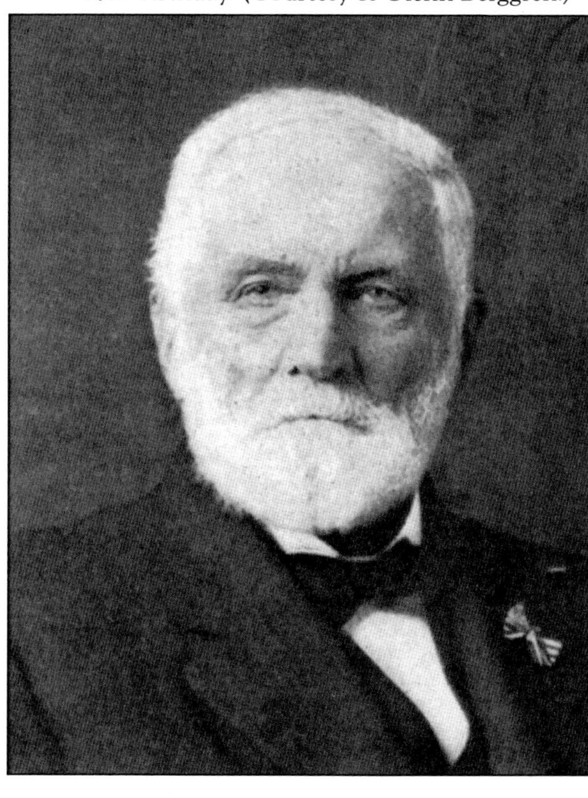

Elizabeth Copeland Kelly, the daughter of Edmund and Sarah Young Kelly, was born August 23, 1872. After her marriage to Franklin R. Stone, son of Hanford and Helen Turner Stone, Elizabeth resided in Pittsford Village. She was active in many organizations, including the Philathea Rebekah Lodge of Pittsford. Elizabeth Kelly Stone died in 1938, and Franklin followed in 1942. They are buried at Pittsford Cemetery. (Courtesy of Cheri Buckley Branca.)

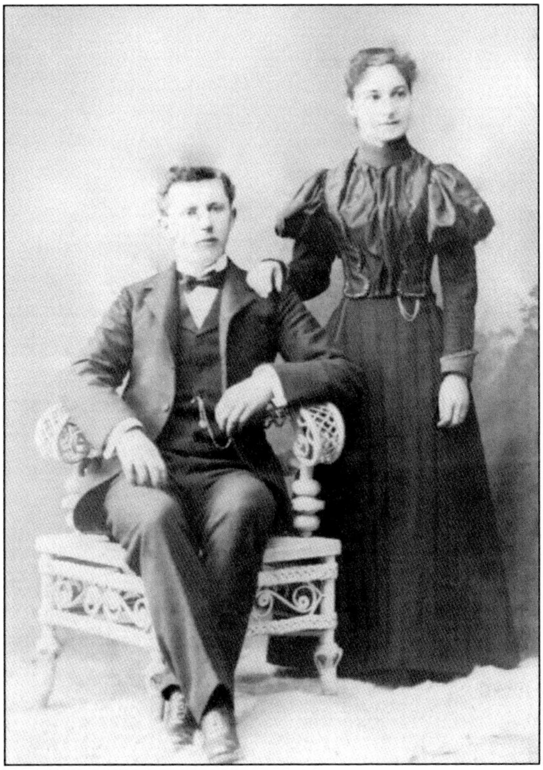

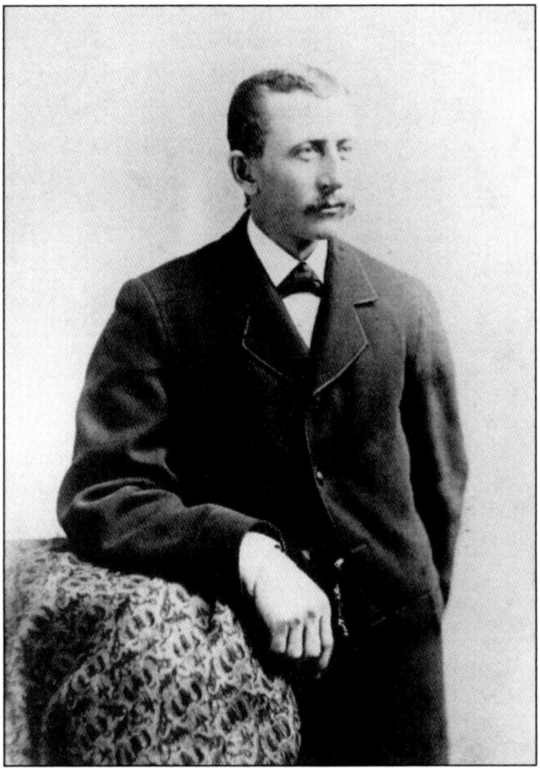

Franklin Benjamin Lusk, the child of Heman S. Lusk and his third wife, Matilda Eckler Lusk, was born July 6, 1852. On March 4, 1874, he wed Addie Lunette Peets in Henrietta, New York. They had three sons, Harry Stephen, Charles Franklin, and Lemuel Heman Lusk. Franklin died in 1910 and was buried at Pittsford Cemetery. (Courtesy of Bill Lusk.)

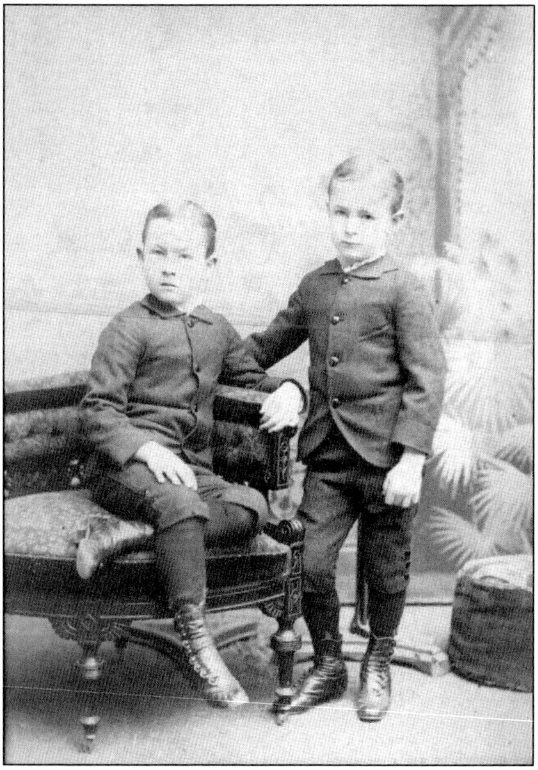

Henry Stephen Lusk, at left, and his brother Charles Franklin Lusk do not seem very happy to be posing for this studio portrait. Henry, or Harry as he was known, appears to be agitated. Charles looks quite tired from standing still so long. The portrait was likely taken about 1881, around the time of the birth of their brother Lemuel. (Courtesy of Bill Lusk.)

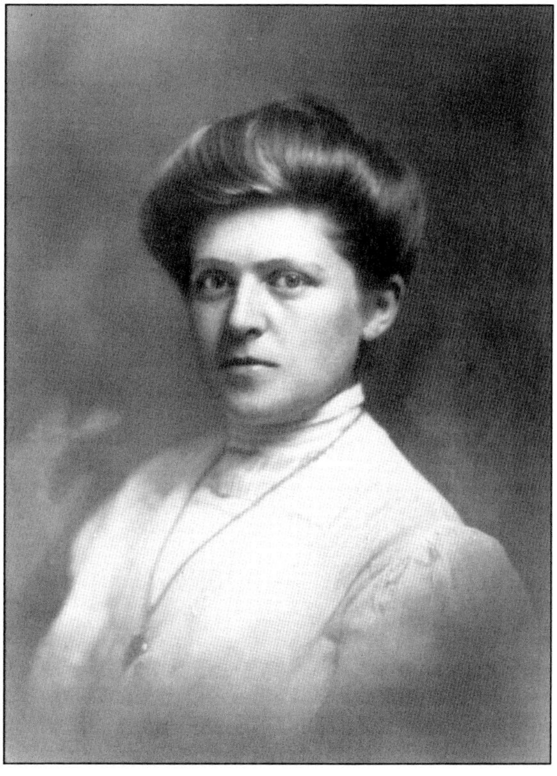

Sarah Ann Willard, the daughter of Oliver Perry Willard and Lucinda Thayer Willard, was born March 29, 1881. Lucinda died when Sarah was just one week old. Sarah married Charles Franklin Lusk on October 19, 1898, at age 17. They had nine children, including two sets of twins. (Courtesy of Bill Lusk.)

Two

Education and Religion

The early residents of Northfield were resolutely determined that their children receive a decent education. As well as clearing the land of first-growth trees and planting crops to feed their families and animals, it was decided that a school be established. The number of families who had children who would attend built a log schoolhouse near Lusk's corner. Each child would be charged $1 per quarter. In 1797, a schoolmaster named John Barrows was hired. He boarded with a different family periodically. That school was known then and now as District No. 1, and it was the only school in the whole territory. Eventually, as other towns were divided from Northfield, additional schools were established. At one time, before the schools were centralized in 1946, there were nine district schools in the town of Pittsford.

Education was important, but religion was equally so to these Yankees. As early as 1803, the Congregational church was organized but soon became Presbyterian. They met originally in people's homes, but a small log building was erected up near the Milepost, near the Pioneer Burying Ground and the Lusk property. That building was eventually sold to the Baptists who had organized in 1807 and had been meeting in members' homes. The Presbyterians decided to build a more elaborate church to the north where the village eventually was located. The log church was razed in 1856 when the Baptist congregation built a more permanent structure in the village. The Methodist circuit riders visited Pittsford on a regular basis, and the sect was organized and a church built around 1815. The Methodist congregation was followed by the Episcopalians, the Roman Catholics, and eventually the German Lutherans. For a while, the town was known as the place of six churches and six saloons.

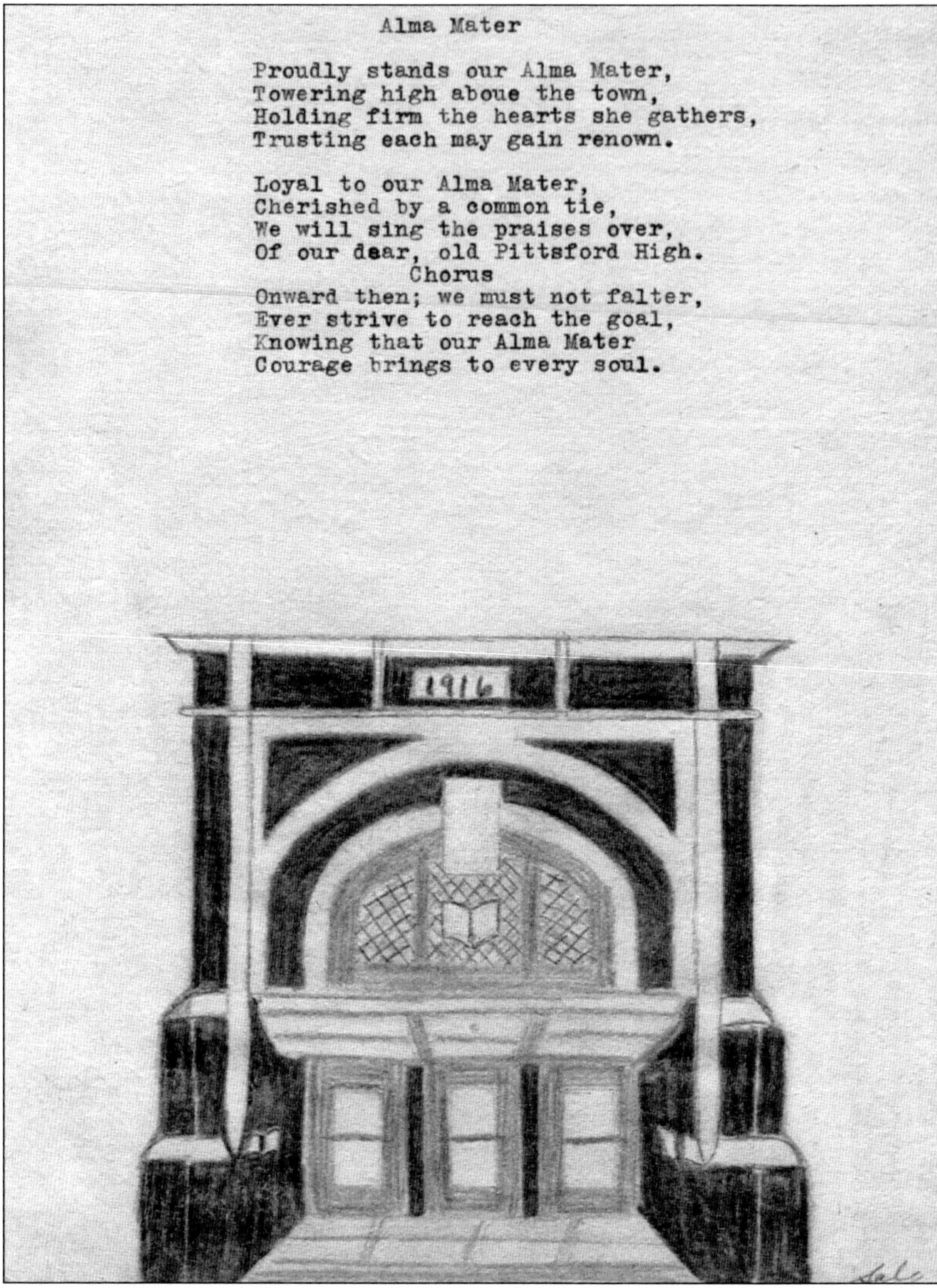

Alma Mater

Proudly stands our Alma Mater,
Towering high aboue the town,
Holding firm the hearts she gathers,
Trusting each may gain renown.

Loyal to our Alma Mater,
Cherished by a common tie,
We will sing the praises over,
Of our dear, old Pittsford High.

Chorus

Onward then; we must not falter,
Ever strive to reach the goal,
Knowing that our Alma Mater
Courage brings to every soul.

Sally Ann Palmer, a member of Pittsford School's class of 1948, sketched the front of the Lincoln Avenue School and typed the alma mater. Sally was the daughter of Jack and Eloise Gruneisen Palmer. She attended college at Plattsburgh, where she received a degree in elementary education. Sally went on to teach Kindergarten for many years. The sketch is signed "Sal." (Courtesy of Jo Anne Gruneisen Shannon.)

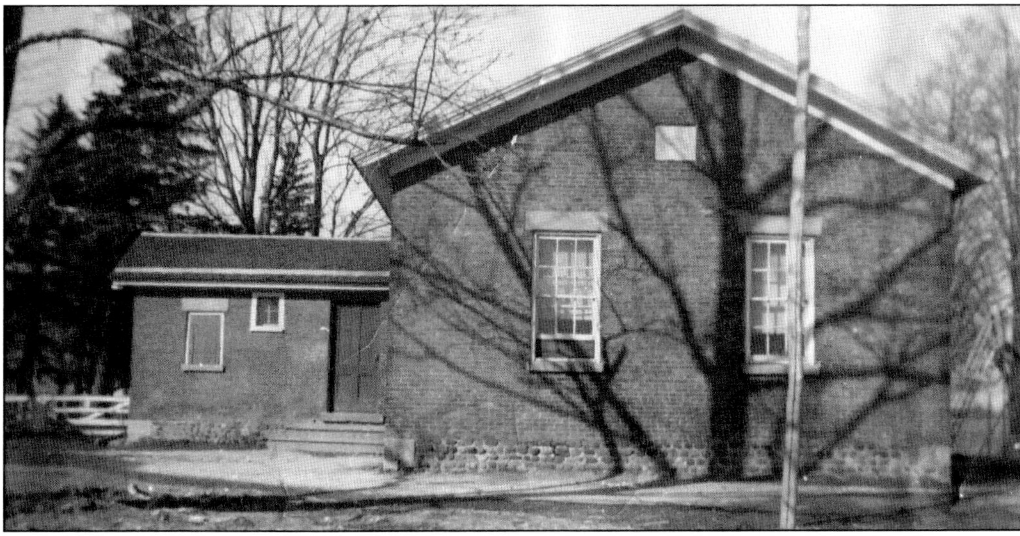

District No. 1 schoolhouse, the Milepost School, is located at 210 Mendon Road and was built in 1826 on land supplied by Simon and Israel Stone. The original school building on this site had been a log cabin, built in 1794. That was replaced in 1806 by a frame building, which was razed in 1826 when this brick structure was built. The town now uses the building as a meeting facility. (Courtesy of Paul M. Spiegel.)

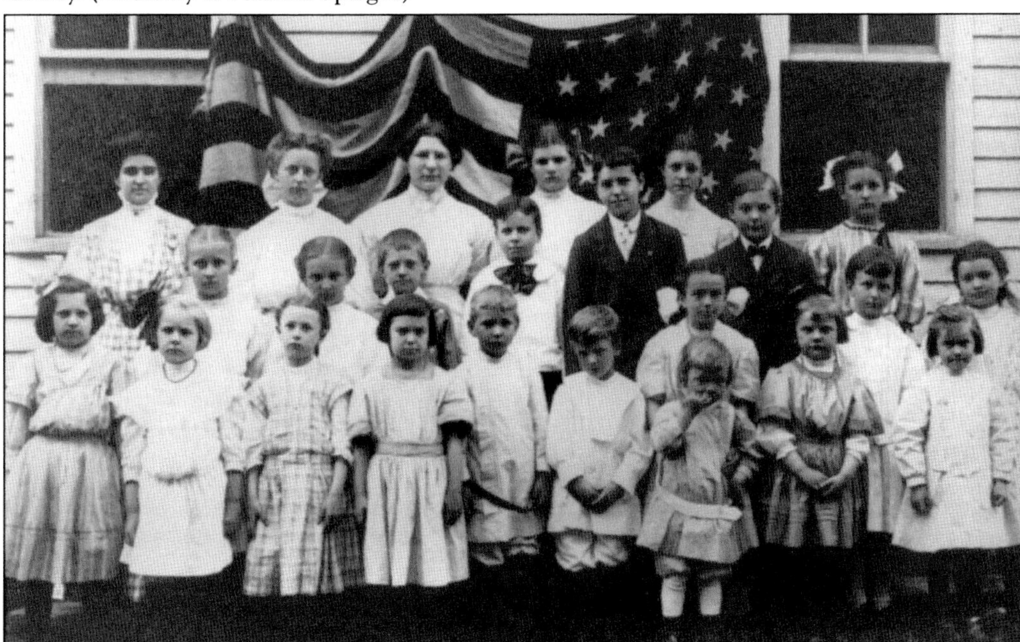

The children of District No. 5 school are shown here about 1910. Donald Girke is in the first row. In the second row, from left to right, are Ruth Merkel, Clarissa Barker, Edna Corby, Jane Hopkins, Louis Girke, Richard Greene, Delora Hopkins, and Emma Lou Barker, and the last girl is possibly Florence Corby. In the third row are Olga Papka, Clara Clawson, Royal Merkel, Phelps Hopkins, Fay Bush, Arlo Barker, unidentified, and Mildred Girke. Standing in the fourth row are the teacher Ella Glotzbach, Dora Papka, May Smith, Bertha Smith, Lorinda Smith, and Florence Papka. (Courtesy of the Engert family.)

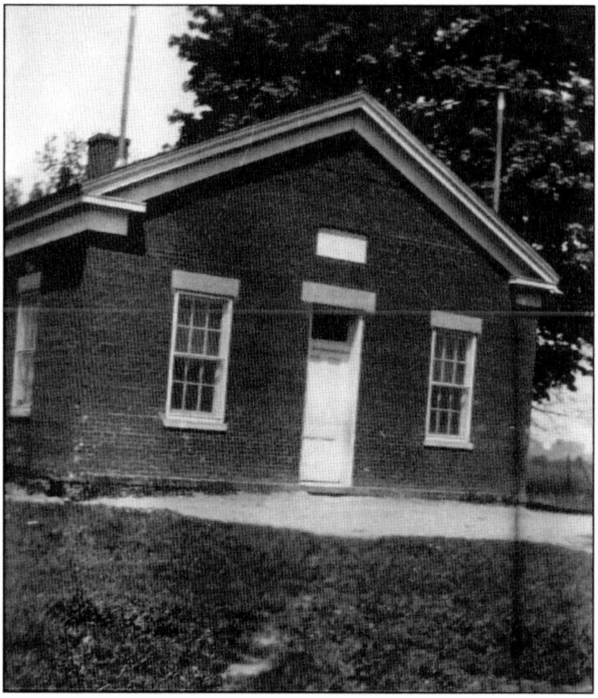

Although it is now a private home, this structure on Marsh Road was once a schoolhouse. The brick and stone building, built in 1856, was originally District No. 13 school but was later renumbered to District No. 9 school. When the Pittsford School District was centralized in 1946, the district schoolhouses, nine in number, ceased to function for that purpose. (Courtesy of Gail Hulbert Esker and Marilyn Hulbert Nielsen.)

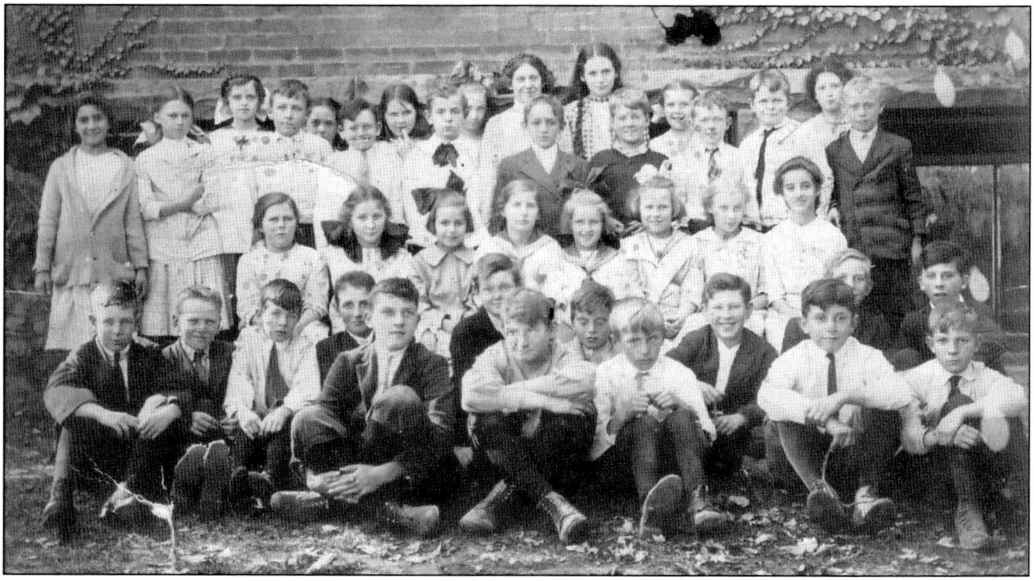

The fifth-grade class is shown here in 1914. The boys seated on the ground are, from left to right, Laurence Williams, two unidentified students, Burt Crumb, Murray Gilbert, Jake Minnamon, Harry Boyce, George Earls, Lou Schwartz, unidentified, John Rand, Bill Stone, Chester Grace, and Ed Miller. The seated girls are Isabelle Cowan, Wava Gruneisen, Florence Schlenker, Alice Roper, Florence Murray, Ada Longyear, Grace Bahringer, and unidentified. Standing in back are Minnie Zampani, Mary Ford, Janice Payne, unidentified, Evelyn Anthony, two unidentified students, George Utz, Marion Thornell, teacher Grace Schad, unidentified, Ella Troughton, two unidentified, Edith Mayo, unidentified, Lawrence Malchow, Sally Rand, and Willis Peck. (Courtesy of the Pittsford Town Historian.)

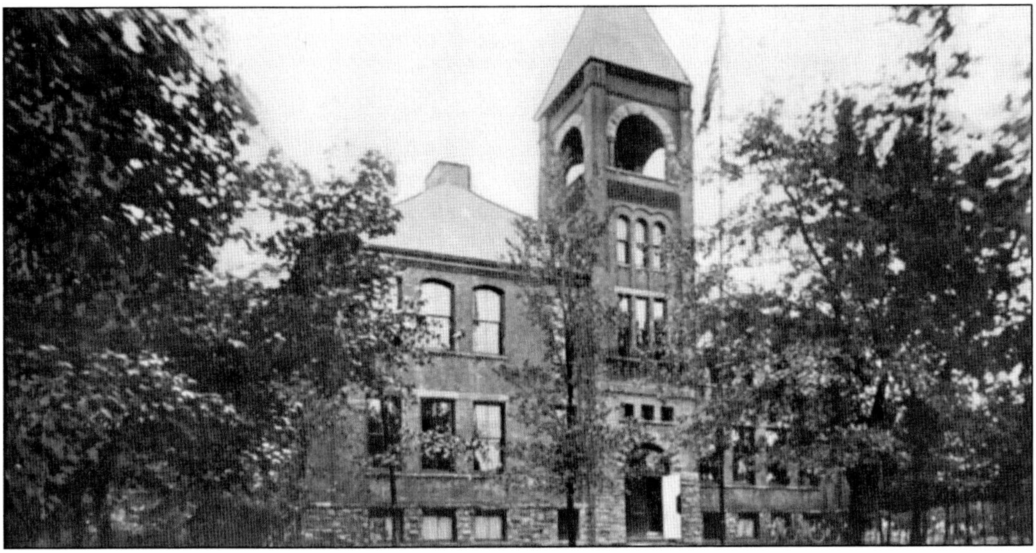

On March 4, 1916, the Pittsford High School on Lincoln Avenue became engulfed in flames. The cause of the fire was unknown, and the building and contents were a total loss. The original building had been built of brick in 1892. A slate roof covered the structure, which contained 12 rooms. An addition, built around 1911, also went up in flames. Over 16,000 books in the library and the third-floor science laboratory were also completely destroyed. The fire displaced 375 students and 11 teachers. A decision was made by the board of education to utilize rooms in the town hall, the Masonic temple, and several churches as classrooms until the school could be demolished and rebuilt. Only one item was saved from the rubble. Student Glen Austin safely removed the school's American flag from the pole out front. (Both, courtesy of Bill Lusk.)

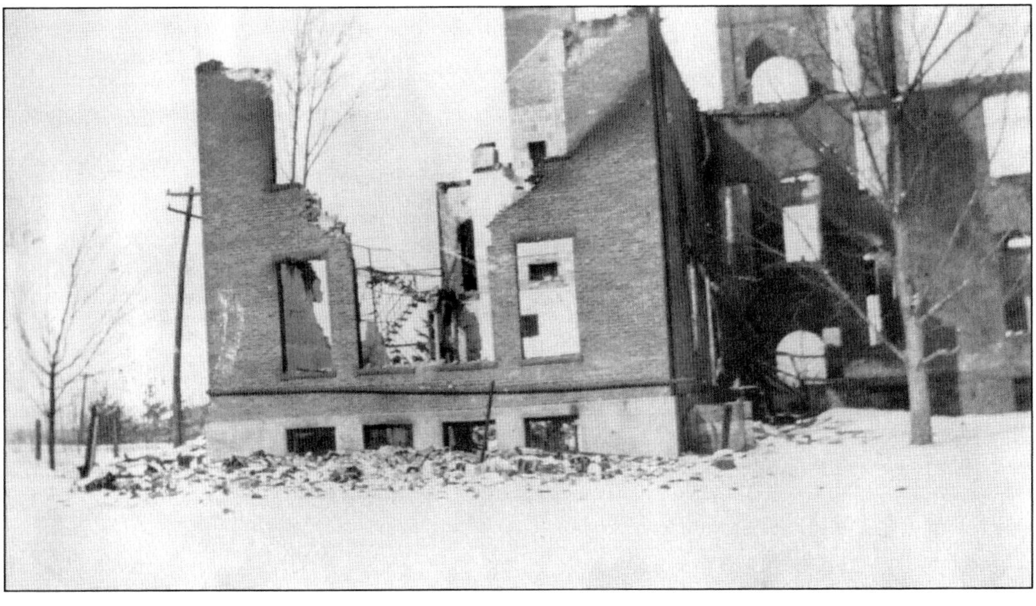

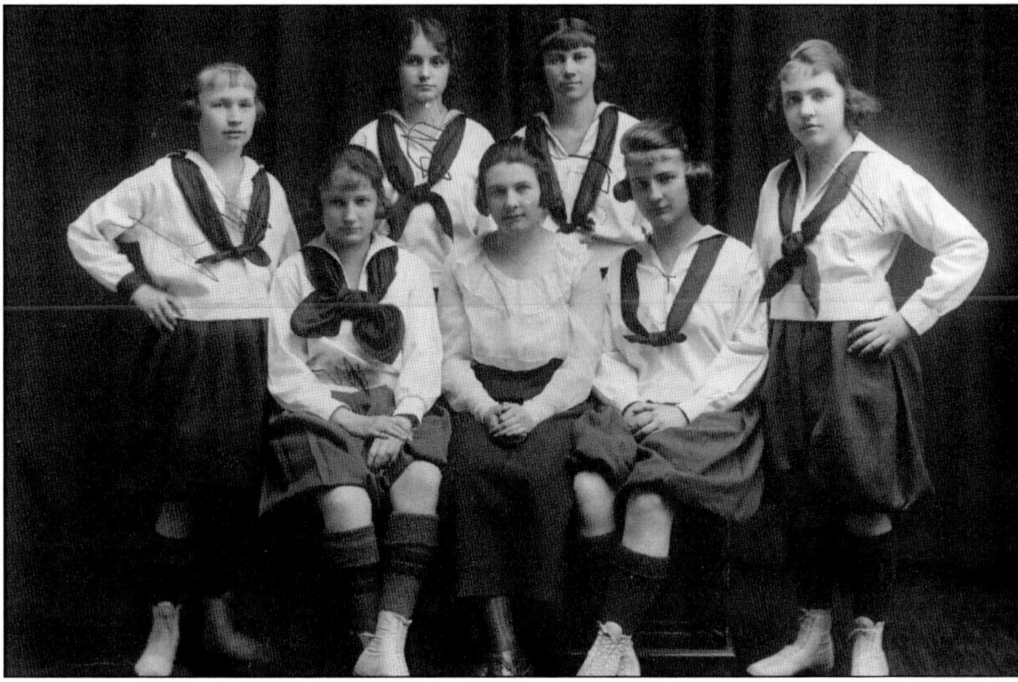

The 1919–1920 Pittsford High School girls' basketball team looks proudly at the camera. Pictured are, from left to right, (sitting) Wava Gruneisen, guard; Mabel Pooler, physical directress; and Evelyn Gates, guard; (standing) Florence Lusk, forward; Eloise Gruneisen, forward; Ruth Merkel, center; and Laura Zeitler, substitute. (Courtesy of Jo Anne Gruneisen Shannon.)

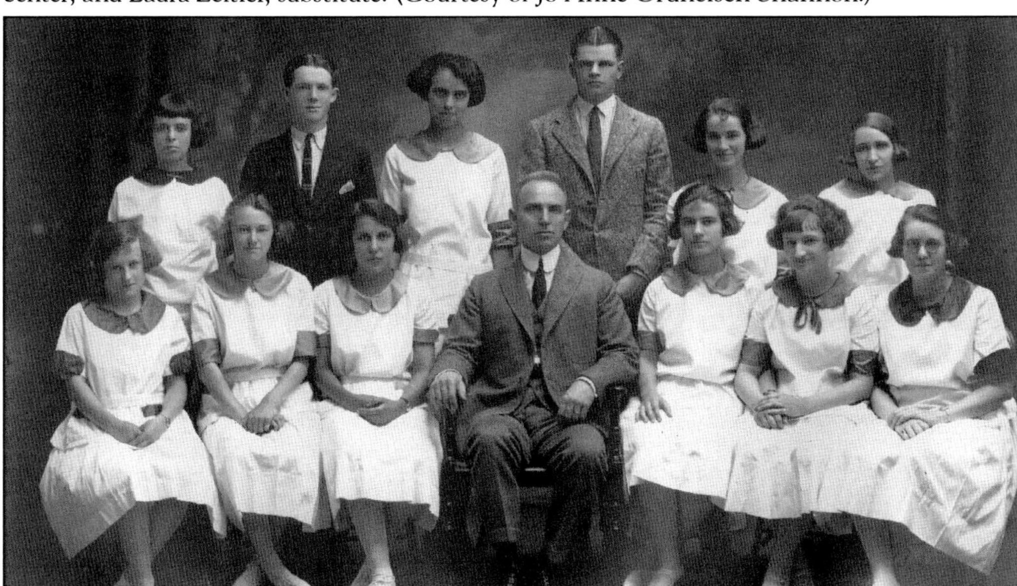

Surrounding Prof. Albert Helmkamp are members of the 1922 Pittsford High School graduating class. They are, from left to right, (sitting) Doris Welch, Mary Ford, Florence Mann, Professor Helmkamp, Phyllis Bolder, Marion Thornell, and Edith Mayo; (standing) Dorothy Thornell, Pat (Leland) Duffy, tentatively identified as Jennie Bisset, Lawrence Malchow, Marguerite Kates, and Tina Utz. (Courtesy of the Pittsford Town Historian.)

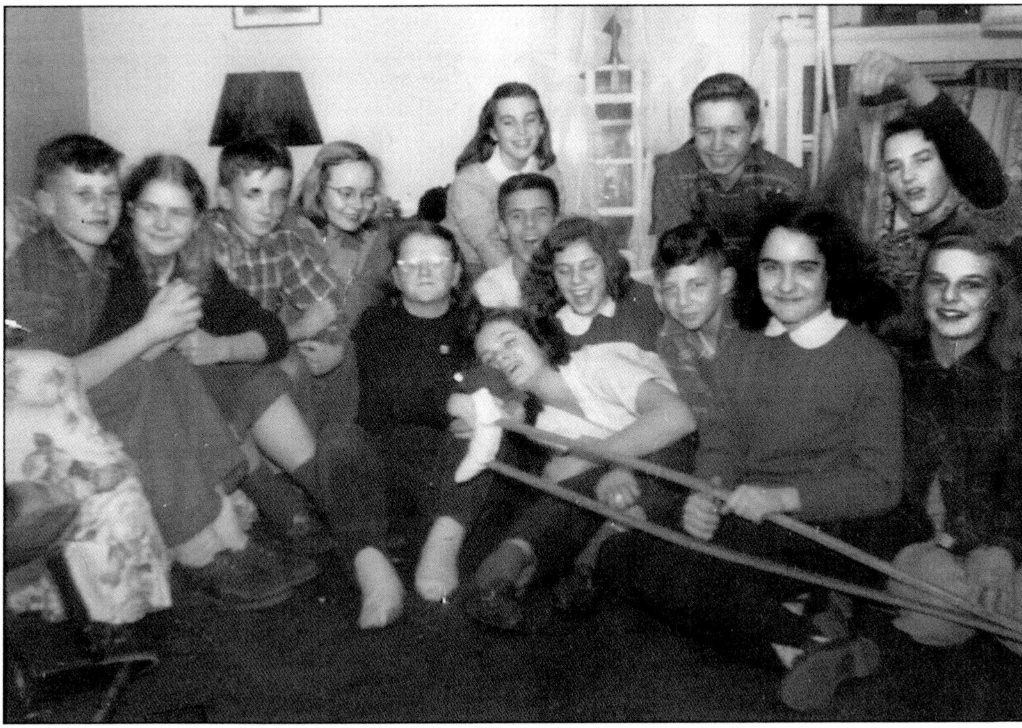

This sixth-grade class, shown in 1946, appears to be having an unofficial get-together at home. On the floor are, from left to right, Liz Jackson, Clark Rumrill, Martha Smith, Betty Brewer, Bob Stone, Jade Hill, and Abbie Brown. Seated on the sofa, from left to right, are Ron Hendee, Adaire Way, Peter Roda, and Kay Utz. Jonatha "Shotsie" Rand, Roy Ruske, and Ron Jabaut survey the group from their chairs. (Courtesy of Jonatha "Shotsie" Rand.)

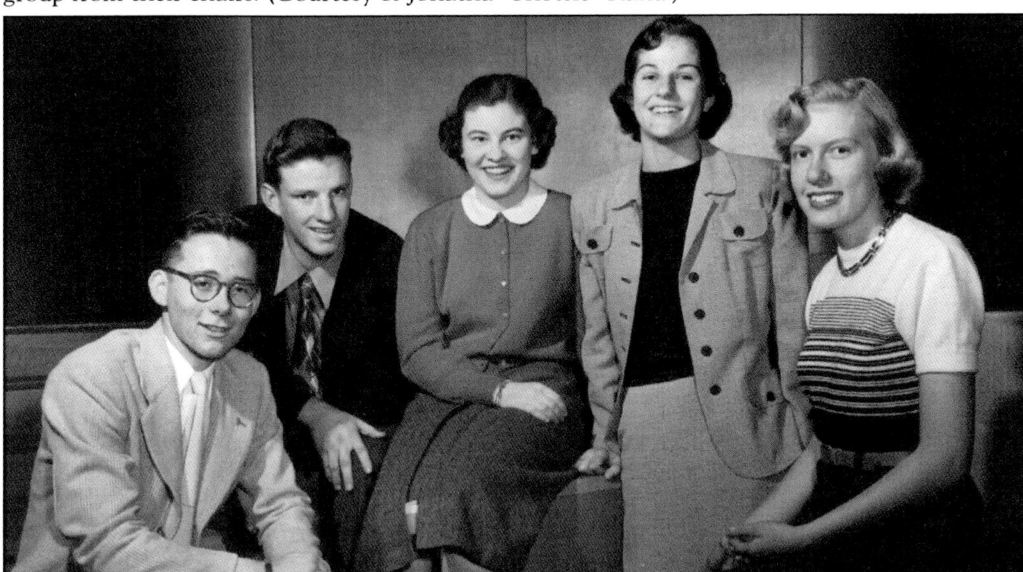

The 1953 Pittsford High School senior class officers are, from left to right, David Foreman, Tom Silco, Barbara Stanton, Eleanor Norfleet, and Marlene Wiegert. (Courtesy of Wenda Tompkins Silco.)

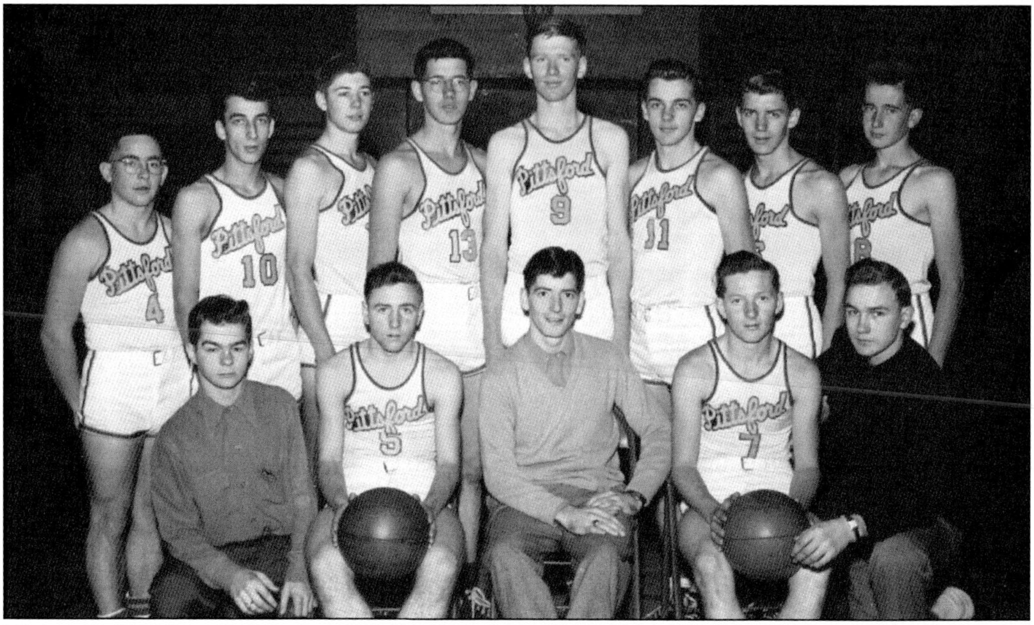

The 1947–1948 Pittsford High School boys' basketball team was the Section V titleholder and also reigned as Class B county champion two years in a row. Coach Lyle Brown's Knights are, from left to right, (first row) Don Smith, John Sens, coach Lyle Brown, Jack Keane, and Bob Jaeschke; (second row) Hank Carter, Steve (Geraci) Zornow, Bob Place, Jim Laurin, John Paul Jones, Dan Tack, Al White, and Bill Patchen. (Courtesy of Bob Place.)

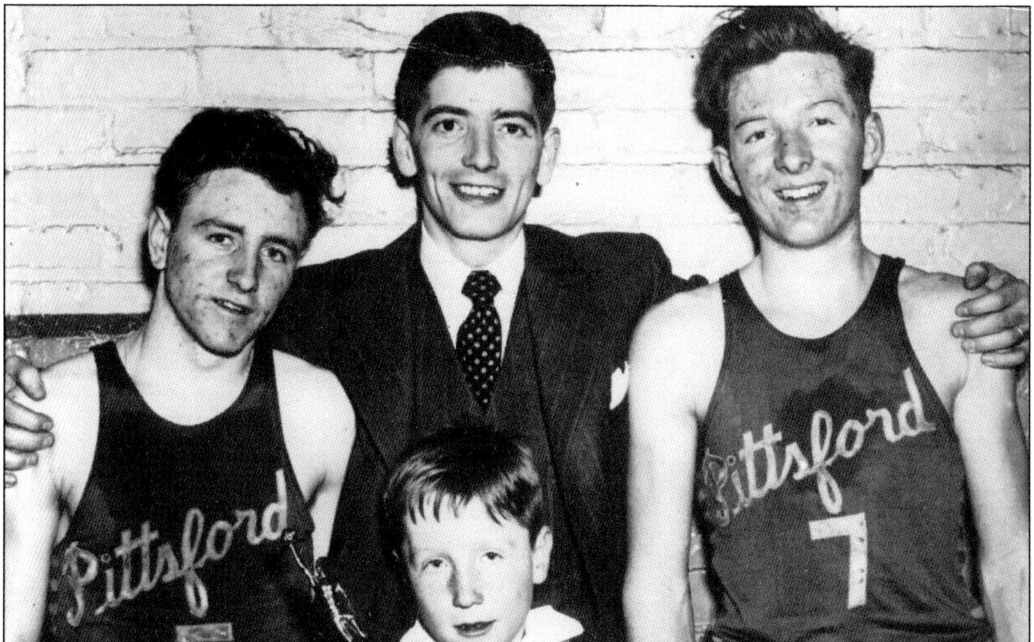

Basketball coach Lyle Brown is shown with several of his Knights. Pictured are, from left to right, John Sens, Coach Brown, and Jack Keane. Standing in front of them is Barry Sens, the unofficial mascot of the team and younger brother of John. (Courtesy of Bob Place.)

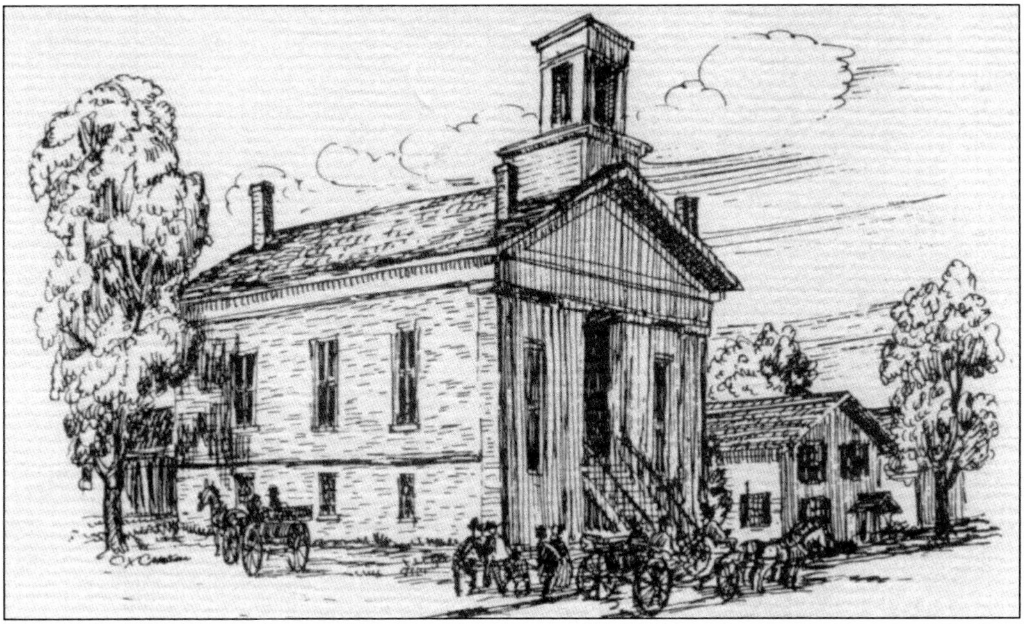

The first Methodist church building was a brick structure built in 1831 on Lincoln Avenue. Just 12 years later, the building was dismantled and rebuilt at the corner of Church and South Main Streets. It remained in that form until 1895, when this new structure, shown below, was built. In 1952, the Methodists joined the Baptists and formed the United Church of Pittsford. The tower was removed, and the building is now commercial space. (Both, courtesy of Paul M. Spiegel.)

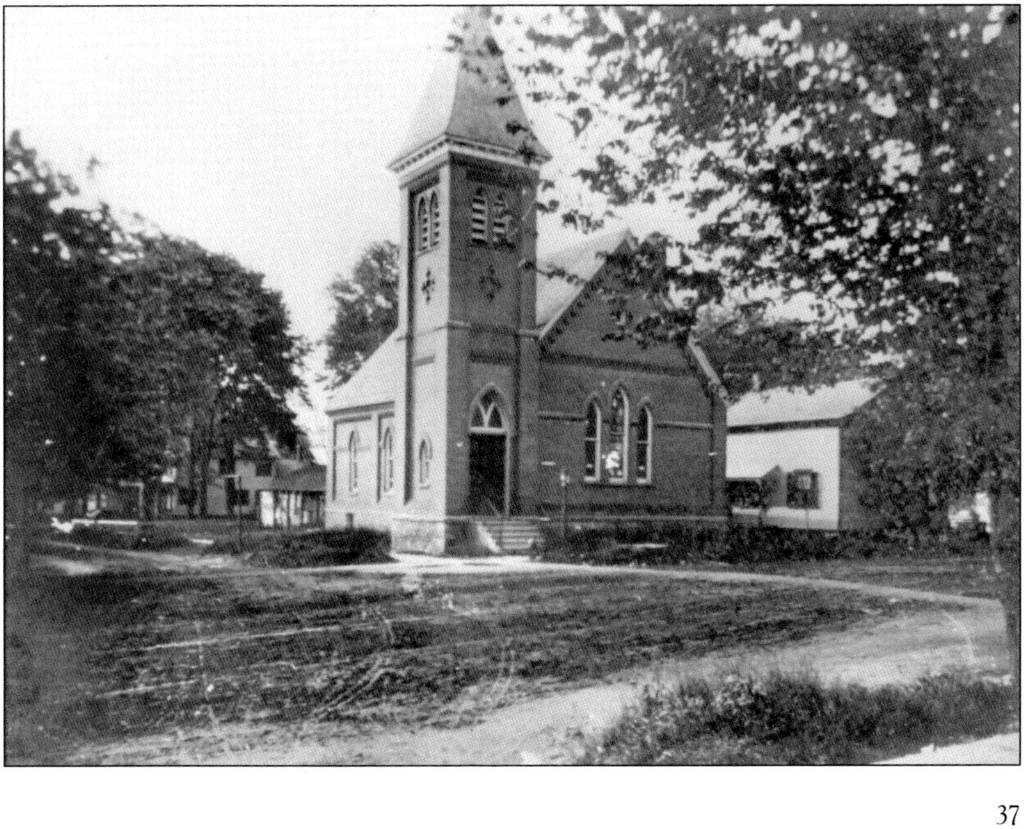

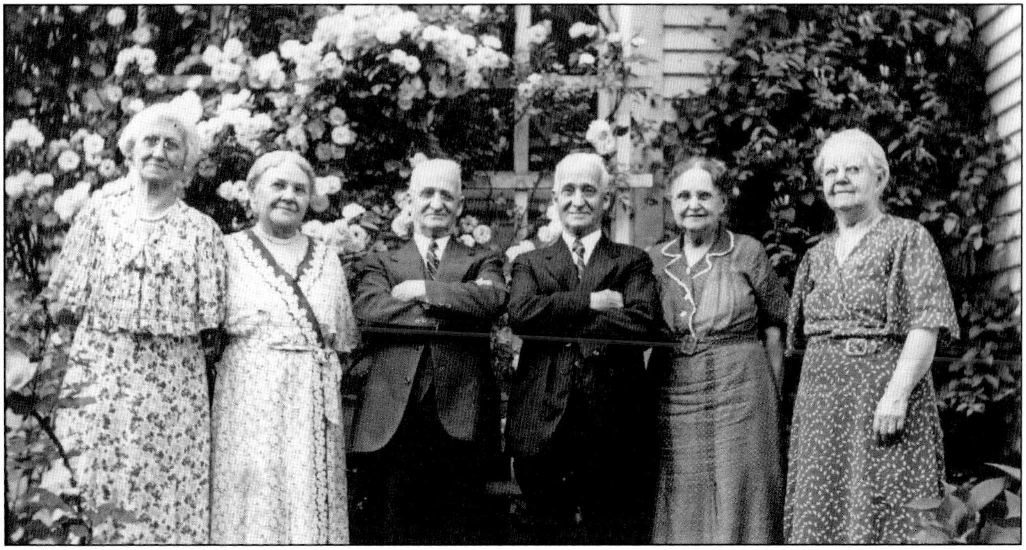

A surprise birthday party was held June 18, 1938, celebrating the 80th birthdays of twins Jerome and Joseph Wood. Jerome was minister of the Pittsford Methodist Church for many years. He and his wife, Grace, lived at 11 Washington Avenue. Shown are, from left to right, Jessie Coe Rogers; Joseph's wife, Stella Wood; Joseph Wood; Jerome Wood; Grace Wood; and Grace's sister Mary Sampson. (Courtesy of Wenda Tompkins Silco.)

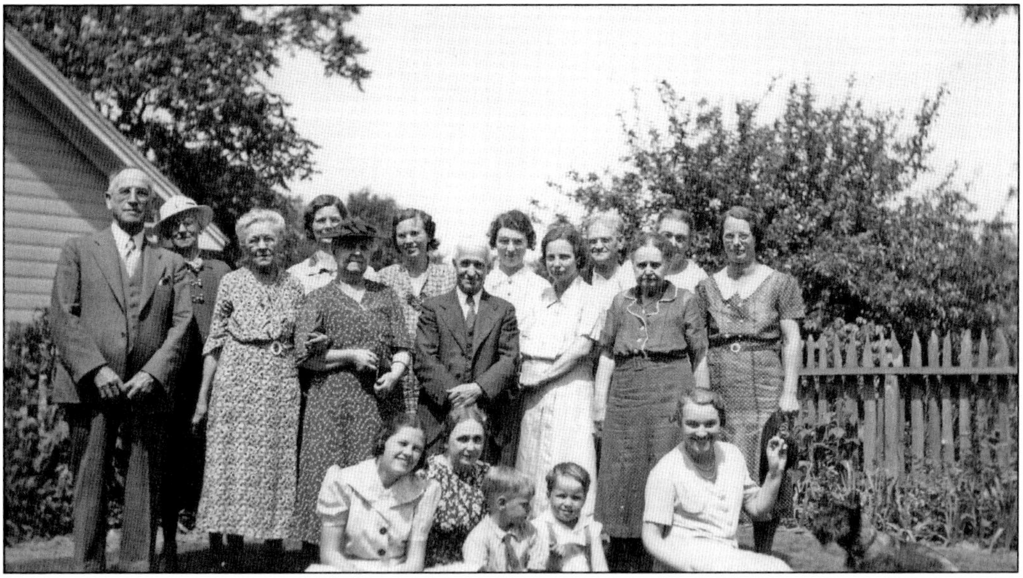

Hester Michael, wife of Oak Hill Country Club superintendent Elmer Michael, hosted a Methodist picnic at her home at 12 Eastview Terrace on June 1, 1938. Identified in the photograph are Dr. L. Lincoln Rogers, extreme left; Jessie Coe Rogers, back row left; Mary Sampson, second row with dark hat; Rev. Jerome Wood, standing center; and Grace Wood, standing second from right middle row. (Courtesy of Wenda Tompkins Silco.)

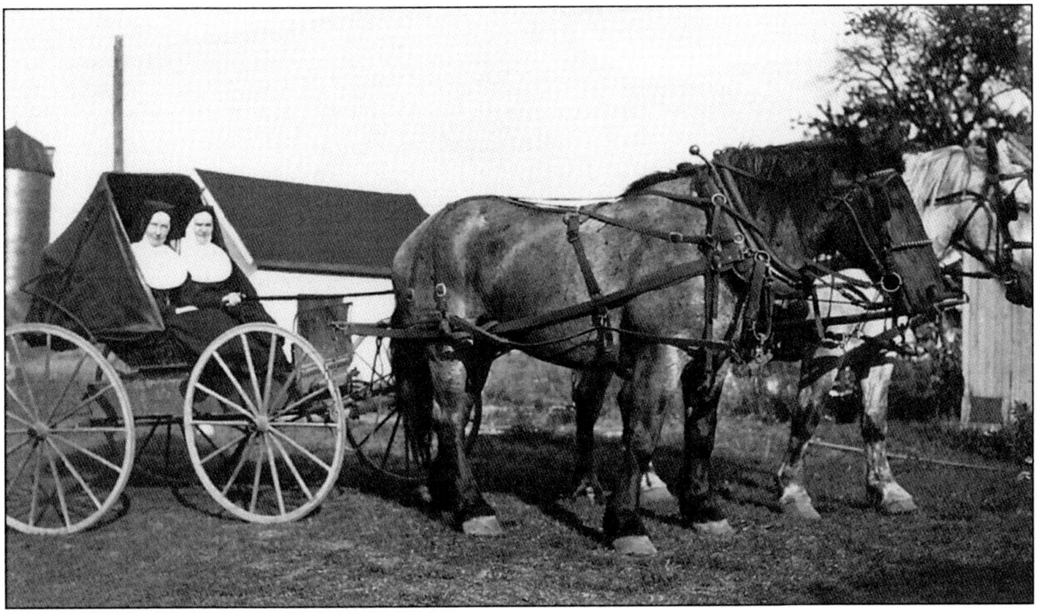

These photographs were taken in the 1930s on the farm owned by the Sisters of St. Joseph (SSJ), located off French Road on the back part of their original property. When the sisters constructed and moved to their East Avenue motherhouse in 1928, the property included a working farm that the congregation operated through the early 1960s. The sisters raised cows, pigs, and chickens and grew crops such as wheat, oats, barley, potatoes, cabbage, turnips, squash, corn, and carrots. Some of the produce was harvested for daily meals at the motherhouse; some was sold to area merchants. The sisters hired a caretaker and other workers for the farm, but they did some chores themselves and were responsible for oversight of the farm's operation. The new SSJ Motherhouse, built in 2002, is located on the site of the farm. (Both, courtesy of the Archives of the Sisters of St. Joseph of Rochester.)

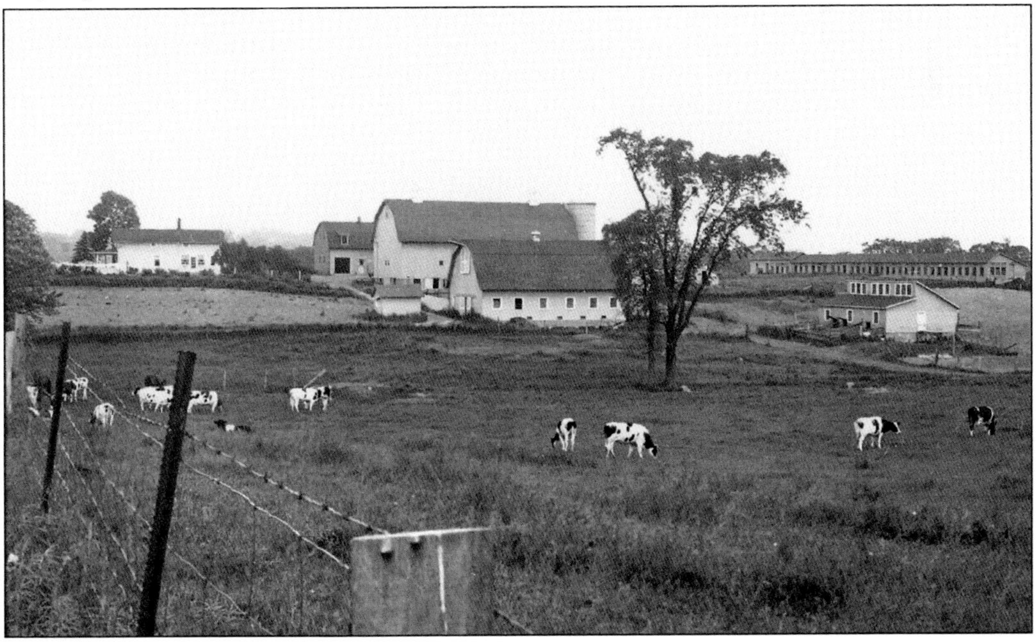

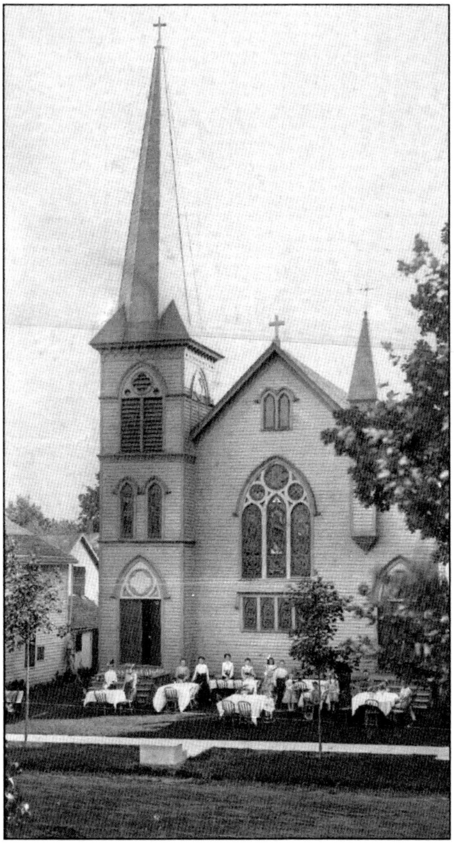

The cornerstone for St. Louis Catholic Church, at that time located on the south side of State Street centered between Main and South Streets, was laid in 1884. The parishioners met here for Masses through 1966, when the church sold the building and moved to their new structure at 64 South Main Street. This building was razed in 1968. (Courtesy of Paul M. Spiegel.)

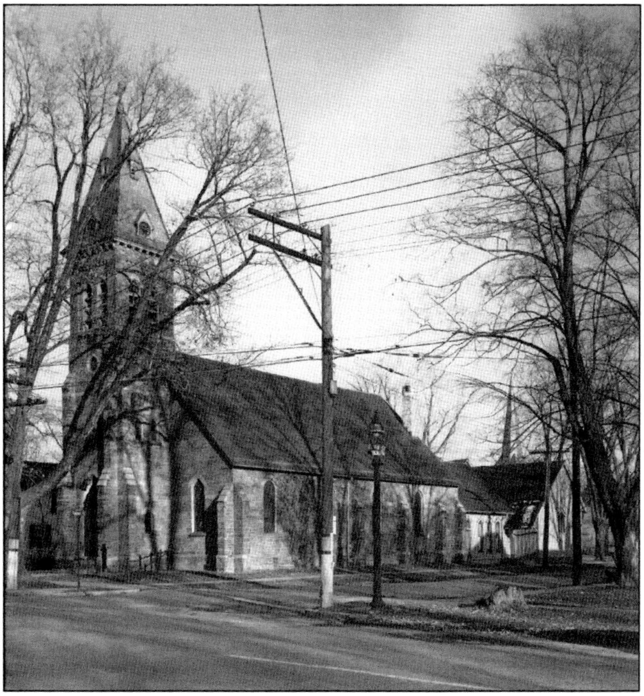

Christ Episcopal Church, now located at 36 South Main Street, was founded in 1846. The congregation originally met at 23 South Main Street, the current Hicks & McCarthy building, before laying the cornerstone for the current structure in 1868. Noted architect A.J. Warner designed the Gothic Revival–style building of Medina sandstone. The square tower features a four-faced Seth Thomas clock, donated by the Hargous family. (Courtesy of Paul M. Spiegel.)

The original building of the First Presbyterian Church of Pittsford, located at this site on 25 Church Street, was built about 1826. That building was struck by lightning and burned to the ground, and the current structure, the only example of Romanesque Revival design in Pittsford village, was built in 1861. The church was again struck by lightning in 2004, but the building was saved and has been beautifully restored. (Courtesy of Vicki Masters Profitt.)

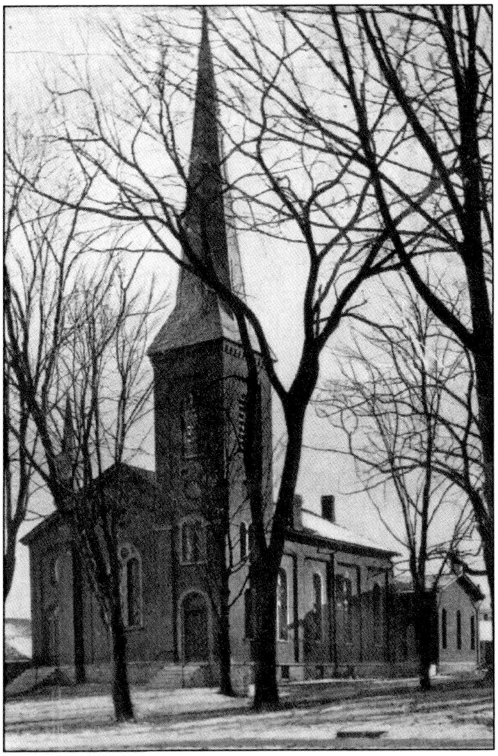

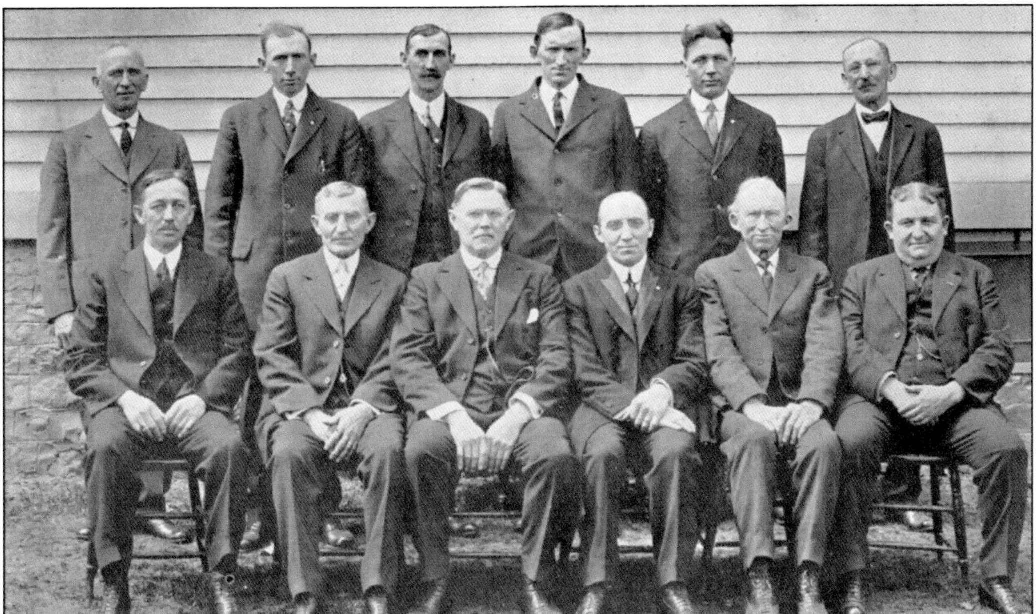

The St. Paul's Church Council had its photograph taken in honor of the church's golden jubilee in 1917. Pictured from left to right are (sitting) Charles Siegel, Charles Schreib, John Steve, Rev. J.C. Krahmer, Charles Grube, and Louis Forman; (standing) Fred Zornow, Daniel Bahringer, George Schoen, Edward Buholtz, George Bluhm, and Charles Ernst. (Courtesy of St. Paul's Evangelical Lutheran Church.)

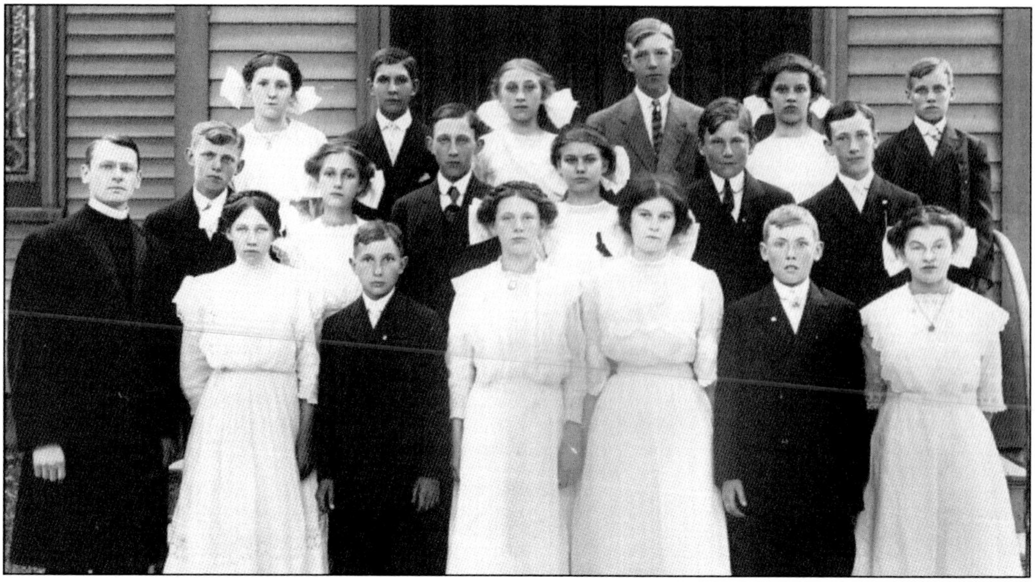

The St. Paul's confirmation class of 1912 stands in front of the church. Pictured are, from left to right, (first row) Rev. Herman Miller, Maude Sackett, Roy Guest, Mildred Holfoth, Ida Ross, Howard Moss, and Mabel Schoen; (second row) ? Koester, Mildred Siegel, Ray Sackett, Bertha Koester, Frank Frohm, and unidentified; (third row) Etta Lehman, unidentified, Elizabeth Steffenhagen, Nelson Ludwig, Mary Koester, and ? Koester. (Courtesy of St. Paul's Evangelical Lutheran Church.)

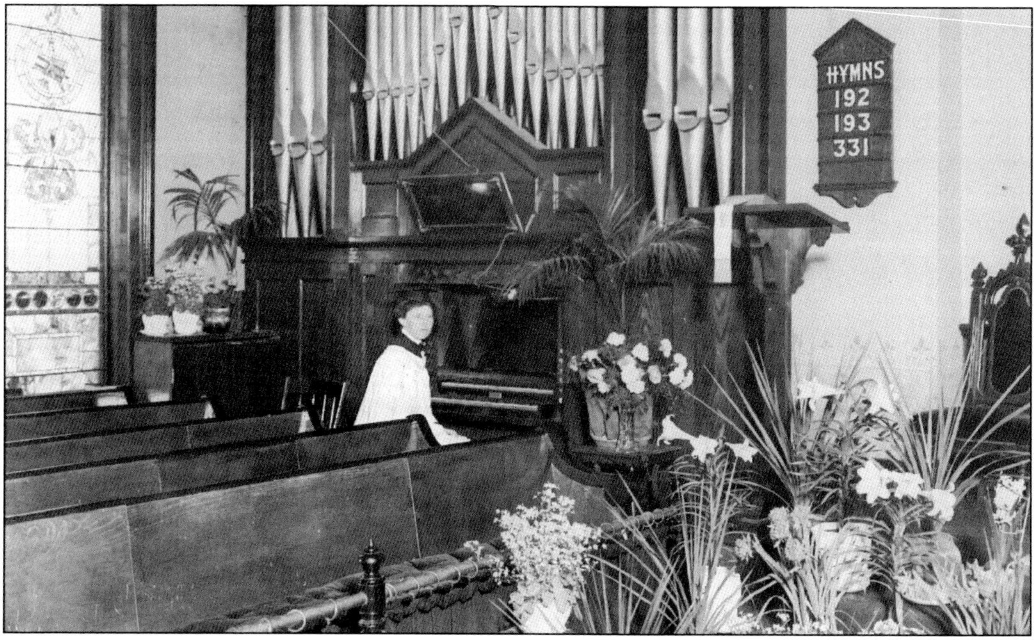

In 1940, Charlotte Steve Snyder celebrated her 40th anniversary as organist for St. Paul's Evangelical Lutheran Church. As a child, Charlotte studied the pump organ with Mina Gomph Utz, and then became the regular church organist on April 22, 1900. As the years went on, Charlotte learned to play the electrified console organ. She is shown here in the early days of her service. (Courtesy of St. Paul's Evangelical Lutheran Church.)

Three

ARCHITECTURE

The town of Pittsford was settled primarily by New England transplants. Therefore, it would be expected that the homes would show that New England influence. Steep roofs, wooden steps, gables, and small paned windows were prevalent.

An early settler named Elihu Doud established a brickyard on his property near the Milepost by District No. 1 school and the Pioneer Burying Ground. Bricks from that yard were used to build homes for the more affluent members of the community. Many of those homes showed the influence of Greek Revival style.

Doud's bricks were used in some of the larger commercial buildings also. The large Federal-style building known as the Phoenix Building was built using his bricks, as well as the large home now owned by the St. Louis Church. Those bricks are arranged in a diamond-shaped pattern.

There is also another style named by an architectural historian as the "Pittsford style." There were four or five of those homes in the village. The style is characterized by four chimneys on the roof of a square building with a one-story ell on the side. The main entrance is on one side of the front and beside two windows. There are three large windows across the front of the second floor, and an elliptical fanlight on the gable ends. Some of those have been remodeled and chimneys removed.

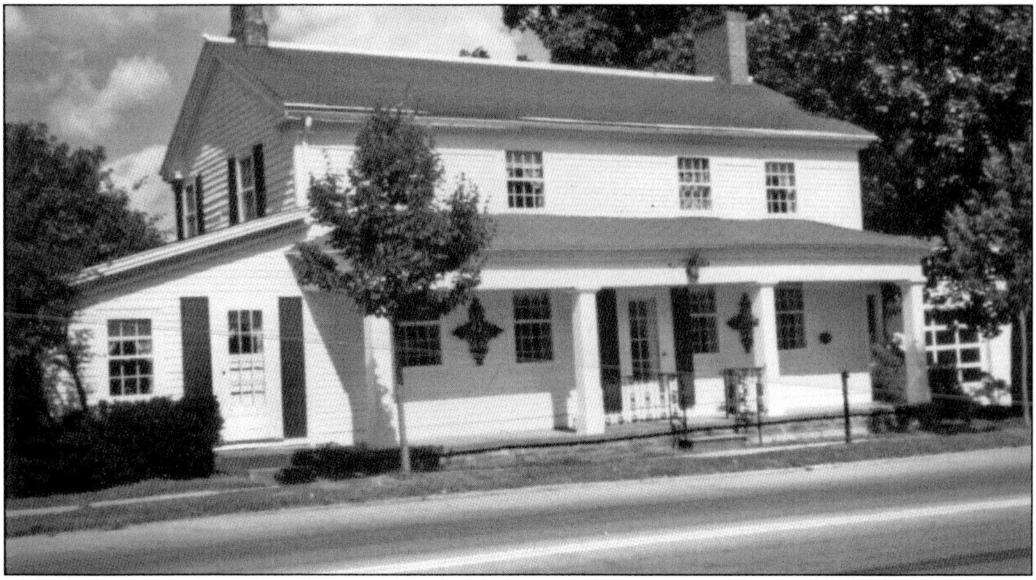

Pittsford's founding father Israel Stone erected a log cabin in 1789 at today's 38 State Street, which was the first structure built in the village. The present wood-frame building located on this site was built in the mid-1840s for Thomas Plumb. Later, the house was sold to the Newcomb family and remained in the family many years. The building now houses Duncan Studio. (Courtesy of the Pittsford Town Historian.)

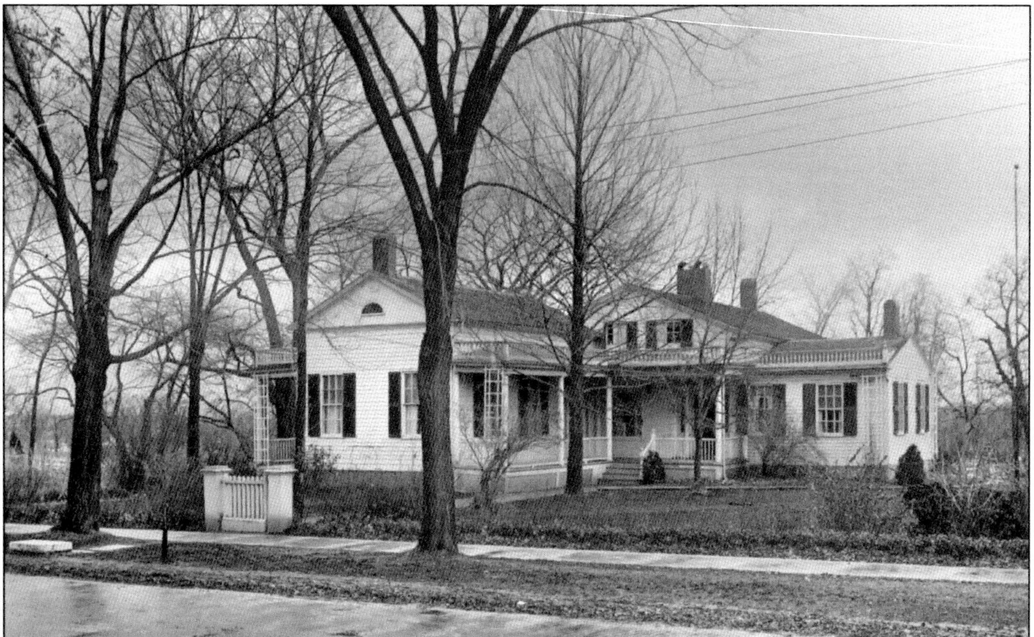

The earliest part of this Federal-style home was built around 1815. Located at 20 Monroe Avenue, the structure is now known as the Potter-Steele-Bolger house. An early owner of the house, businessman Henry S. Potter later sold it to John M. Steele. The house remained in the Steele family for nearly a century. Renowned landscape architect Fletcher Steele, John's grandson, owned the home until his death in 1971. (Courtesy of the Perinton Historical Society, Karl Jost Collection.)

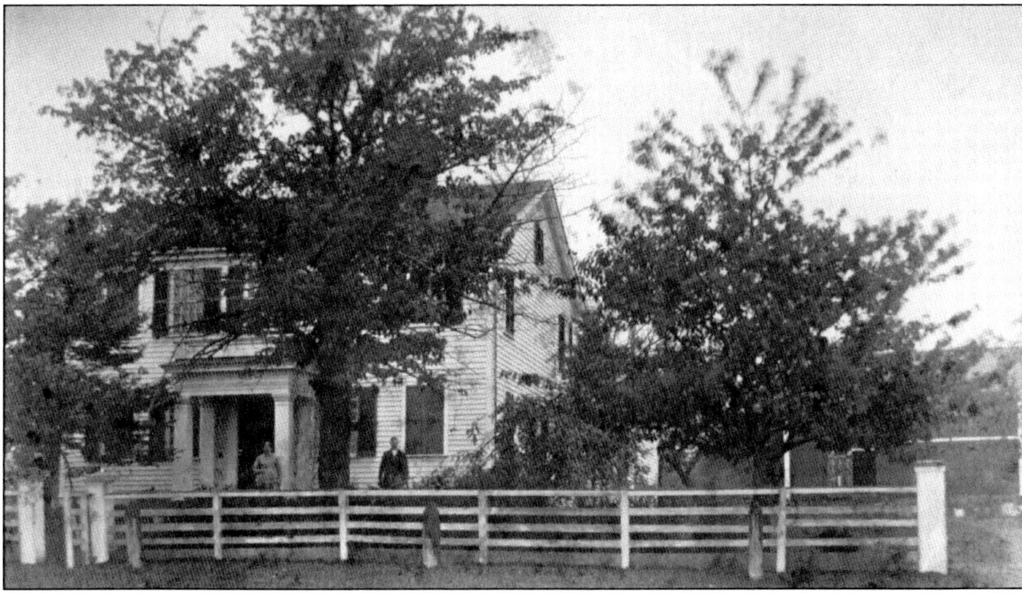

Caleb Hopkins built the Hopkins homestead, located at 3151 Clover Street, about 1816. Featuring a gable roof and a hewn-timber frame, the house was constructed in a variation of the Federal style. The house is situated on the original 150 acres purchased by Caleb Hopkins in 1813. Additional land and buildings were purchased in later years. In 2000, the Hopkins farm and homestead was listed in the National Register of Historic Places. (Courtesy of Mark Greene and John Hopkins.)

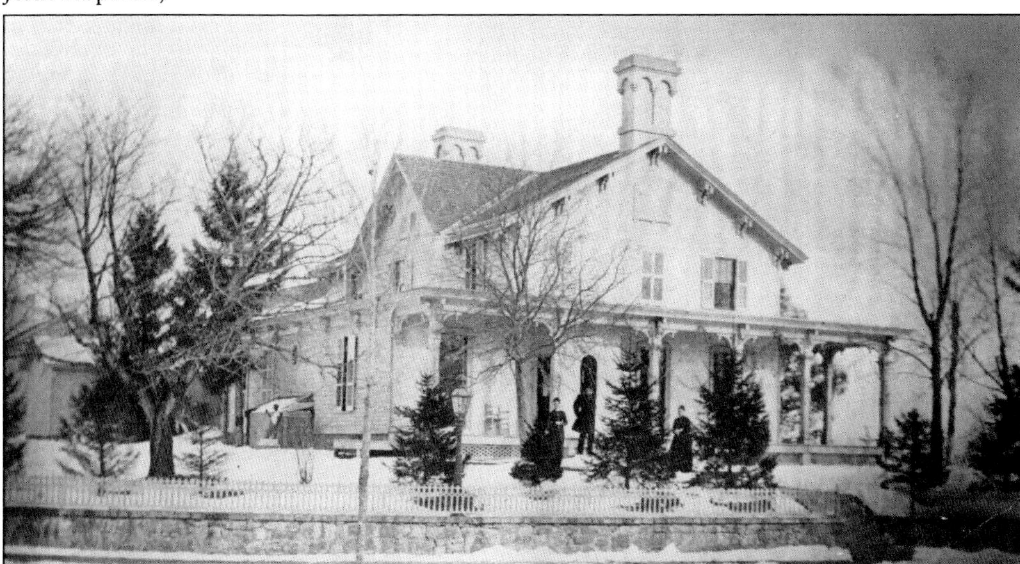

Entrepreneur Samuel Hildreth built this house at 44 North Main Street around 1820. Originally designed in the Federal style, the house has evolved into an Italianate style. Jarvis Lord, a member of the New York State Assembly and Senate, owned the house from the 1860s until his death in 1887. The house was then sold to Frank Hawley and ultimately to the Zornow family. The Corby family, proprietors of the adjoining Pittsford Farms Dairy, owns the home today. (Courtesy of the Pittsford Town Historian.)

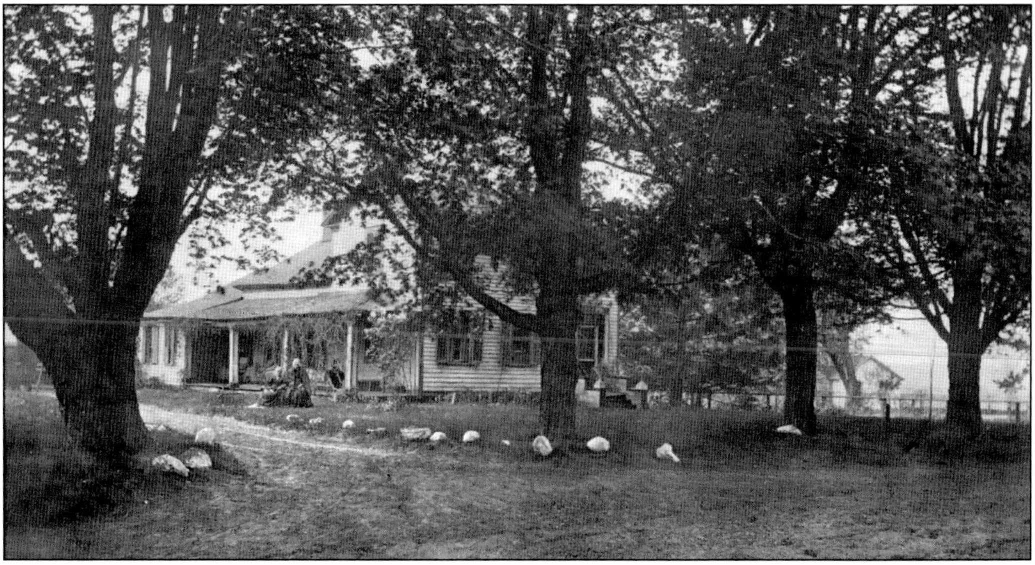

The Shepard-Light homestead was located on the west side of East Avenue, approximately between today's Kilbourn Road and Ellingwood Drive. Established by Sylvester and Matilda Palmer Shepard in the 1820s, the homestead remained in the family for over 100 years. Their daughter Mary Helen Shepard lived in the house after her marriage to Harvey E. Light in 1861. Mary Helen is shown, sitting at left, in the above photograph. The woman beside her is unidentified, but may be her elder sister Catherine Shepard Hinds. Frances Light, daughter of Arthur and Maude Merritt Light and granddaughter of Mary Helen and Harvey, was born here in 1903. The photograph below, taken later, shows a remodel that included a wraparound porch. The four women and one boy are unidentified. After Harvey's death in 1921, 77 acres of the Shepard-Light homestead remained. The house was razed, and the acreage was sold to make way for Oak Hill Country Club and the new subdivisions along East Avenue. (Both, courtesy of Glenn Berggren.)

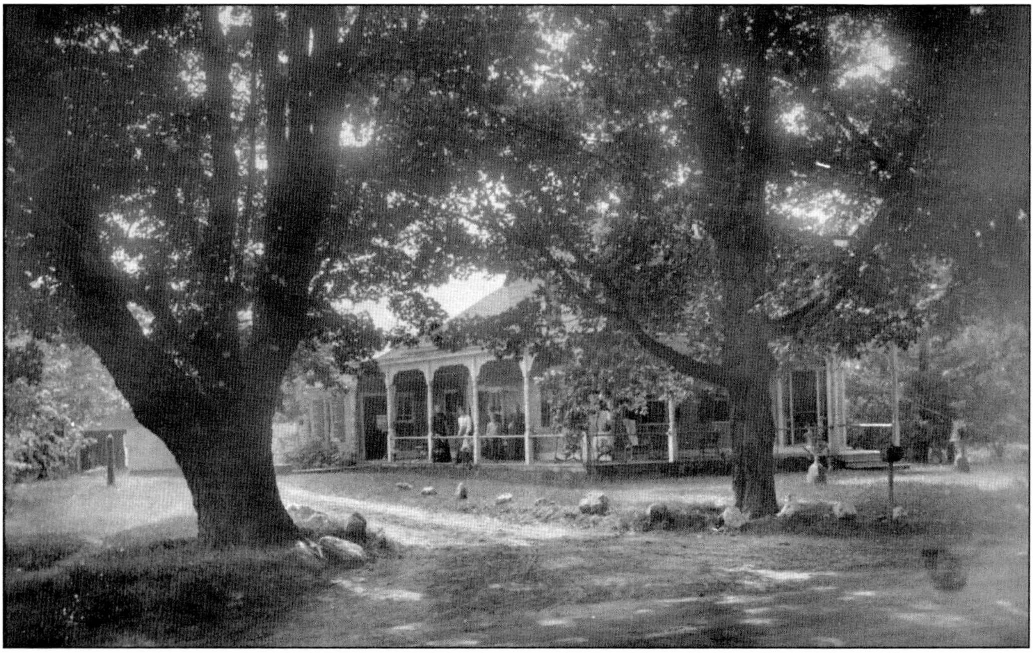

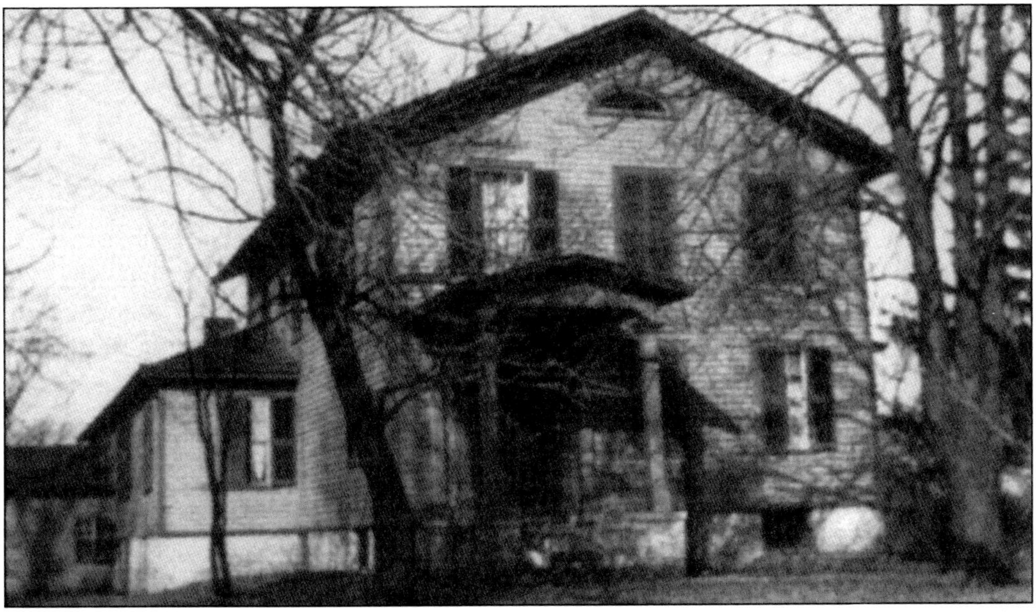

The house at 42 Monroe Avenue was built in the early 1820s for David Sutherland on land ceded to him by Glover Perrin. Several generations of Sutherlands occupied the house for nearly a century before it was sold. The property was also gradually sold off, some of which became Sutherland Street. The deep lot backs to the Erie Canal. (Courtesy of Charles Lenhart.)

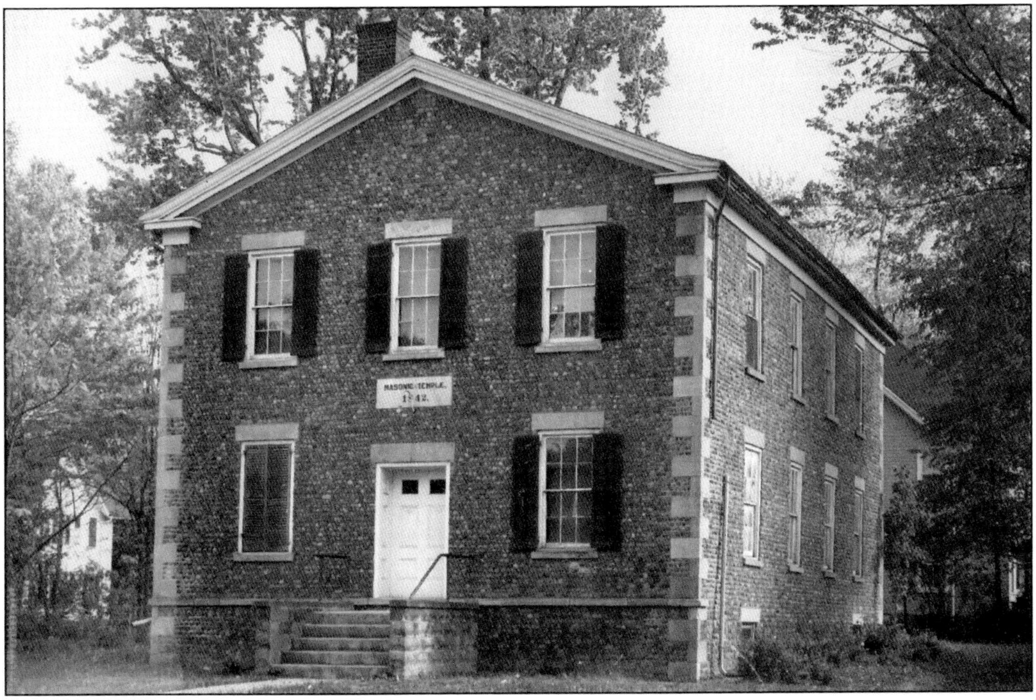

Samuel Crump constructed this cobblestone structure, located at 17 Church Street, in the 1840s for use as a school. The children of the village attended school in this District No. 6 schoolhouse until the 1890s, when the new school on Lincoln Avenue was built. The cobblestone building is now owned and maintained by the Northfield Masons F&M Lodge No. 426. (Courtesy of Paul M. Spiegel.)

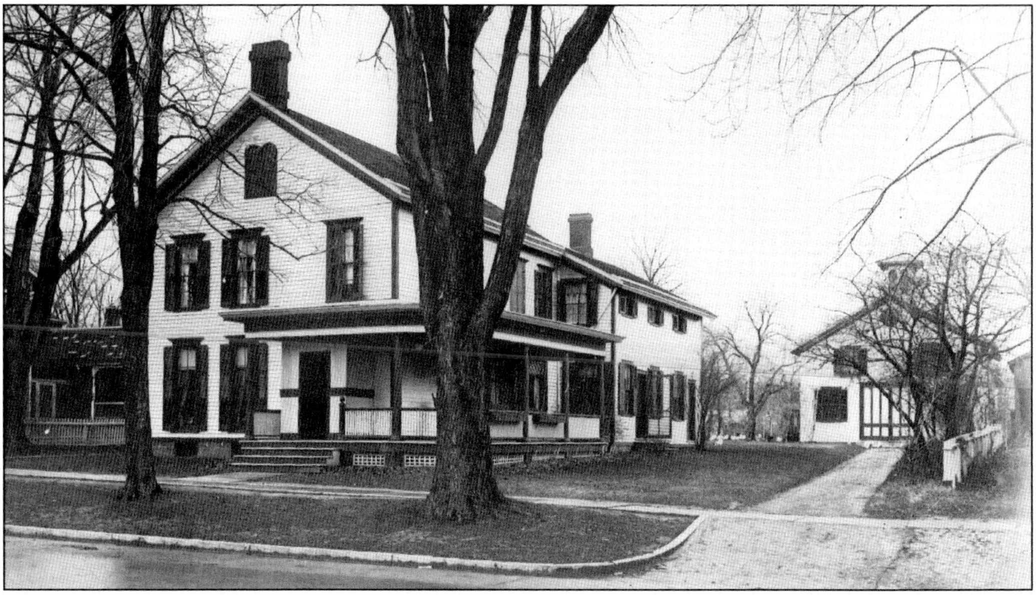

Now known as the Wadhams house, this building stands at 19 North Main Street. The original structure was built in the mid-1850s, although several people owned the land before that. James Martin Wiltsie, the proprietor of the Wiltsie & Crump store, purchased the house in 1869. After James's death in 1901, it was passed down to his daughter Mary Antoinette, wife of W. Grant Wadhams, and is now owned by the Pittsford Fire Department. (Courtesy of the Perinton Historical Society, Karl Jost Collection.)

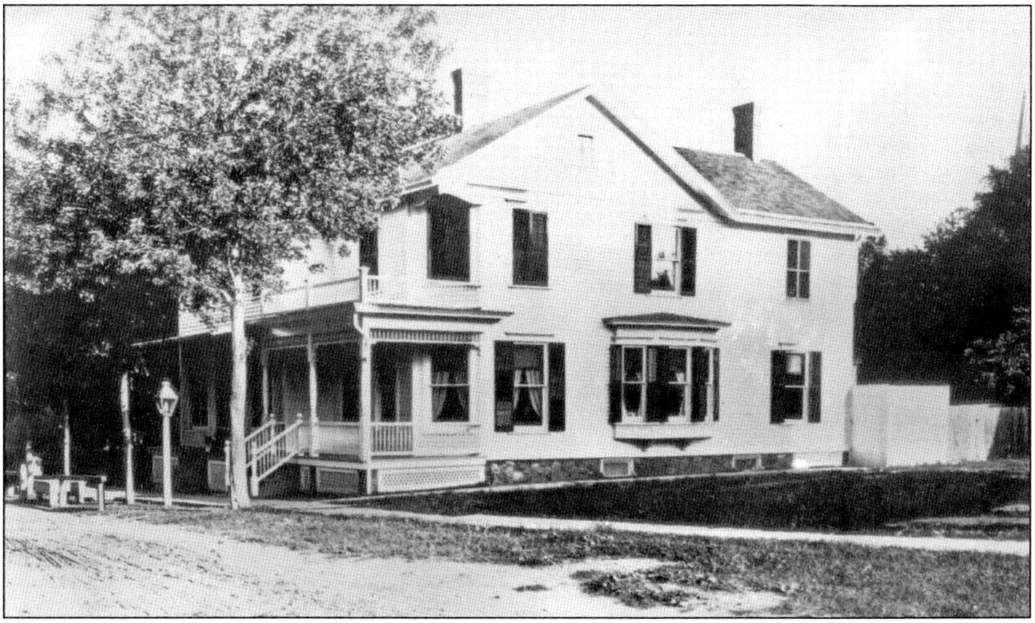

Isidor Harscher was born in Germany in 1837. At 20, he immigrated to America and set up business in Pittsford as a harness maker. The shop was based out of his home on State Street, not far from the Phoenix Building. Isidor and his wife, Carolina Weishar, had four children, Amelia, Alfred, Edward, and Charles. Edward worked as a harness maker alongside his father. The house was razed. (Courtesy of the Pittsford Town Historian.)

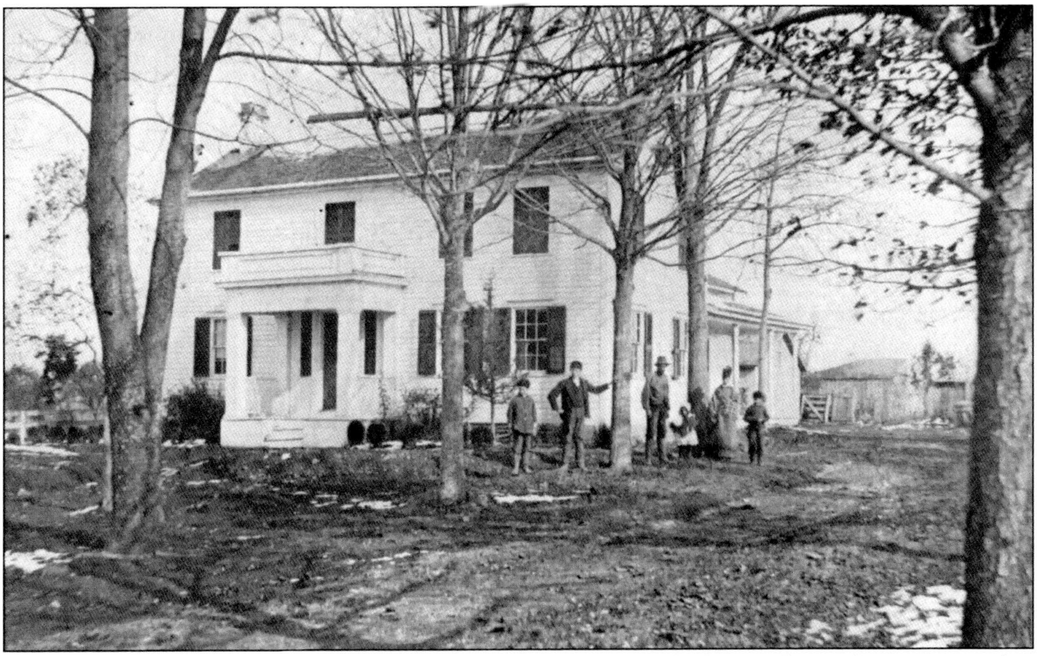

The Pugsley-Goodenough house is shown here about 1877. The house, located at 648 Mendon Road, was the home of James and Matilda Mann Pugsley and their four sons, Torrence, Orville, Frank, and Floyd, for over 30 years. Later, Swayne and Ruth Thompson Goodenough raised their three daughters in the house. (Courtesy of Bob Place.)

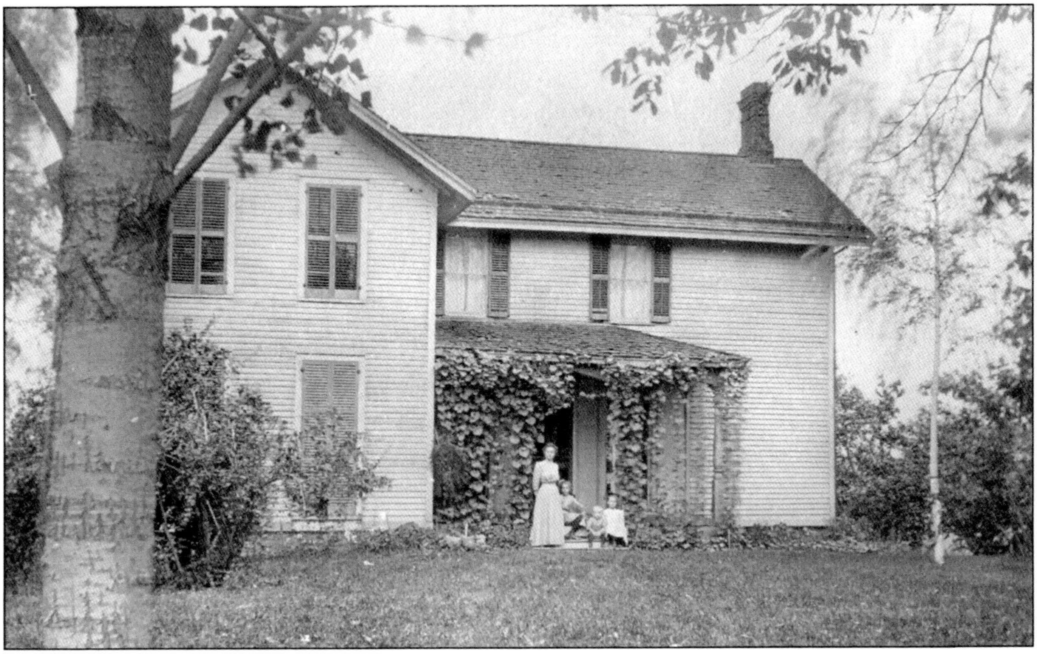

Nathan Elmer Welch, born in 1871, was the son of Lyman and Alice Abbott Welch. His home on East Street still stands but has been extensively remodeled. Nathan married Mabel Hughes, and they had five children, Helen, Alice, Lillian, Lyman, and Leah. This photograph was taken on October 3, 1911. (Courtesy of the Pittsford Town Historian.)

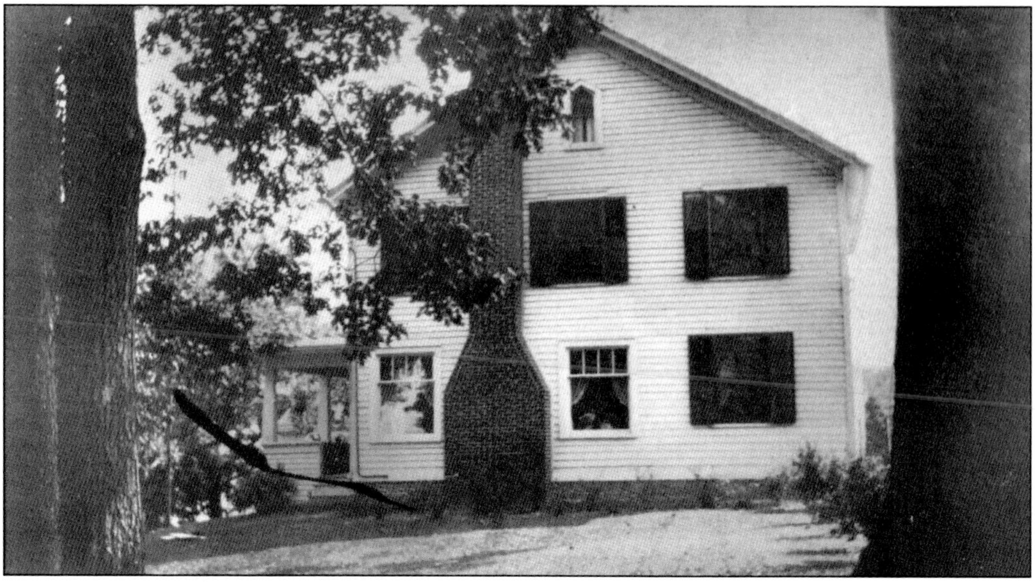

James M. Knickerbocker owned this home at 173 Knickerbocker Road for many years. The home and surrounding acreage have been in the family since the mid-1800s. (Courtesy of Mary Knickerbocker Menzie.)

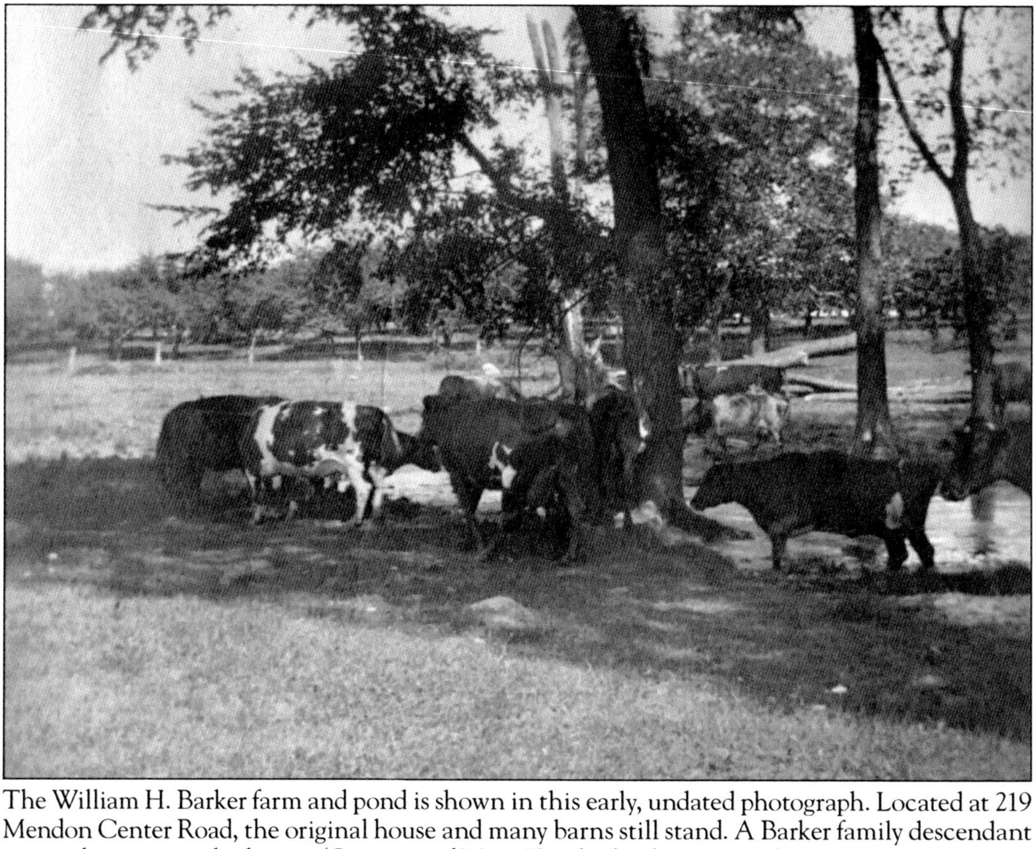

The William H. Barker farm and pond is shown in this early, undated photograph. Located at 219 Mendon Center Road, the original house and many barns still stand. A Barker family descendant currently occupies the home. (Courtesy of Mary Knickerbocker Menzie.)

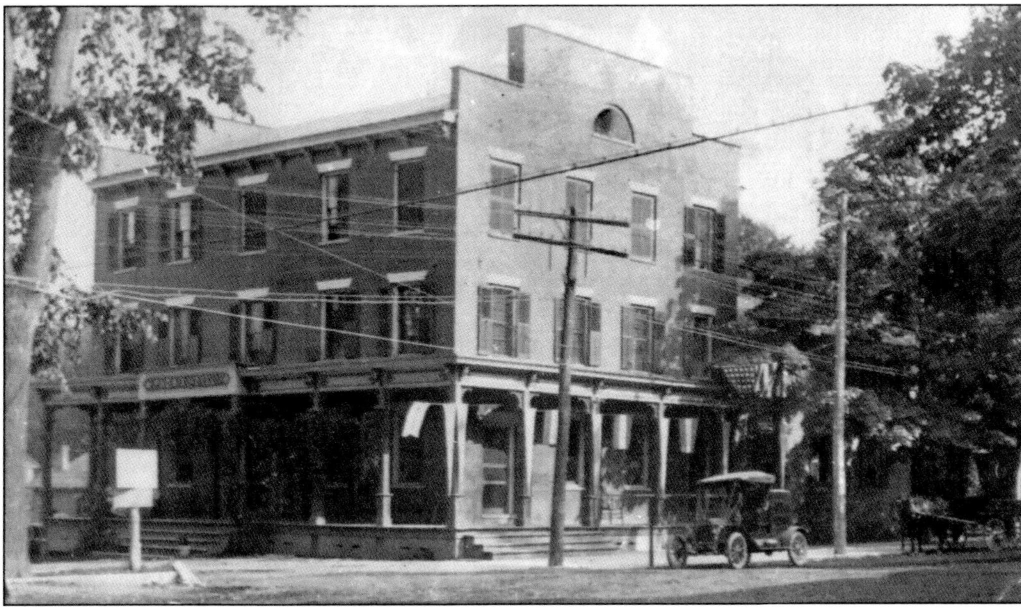

The Phoenix Building, located at 4 South Main Street, has been a mainstay at the four corners of Pittsford for nearly 200 years. In the first decade of the 19th century, Glover Perrin owned a frame building at this location that later burned. The current brick structure was built in the Federal style sometime between 1814 and 1824. For many years, the Phoenix was a tavern and an inn, a restaurant, and a newspaper office. Today, it houses Mitchell Pierson Realtors. (Courtesy of Bill Lusk.)

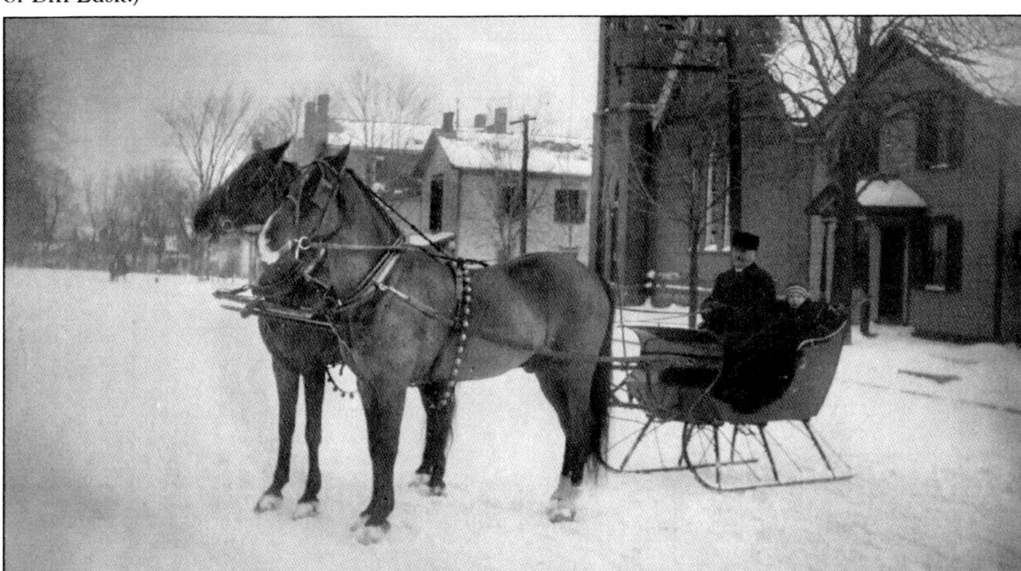

In a photograph taken about 1902, James M. Knickerbocker takes his team, Jim and Gussie, and his grandson H. Harlan Knickerbocker for a drive on South Main Street. The Methodist church is visible, center right. James was known to race his team on Saturday afternoons in the village, starting at Jefferson Road and heading up Main Street to the canal. The photographer was Lillian Hartman, the first licensed woman pharmacist in New York State. (Courtesy of Mary Knickerbocker Menzie.)

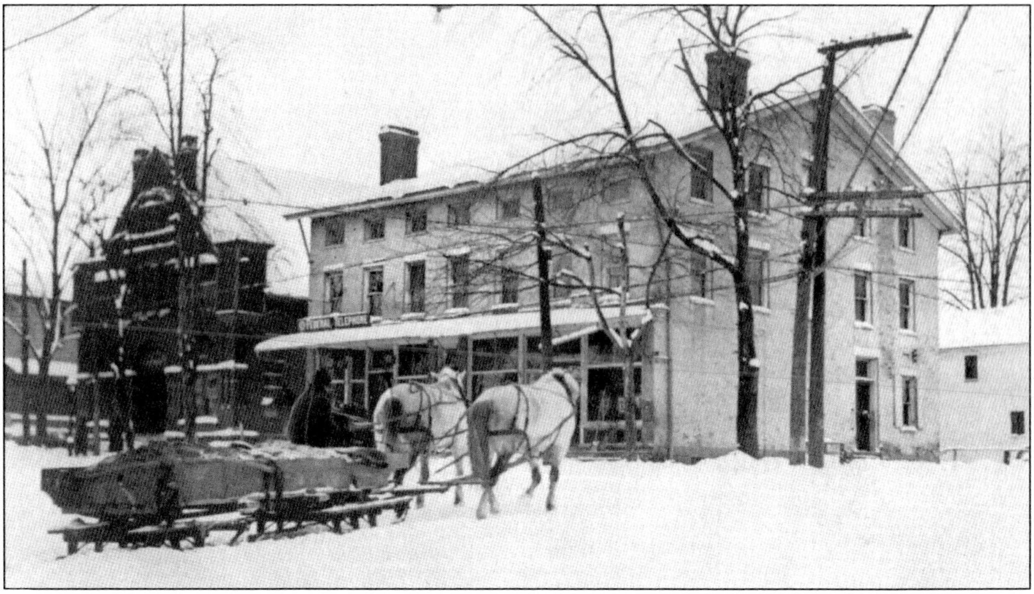

This beautiful winter scene features the town hall and the Parker Building at the corner of Monroe Avenue and South Main Street. A sign for Federal Telephone is clearly visible in the location, which, until recently, was occupied by Ben & Jerry's. The brick structure now housing Sissy's Country Gallery had not yet been built between the town hall and the Parker Building. (Courtesy of Bill Lusk.)

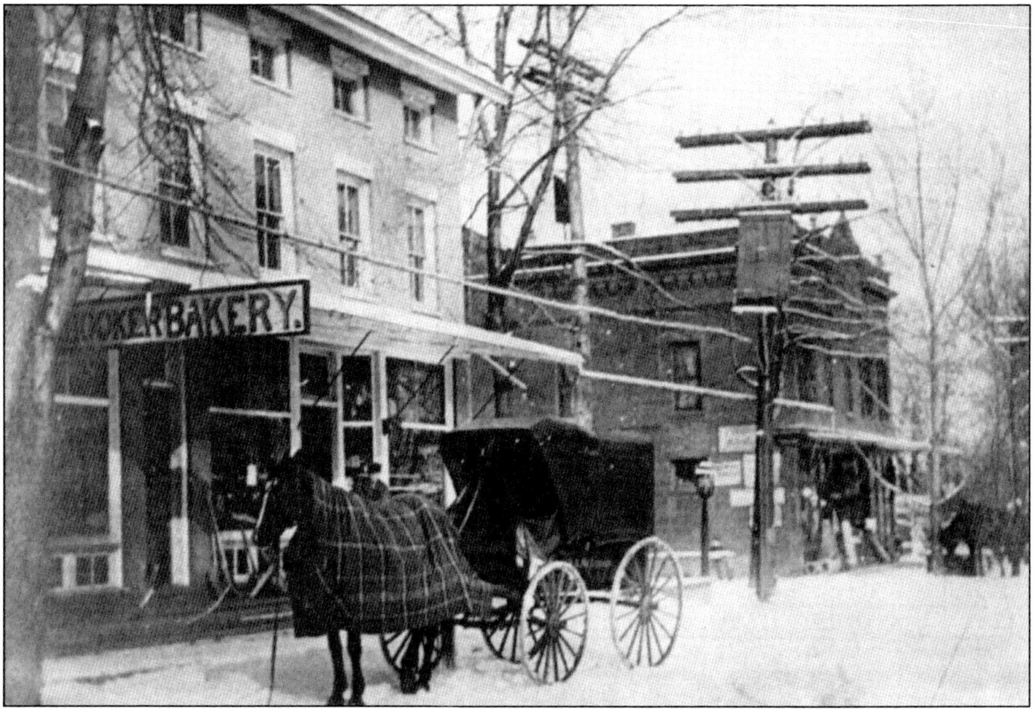

Another wintry scene, taken around 1902, shows a well-clad horse waiting patiently for its owner, who appears to have stepped inside the Hooker Bakery for some treats. The Wiltsie Building is to the right, looking much as it does today. (Courtesy of Paul M. Spiegel.)

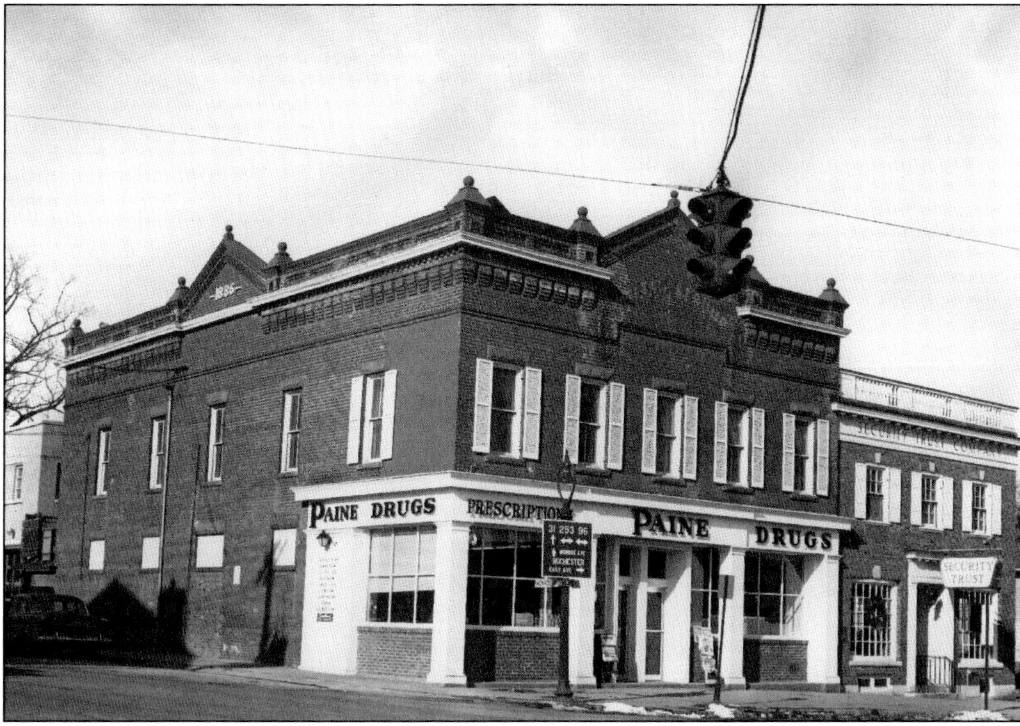

The Wiltsie & Crump Building has been in its present form since 1886. Slight changes through the years have been made with awnings and covered porches, but the building itself is always recognizable. The building, at 1 North Main Street, has housed a pharmacy and a delicatessen, but in recent years, Embrasse Moi lingerie and James Salerno jewelers have called it home. (Courtesy of Paul M. Spiegel.)

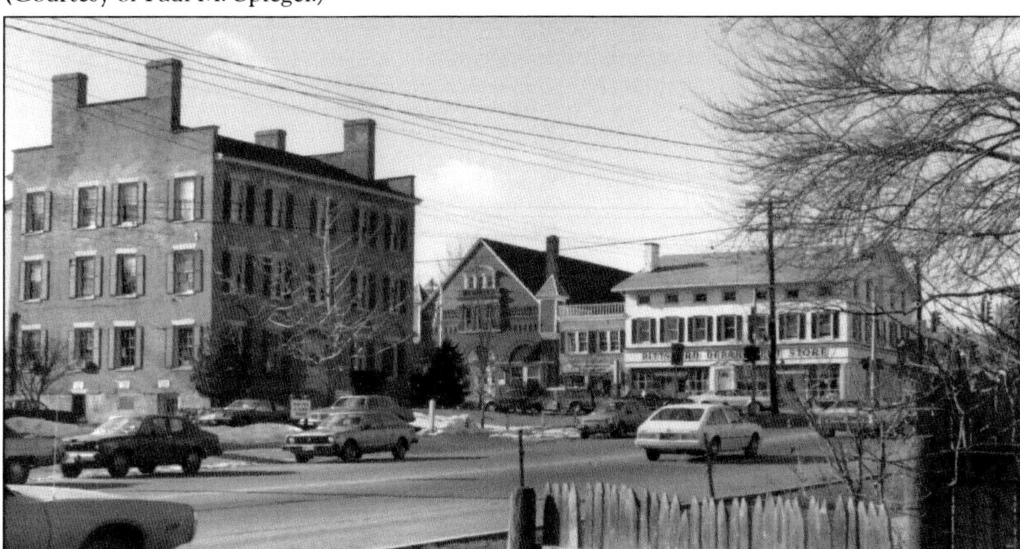

The Phoenix Building, town hall, and Parker Building stand proud in this unique view of the four corners looking southwest from Copper Beech Park on State Street. (Courtesy of the Pittsford Town Historian.)

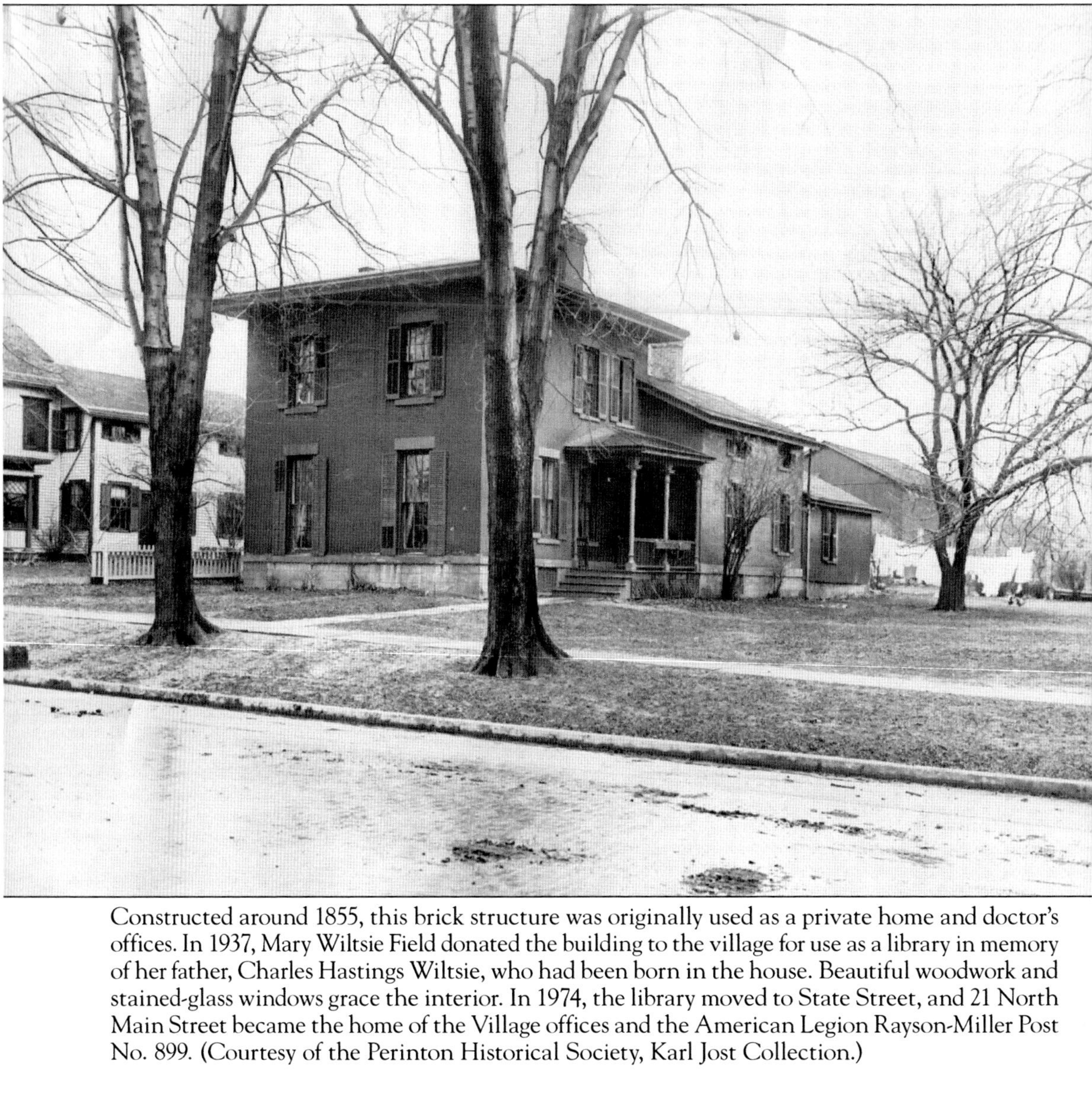

Constructed around 1855, this brick structure was originally used as a private home and doctor's offices. In 1937, Mary Wiltsie Field donated the building to the village for use as a library in memory of her father, Charles Hastings Wiltsie, who had been born in the house. Beautiful woodwork and stained-glass windows grace the interior. In 1974, the library moved to State Street, and 21 North Main Street became the home of the Village offices and the American Legion Rayson-Miller Post No. 899. (Courtesy of the Perinton Historical Society, Karl Jost Collection.)

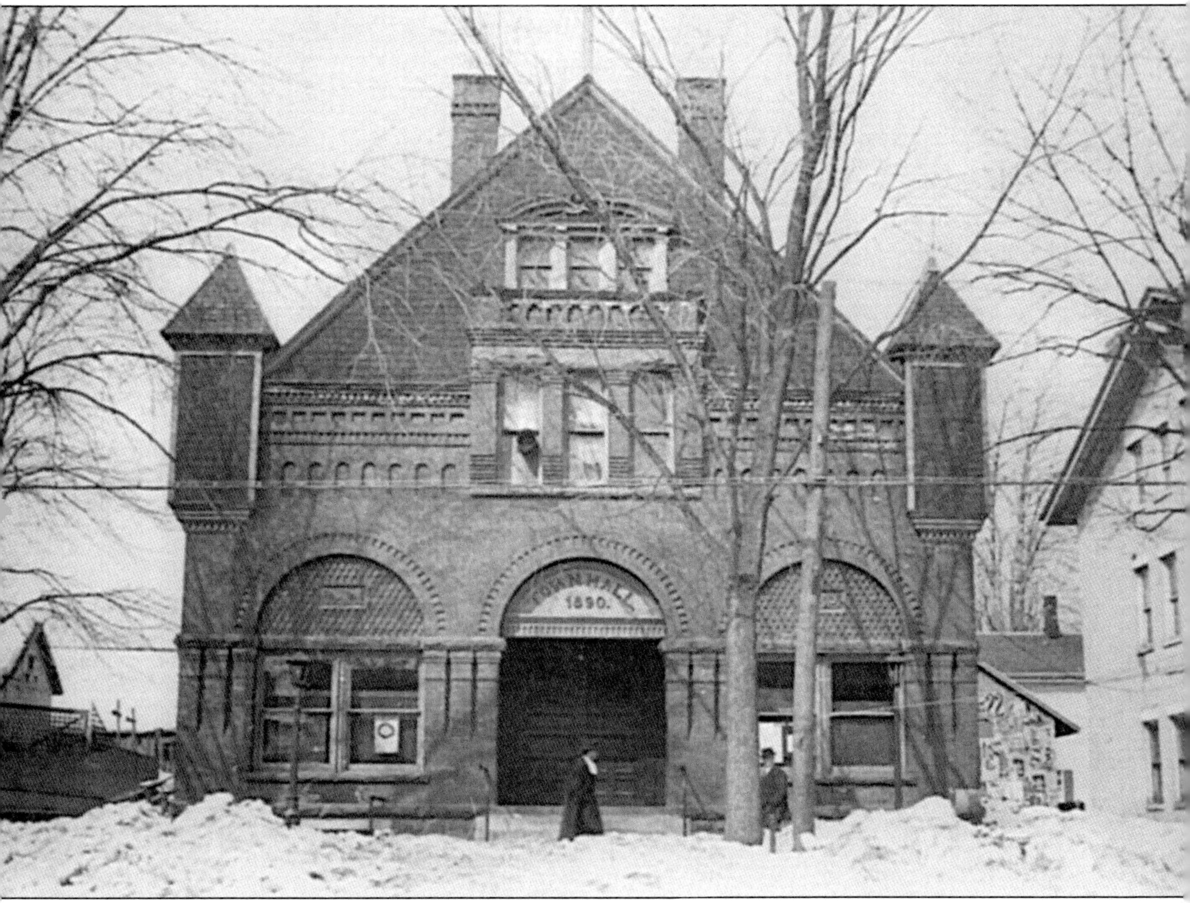

It is incredible to think that the town of Pittsford had been organized in 1796 but had no town hall building of its own until 1890. Before this brick and stone structure was built, the town meetings had been held in businesses and churches throughout the area. Once the site was located, Edward W. Gaskin and William Agate won the contract, and ground was broken at 11 South Main Street in June 1890. The Northfield Masons F&M Lodge No. 426 laid the cornerstone of the new building. The structure has been remodeled several times, each time adding more modern necessities and conveniences. (Courtesy of Paul M. Spiegel.)

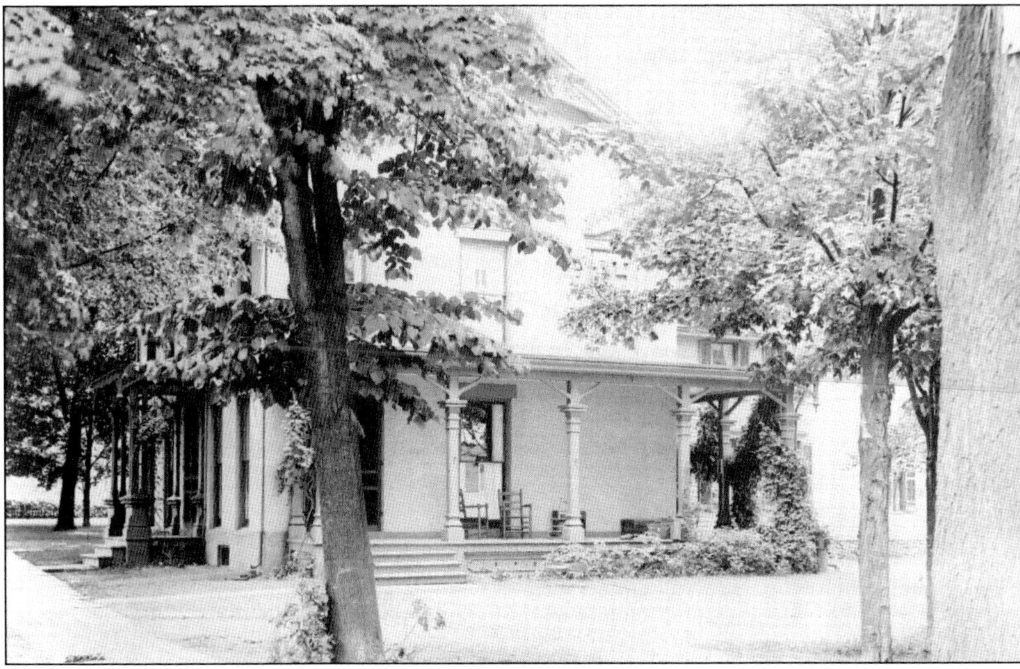

William Agate lost his business and his home to the enlargement of the canal in 1910. His house, which sat on North Main Street immediately south of the canal, was dismantled piece by piece. The above photograph shows the beginning stages of the demolition. As the work progressed, trees were cut down, and the work continued until the process was complete. William's brother John was more fortunate. The canal enlargement did not take his house, which sat beside William's and is now the Canal Lamp Inn. (Both, courtesy of Connie Wilson, Ralph Parker Collection.)

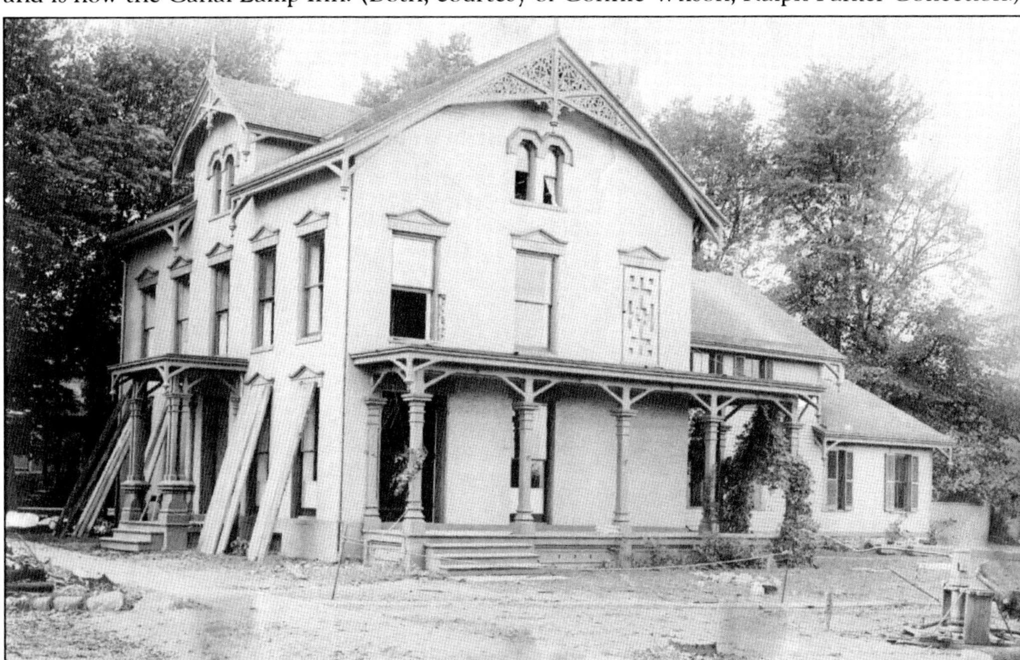

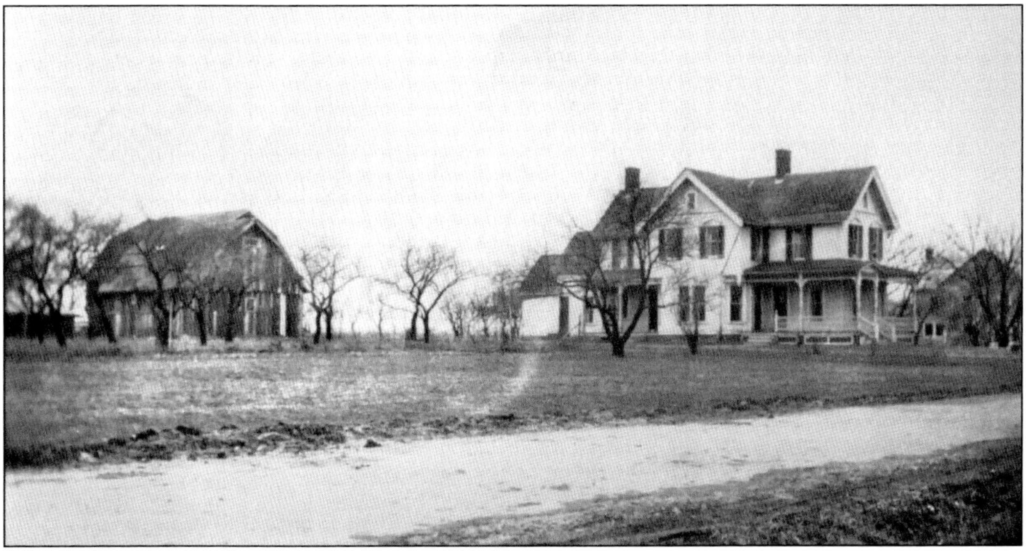

Earl W. Place purchased the Charles Zornow house, located at 149 West Jefferson Road, in the mid-1920s. At that point, West Jefferson was a dirt road, and Sunset Boulevard was not yet built. Earl lived in the house with his wife, Florence, and their three sons. The house remained in the family for the next 50 years. (Courtesy of Bob Place.)

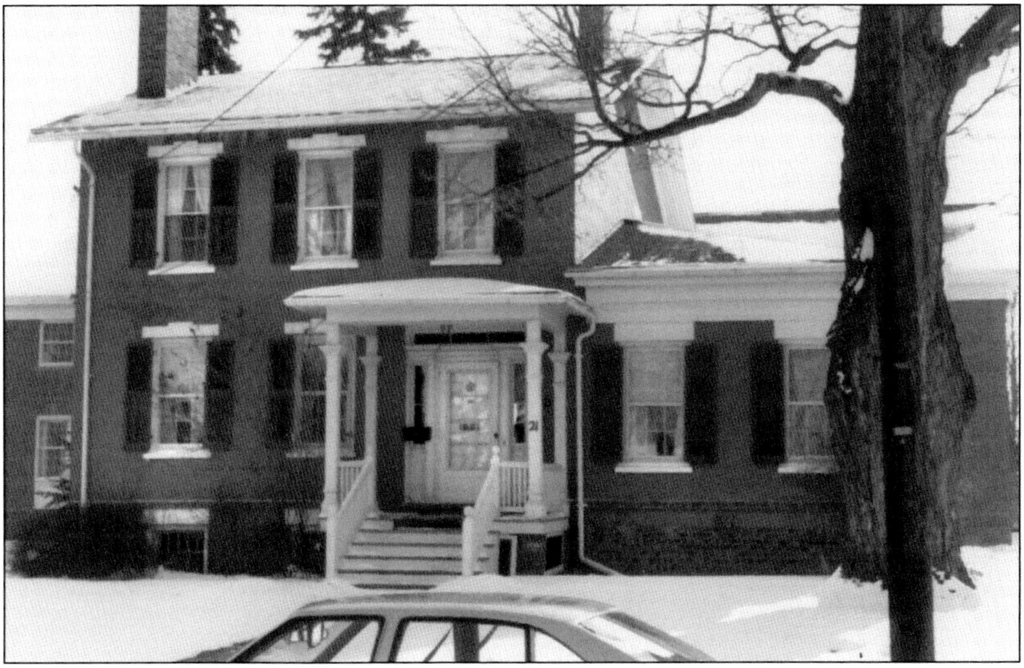

This beautiful brick structure, located at 21 Church Street, now houses the offices of the First Presbyterian Church of Pittsford. The building was constructed about 1816 for Dr. John Ray, Pittsford's first physician. It is the oldest example of Pittsford-style architecture, which is characterized by four chimneys and a main entryway set off to the side of center. The building served as a parsonage for many years in the 1800s until Robert Rand occupied it in the early 20th century. William H. Guetersloh owned the house from 1921 until his death in 1961. Shortly afterward, First Presbyterian purchased the house. (Courtesy of the Pittsford Town Historian.)

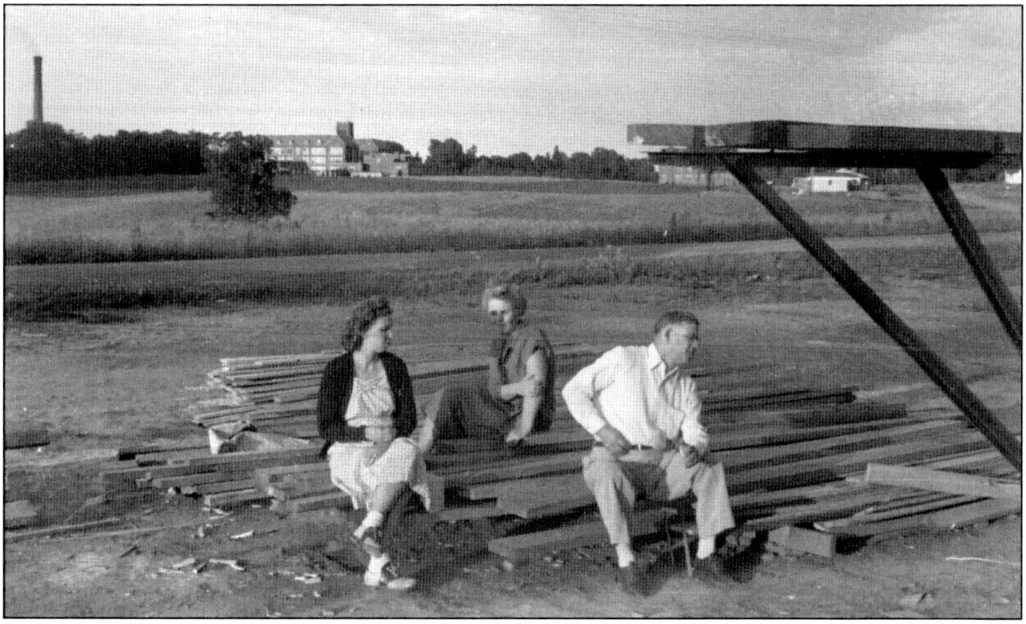

It is difficult to imagine French Road devoid of houses, but that was exactly what the landscape in the area looked like before 1949. Until then, Civil War veteran Marvin French's home at 60 French Road was the only house for quite a distance down the road. In 1949, Don and Jean Taylor began construction on what became 109 French Road. The Administration Building of Nazareth College is clearly visible in the distance. After the 1,400-square-foot Cape Cod was completed in the fall, the Taylors moved in and lived there 56 years before selling to the current owners. Jean Taylor is seated at left beside her sister. Don Taylor is to the right. (Both, courtesy of MaryBeth Andersen and Gordon Graham.)

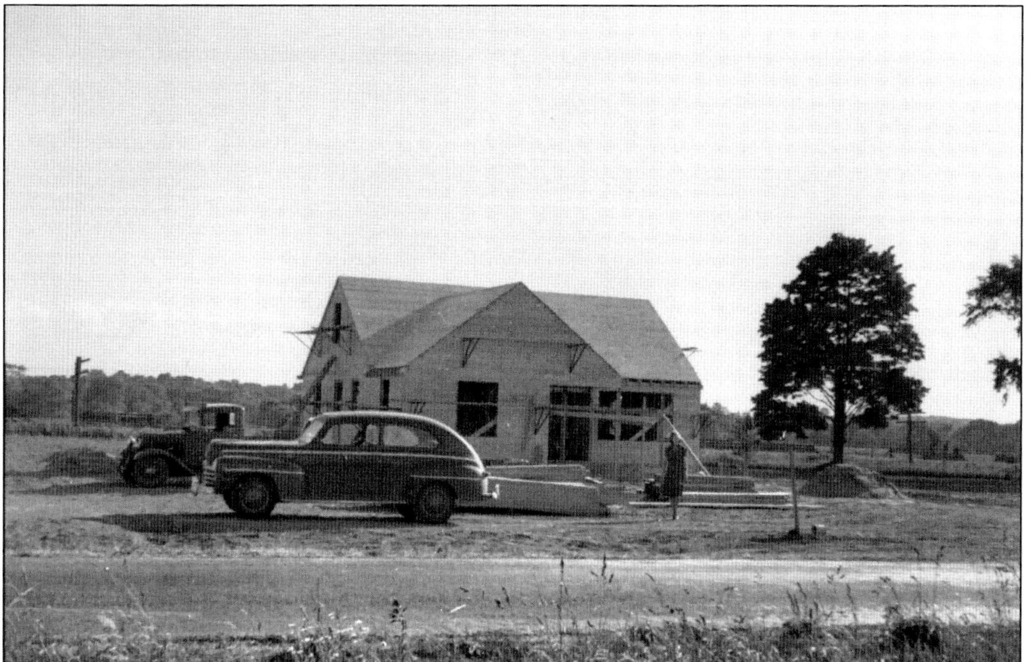

Four

COMMERCE AND AGRICULTURE

Pittsford was settled by farmers and established as an agrarian community. The land was very rich and produced excellent wheat used locally and shipped across the state and the country to be made into flour. At one time, Pittsford was called the "bread basket of the country." Mills were established here and in the neighboring city of Rochester, which, at one time, was known as the Flour City before it became touted as the Flower City.

As more settlers came to this western town, trades people were needed and stores and shops were established. Horses were the main means of transportation, and so of course, businesses that supported husbandry, like wagon shops and wheelwrights, sprouted. Later on, when the automobile became the popular mode of travel, trades that went hand in hand arose.

In 1822, the Erie Canal was completed through Pittsford and into Rochester. Industries changed, and barges could ship products manufactured here to other communities. The mill flourished; a pickle factory was born; goods from afar could be brought in to this community. Pittsford was busy. One of the farms, as well as producing crops and dairy products, was also known for its celebrated Shetland ponies. A racetrack for trotters was created by a wealthy landowner and brought many a horse fancier. Later in the 20th century, an airfield was created.

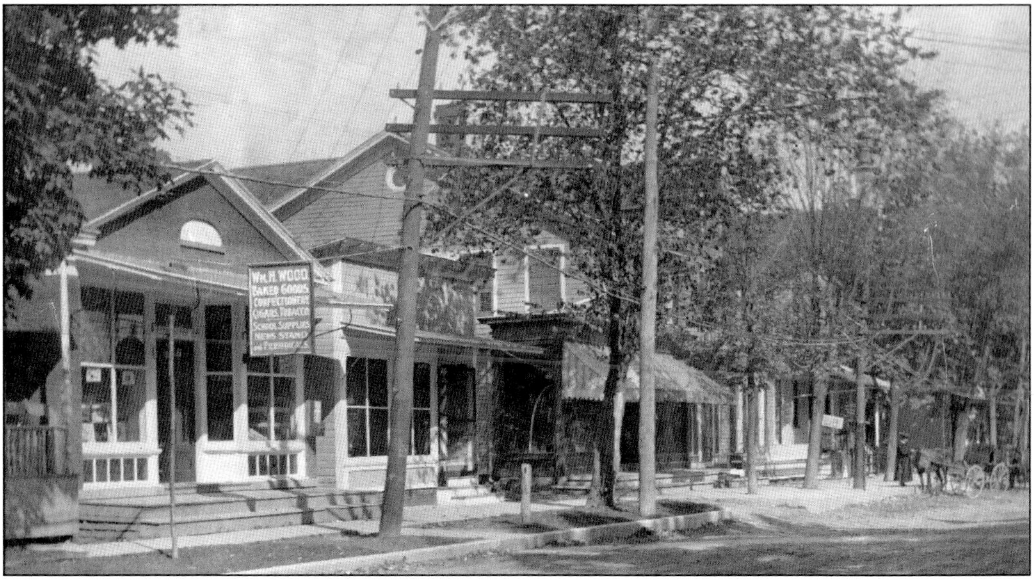

William H. Wood's confectionery was located at 23 South Main Street in the building that later became Hicks & McCarthy. By trade, William made paper boxes and moved often. Using census records, this photograph dates to about 1910, which was the only year in which William's trade was listed as "confectioner." (Courtesy of the John Bacon family.)

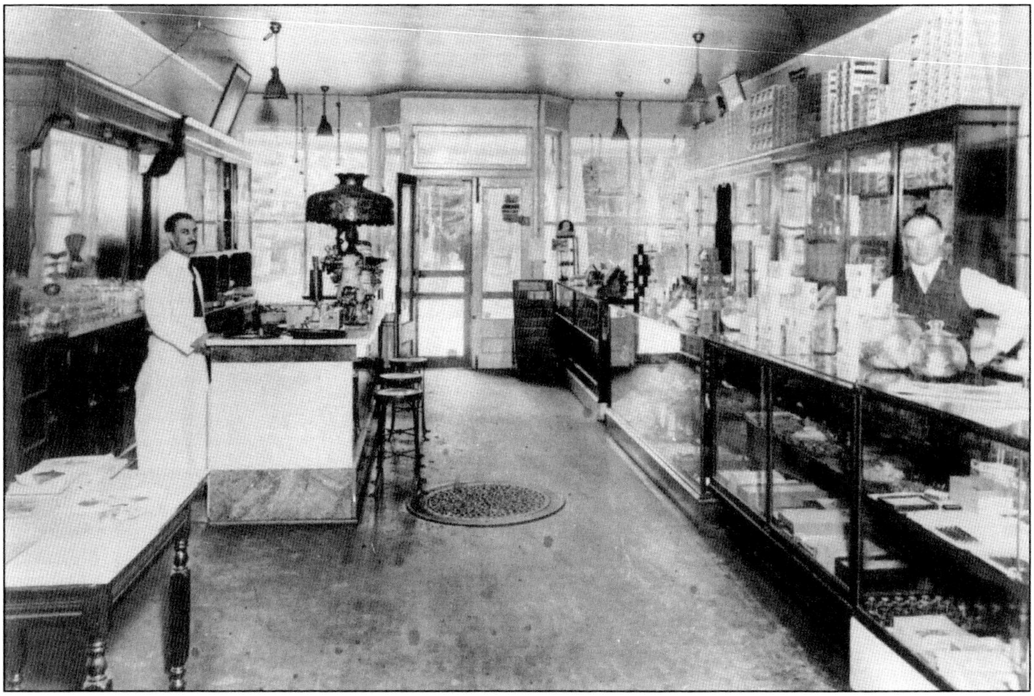

Hicks & McCarthy has been a fixture at 23 South Main Street for a century. Isaac Hicks, also called Ike, and John McCarthy opened the business in 1913 after purchasing several ice cream stores in the area. Ike and John were brothers-in-law, having married Anna and Ella, the youngest daughters of Thomas and Margaret Finucane. The Hicks & McCarthy name has survived through several successive owners. (Courtesy of Paul M. Spiegel.)

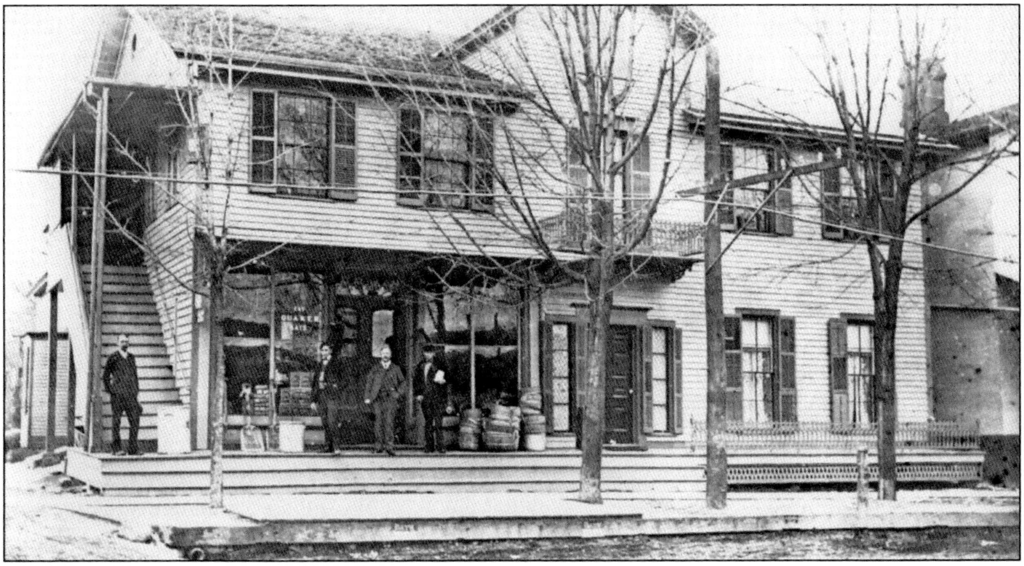

In 1884, John Buckley Bacon and his brother Conrad purchased this general store at 19 South Main Street from Charles Armstrong. Conrad returned to Connecticut, but John stayed, and his business flourished. An explosion in 1904 in a cobblestone structure at the back of the store injured clerk E.T. Tracy and may have been the impetus for John's retirement the following year. John Buckley Bacon stands second from right. (Courtesy of the Pittsford Town Historian.)

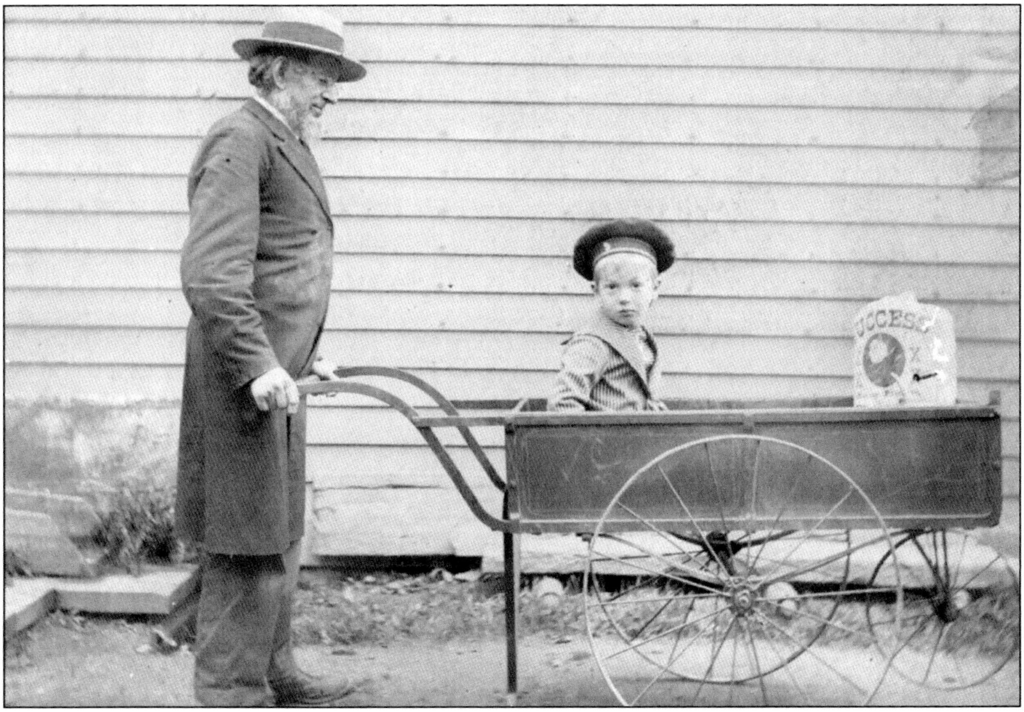

A notation on the back of this photograph states, "Walter Rose delivering groceries for John B. Bacon store. Always had room for Howard R. Bacon in the cart." Howard was John Buckley Bacon's only child. Judging by Howard's age, this photograph was probably taken about 1893. (Courtesy of the John Bacon family.)

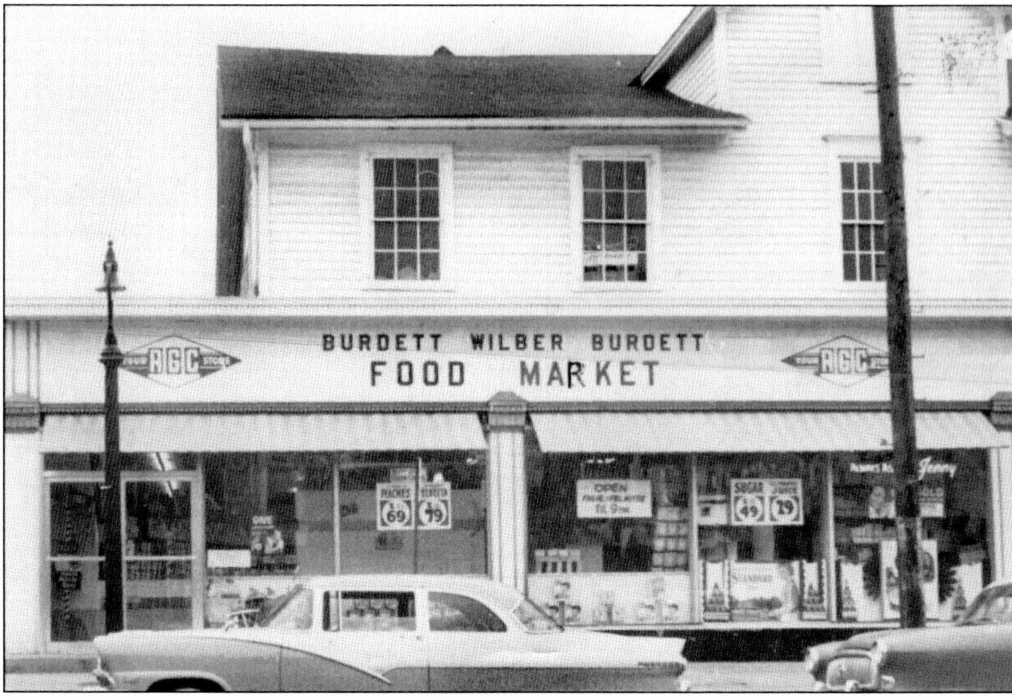

The building at 19 South Main Street has housed many businesses in the past. Samuel Hildreth, a prominent merchant who arrived in Pittsford in 1814, built the "Pittsford House" before his death in 1824. Through the years, Charles Armstrong, John Buckley Bacon, Phillips and Agate, and Zeitler and Berg all ran stores in the building. Arguably, the most well-known occupant of this building has been Burdett's Food Market, which operated for many years in Pittsford under the ownership of James Burdett Sr. and his sons James Jr., Robert, and Richard. (Both, courtesy of the Burdett family.)

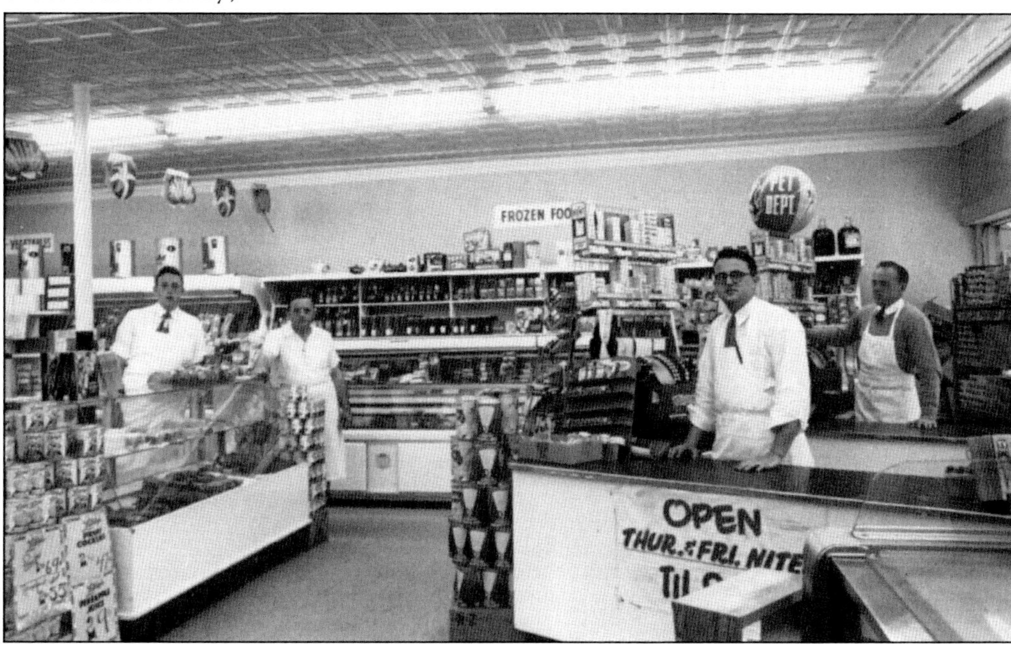

James Burdett Sr. and his sons James Jr., Robert, and Richard, operated Burdett's Food Market on South Main Street for many years. Jim Sr. was a butcher, a position his youngest son Richard shared. Oldest son James Jr. managed the groceries and produce, and Robert was the business and marketing manager. (Courtesy of the Burdett family.)

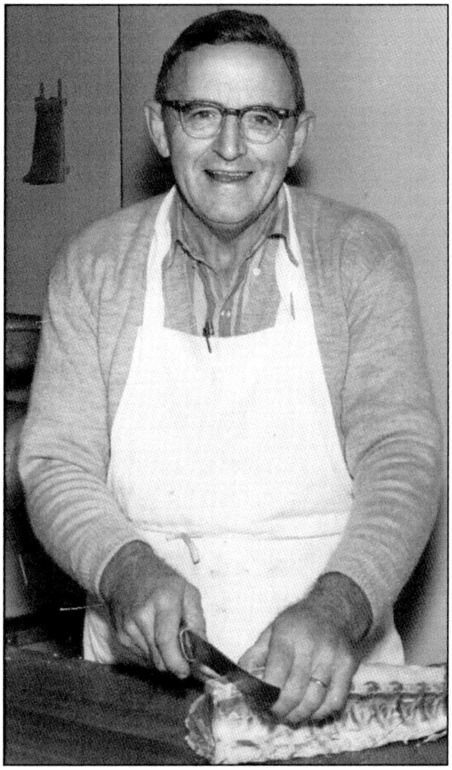

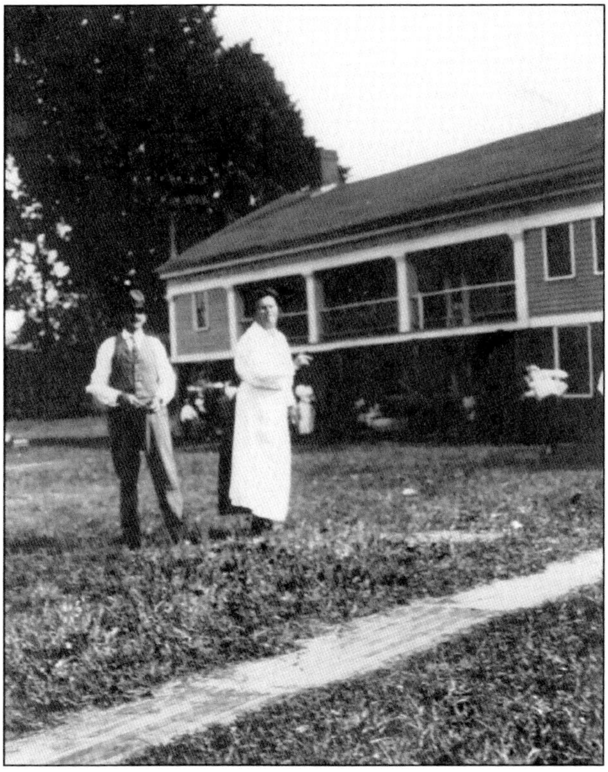

Fred Gerlach and Adelhest Guest Schrader stand in front of 1474 Marsh Road in 1916. The structure, now known as Richardson's Canal House, was built around 1818 as an inn. Although it had many owners through the years, the inn proprietors at this time were John and Christina Klitzing Kossow, Fred's in-laws. They owned the hotel for about 20 years in the early 1900s. The building was abandoned in the 1960s but purchased and restored by Andrew and Vivienne Tellier Wolfe in the 1970s. It remains a popular restaurant. (Courtesy of Cheri Buckley Branca.)

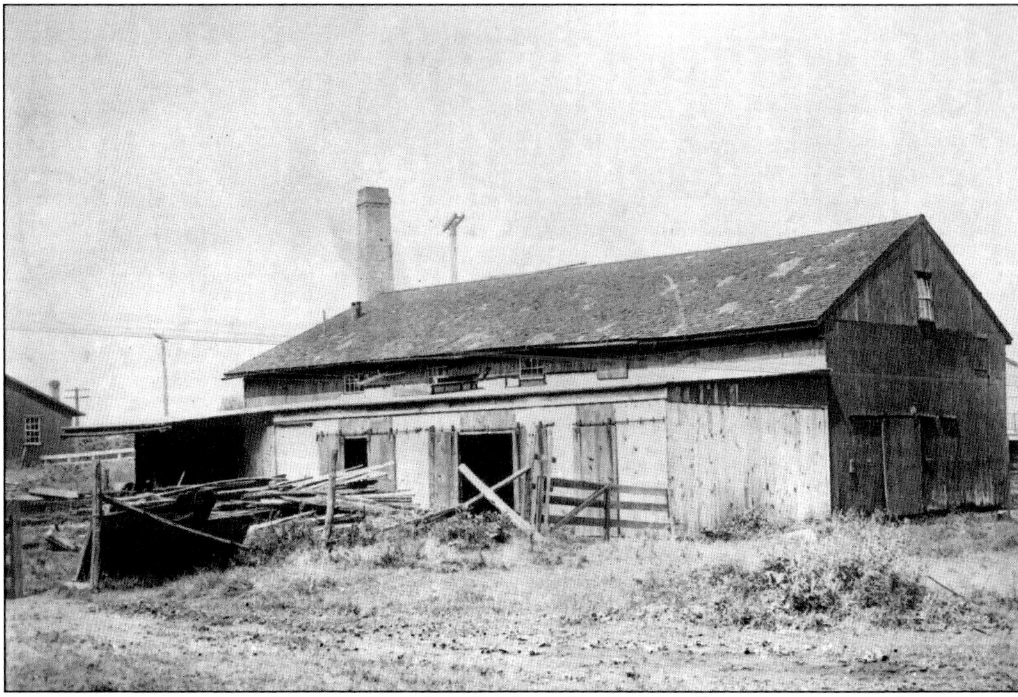

W. Grant Wadhams and Andrew Whitlock formed the Wadhams and Whitlock lumber mill. The mill was originally located south of State Street near Boughton Avenue. In 1911, the mill moved to the east end of Schoen Place, now known as Northfield Common, when the canal was widened. In the 1920s, Andrew Whitlock retired from the mill. W. Grant Wadhams had also worked with the Despatch Lumber Company. (Courtesy of Paul M. Spiegel.)

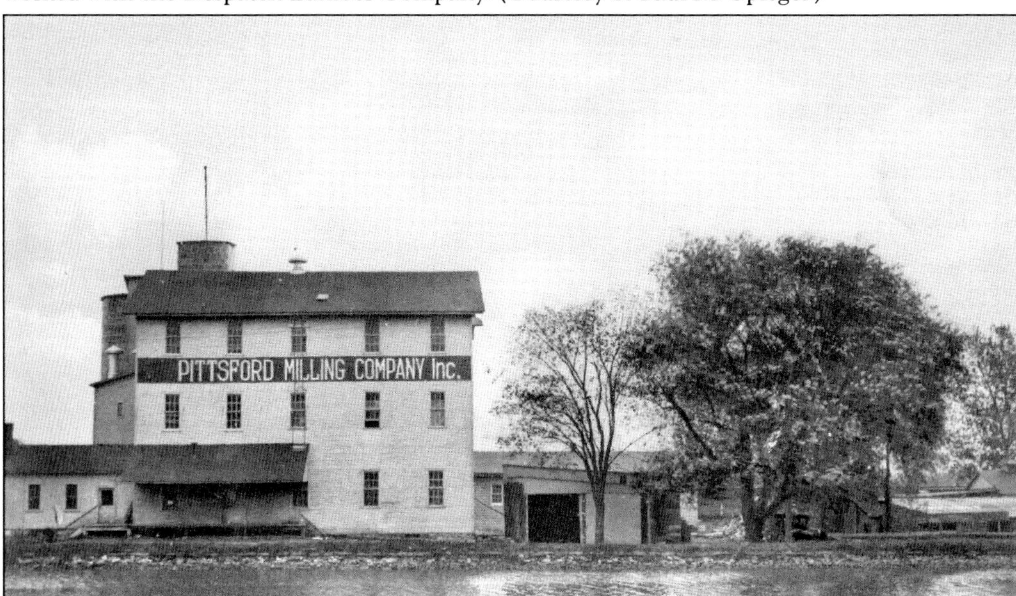

The Pittsford Milling Company sits along the north bank of the Erie Canal on Schoen Place. The three-story wood-frame structure was built in the mid-1800s as a flour mill. At one time, Grandin Vought, who later sold it to Henry Perrigo, owned the mill. (Courtesy of Paul M. Spiegel.)

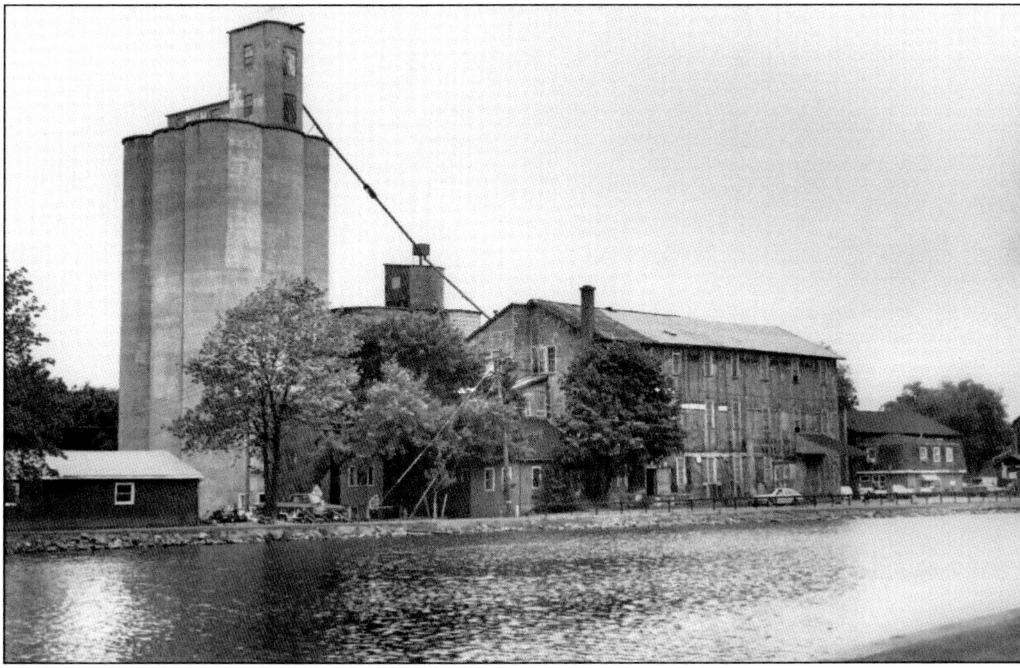

The grain elevator, constructed of cement, has been a fixture at Schoen Place on Pittsford's canal waterfront for nearly 75 years. Standing 130 feet high, the elevator was built in 1939 beside a flour mill, which was part of the Pittsford Milling Company complex. In 2004, Schoen Place LLP purchased the complex and began the process of restoring it to its original glory. Since then, the main mill building and the grain elevator have been converted to office space. The Providence Socony tank barge, shown below, passes by the grain elevator heading west on the canal. (Both, courtesy of the Pittsford Town Historian.)

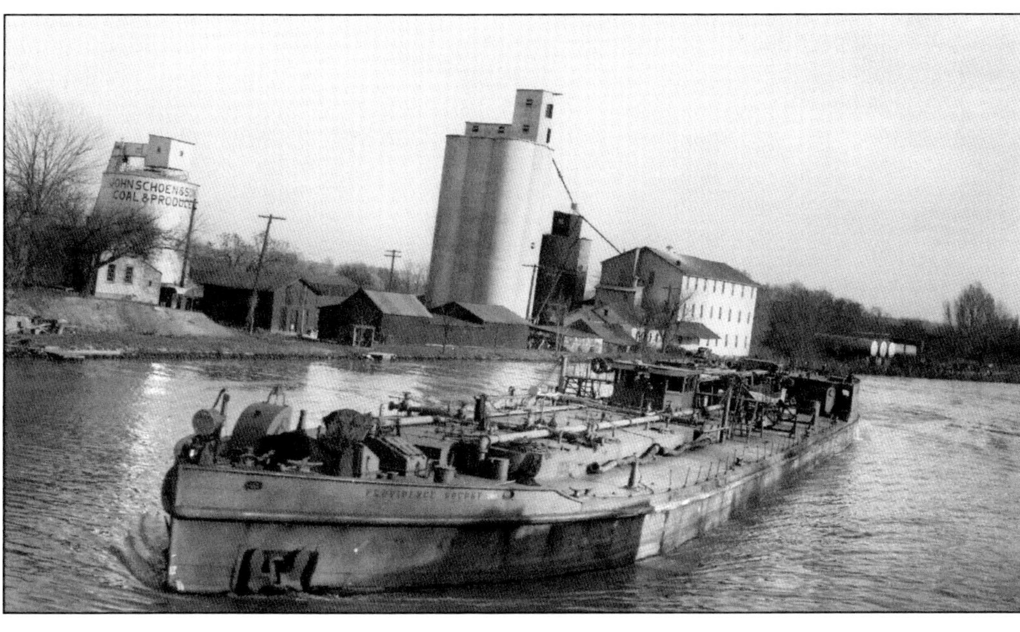

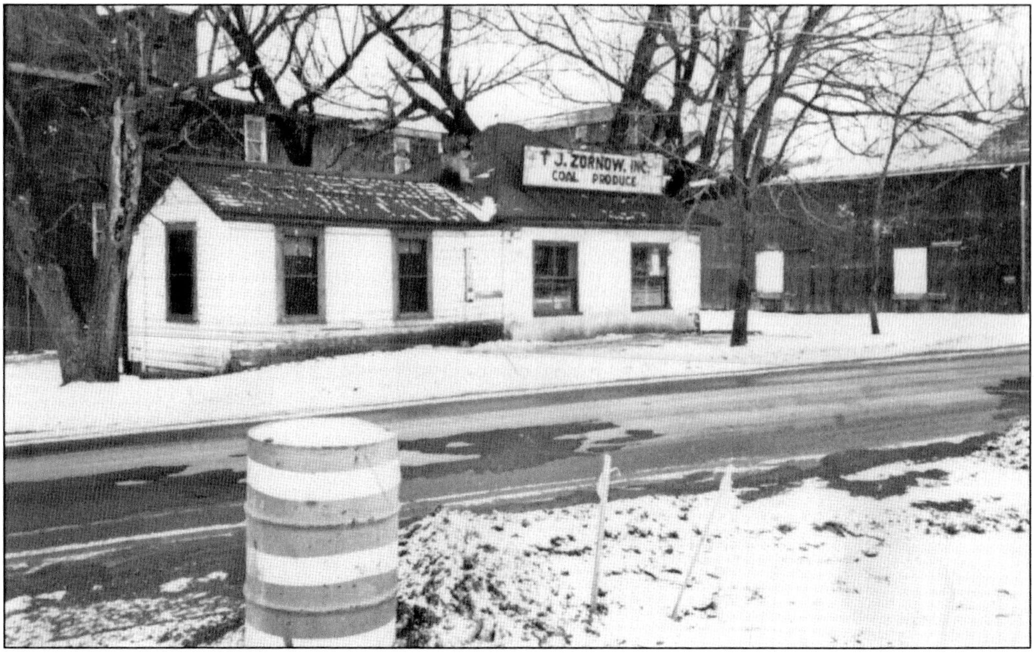

In the early 1950s, Theodore J. Zornow, a grain wholesaler, purchased the Pittsford Milling Company complex, consisting of the Pittsford Milling Building, the grain elevator, and the coal tower. His business also supplied coal to the chutes located across the canal; the passing tugboat operators and local citizens purchased the coal. (Courtesy of Paul M. Spiegel.)

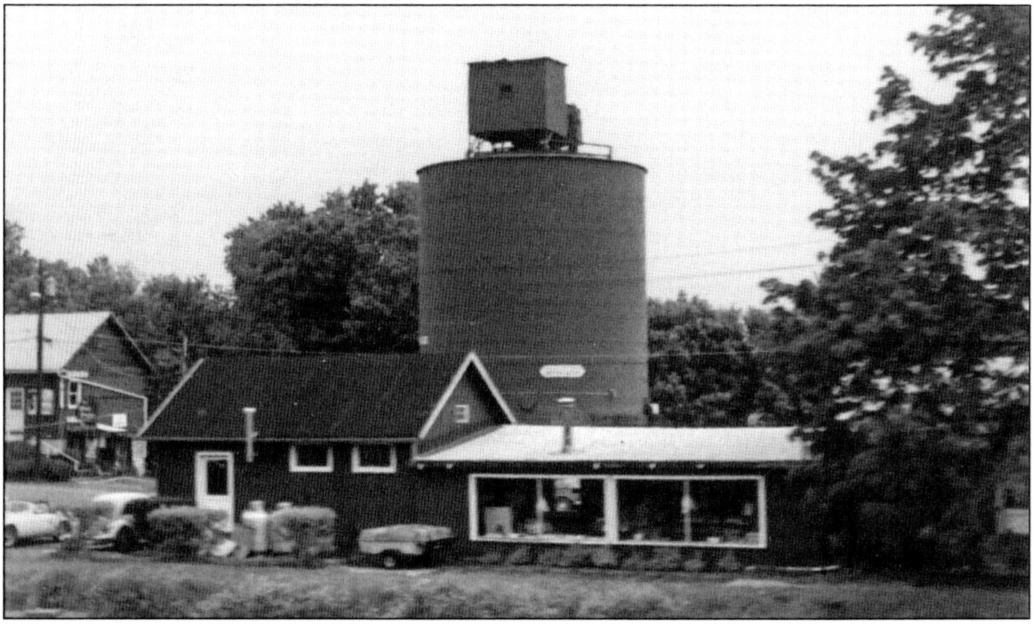

The coal tower is a distinctive landmark in Pittsford. Sitting along the canal on Schoen Place, the tower was constructed in the 1920s by the Schoen brothers, and supplied many businesses, homes, and tugboat operators with coal. In 1976, the structure was repurposed and became the well-known Village Coal Tower restaurant, which it remains today. (Courtesy of the Pittsford Town Historian.)

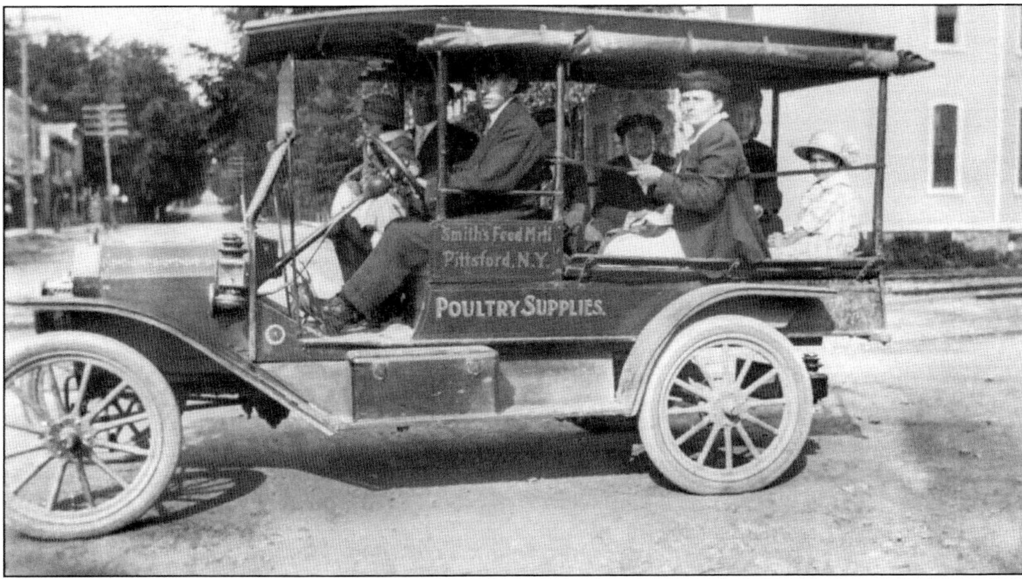

Gordon Earl drives the Smith's Feed Mill truck about 1918. His father, Charles Earl, is seated beside him holding the small child, tentatively identified as Evelyn Earl. Riding in the back are Gordon's brothers Elmer Earl and Howard Earl. Gordon's mother, Emma Chase Earl, is seated closest to the camera. The little girl in back is likely Gordon's sister Ruth Earl. The older woman is unidentified. (Courtesy of Lindsay Bach, D. Gordon Earl Collection.)

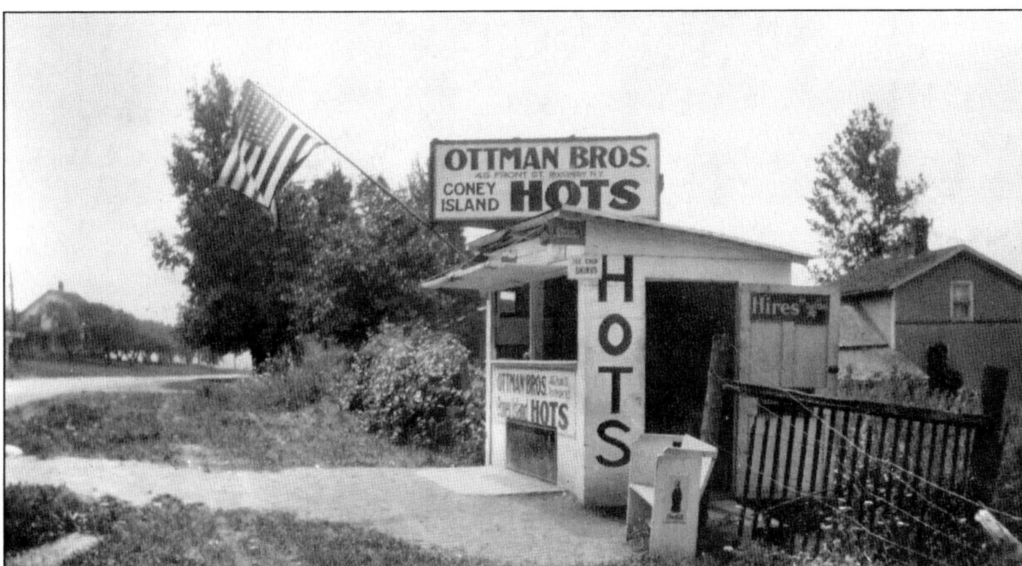

A hotdog stand opposite the Pioneer Burying Ground on Mendon Road may seem like an odd location, but it served to put E. William Place through college at the University of Rochester. William owned the stand for several years in the 1920s. Ottman Bros., a sausage-manufacturing plant, was established in Rochester in 1871 and survived until 1960 when the corporation was dissolved. (Courtesy of Bob Place.)

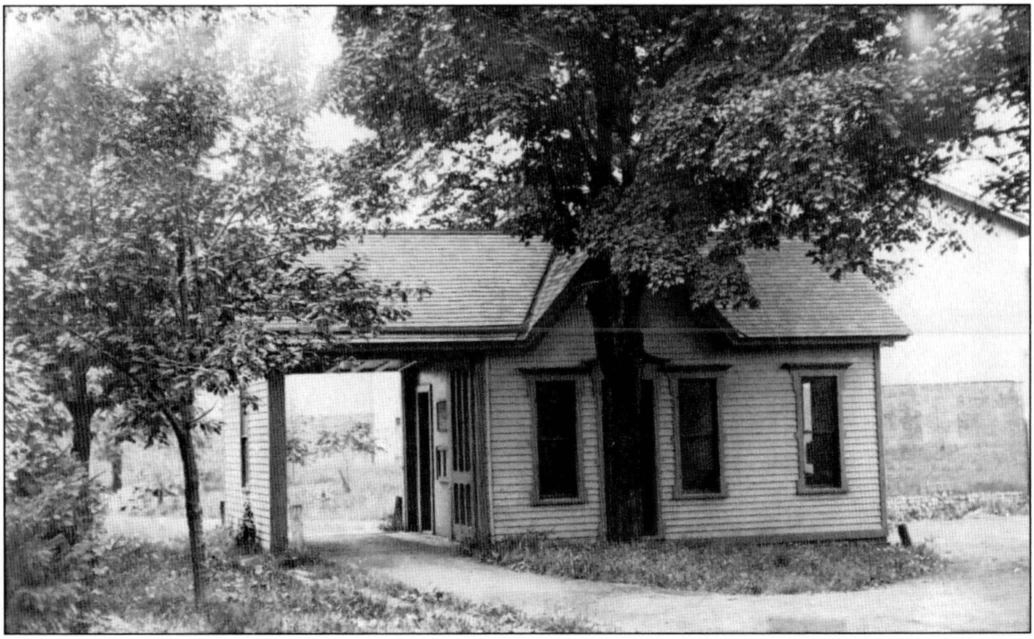

The Agate complex sat at on the south bank of the canal just west of the North Main Street Bridge. Owned by brothers John and William Agate, the complex included a malt business and gristmill. William Copsey photographed the Agate office, scales, malt house, and flour mill shown here on August 18, 1910. As the plans for widening the canal moved forward, the homes and businesses along the canal were documented in photographs such as these for compensation purposes. (Both, courtesy of Connie Wilson, Ralph Parker Collection.)

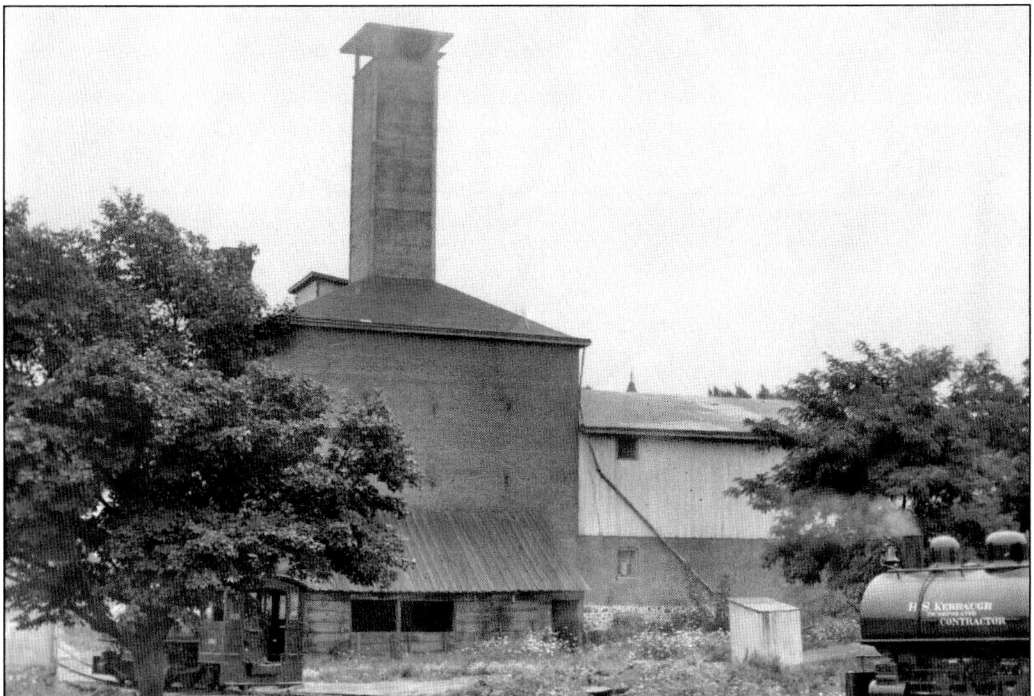

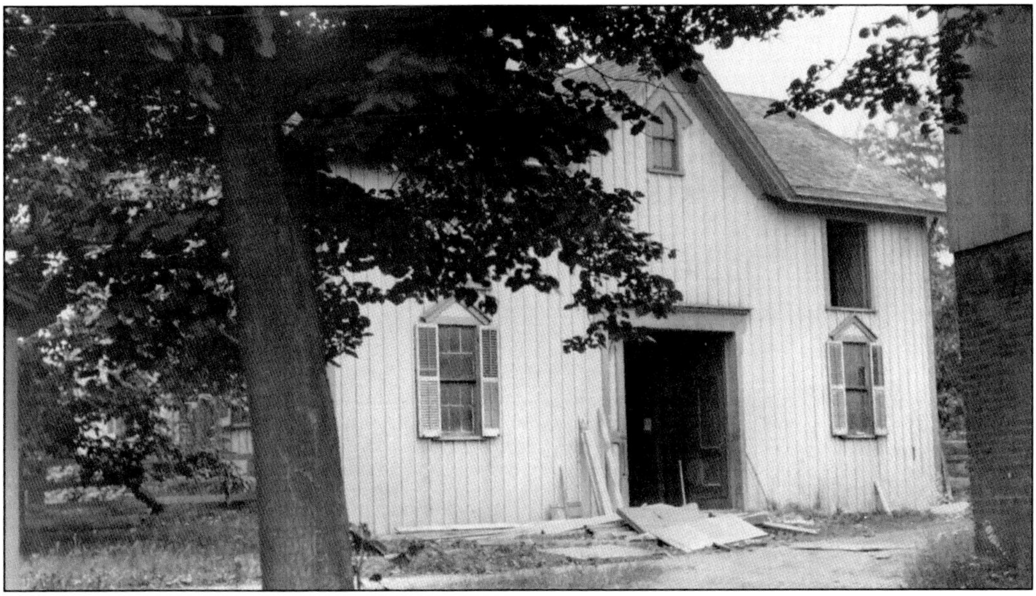

The Agate barn, in the process of dismantling, is shown above in this 1910 photograph by William Copsey. The same photographer captured the Agate mill and shed. The sign on the building advertises, "Corn meal & shorts. Corn & oats." The enlargement of the canal as a whole began in 1903 and was completed in 1918. In 1910, Pittsford was affected when the state engineers employed local citizens J. Monroe Knickerbocker, J.S. Ford, Burton Wiltsie, and William Anscomb to appraise the properties to be taken for the Barge Canal. Along the four-mile route from King's Bend to Bushnell's Basin, the following properties were slated for demolition: Agate's malt house, William Agate's home, Samuel Hutchinson's warehouse on Main Street, the Wadhams and Whitlock planing mill, the Enos and Samuel Salter house, Chester Austin's home, the former Bennett warehouse, and Jaeschke's millpond. (Both, courtesy of Connie Wilson, Ralph Parker Collection.)

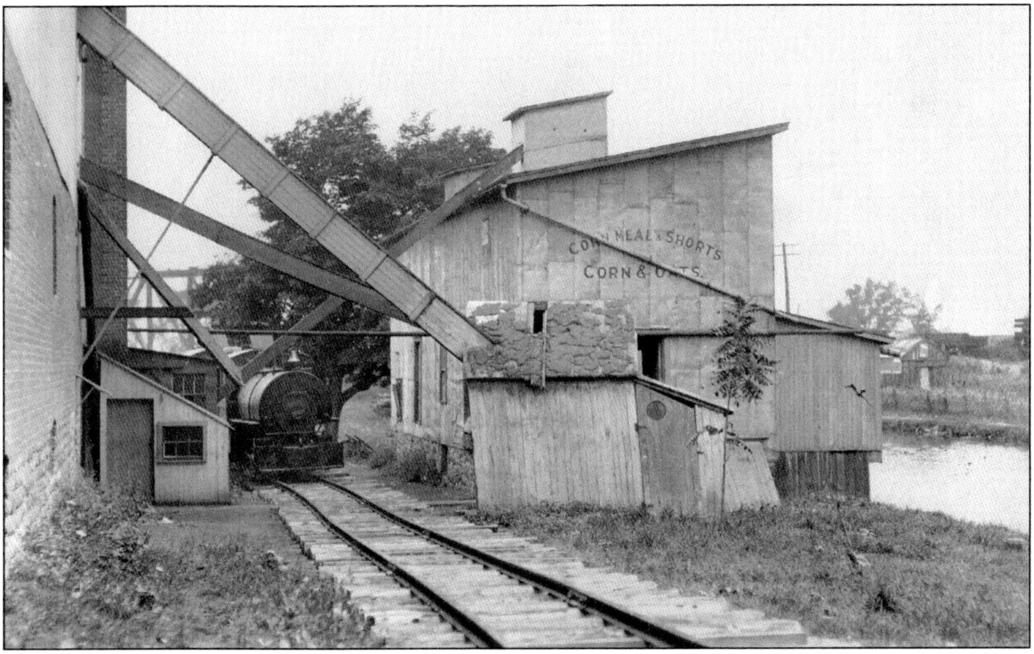

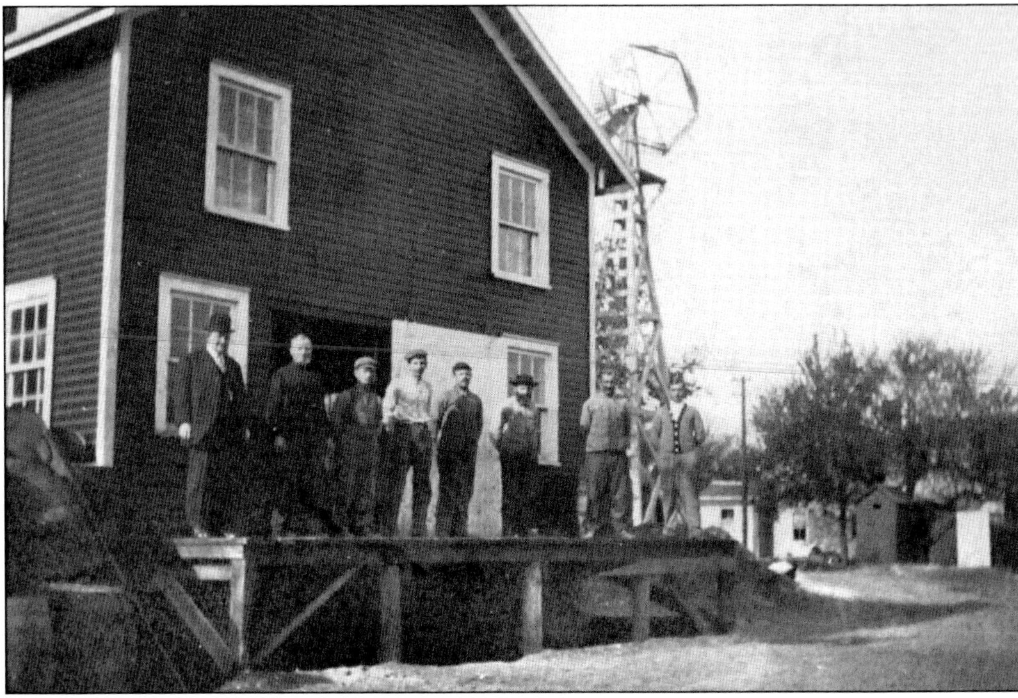

William A. Loder began his pickle manufacturing business as early as 1885. By the time of this photograph, about 1911, he was well established in the industry, as evidenced by the large number of employees shown here at the East Avenue plant. From left to right are the following: Louis Forman, Will Schwartz, unidentified, Albert Hegeman, Charles Chesterman, George Harmor, George Smith, and Albert Forman. William Loder continued his business well into retirement years. (Courtesy of Paul M. Spiegel.)

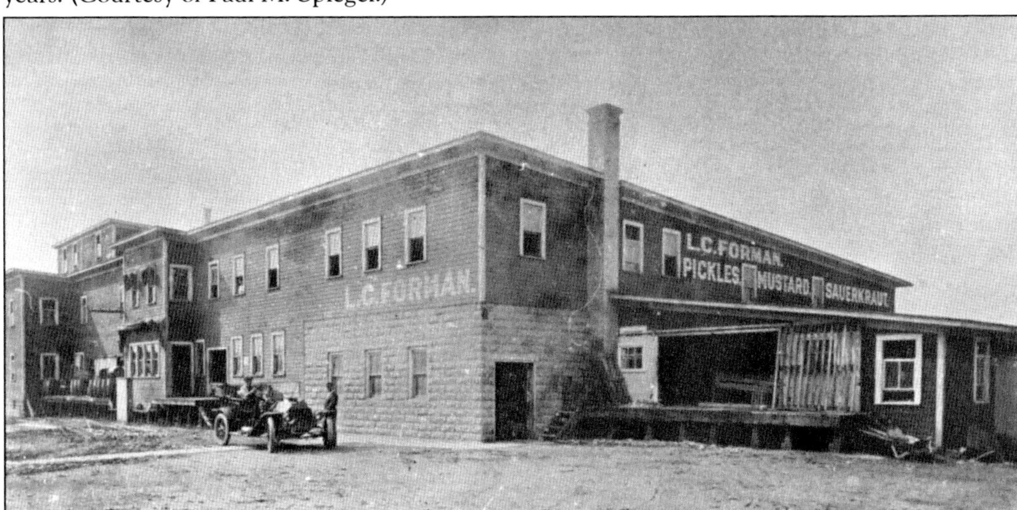

Louis C. Forman learned the pickle business while employed at Loder's pickle factory. He began selling pickles out of his home on East Avenue. When the house burned down in 1913, Louis found a new location for the business. The structure was built at Grove Street and is now known as the Pickle Factory. The Forman family sold to the R.T. French Company in 1960. The Pickle Factory is now an office building. (Courtesy of Paul M. Spiegel.)

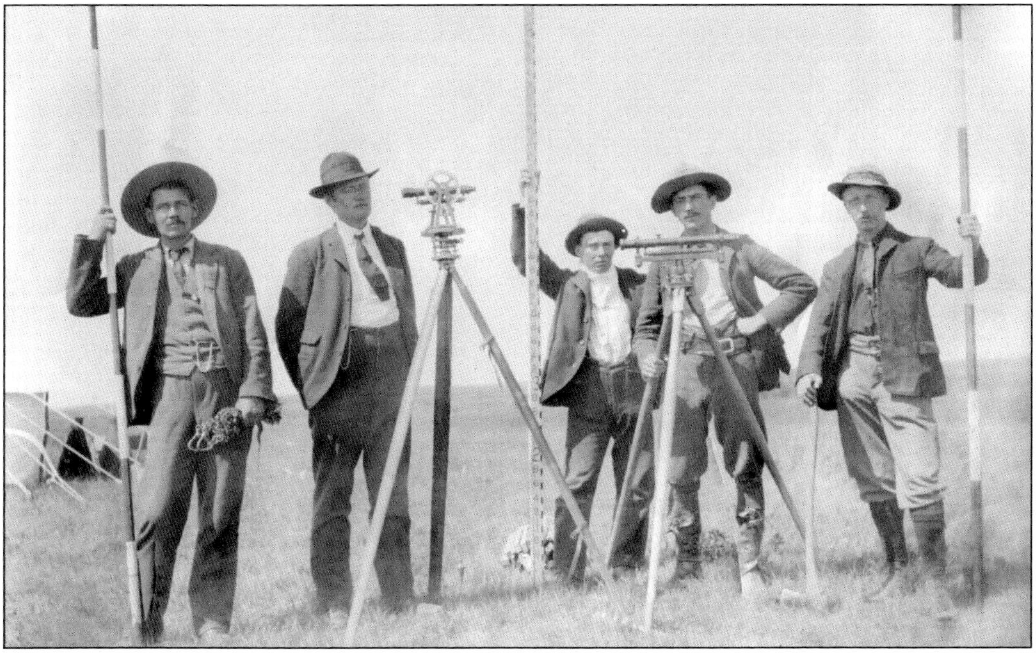

Elroy Agate, shown second from left, was a civil engineer by trade. Here, Elroy is conducting a survey in an undisclosed location with men identified only as Warren, Taylor, Cauchon, and Street. Elroy was the second child of John and Mary Jane Austin Agate. He married Emma Sikes later in life and died in 1952. (Courtesy of Connie Wilson, Ralph Parker Collection.)

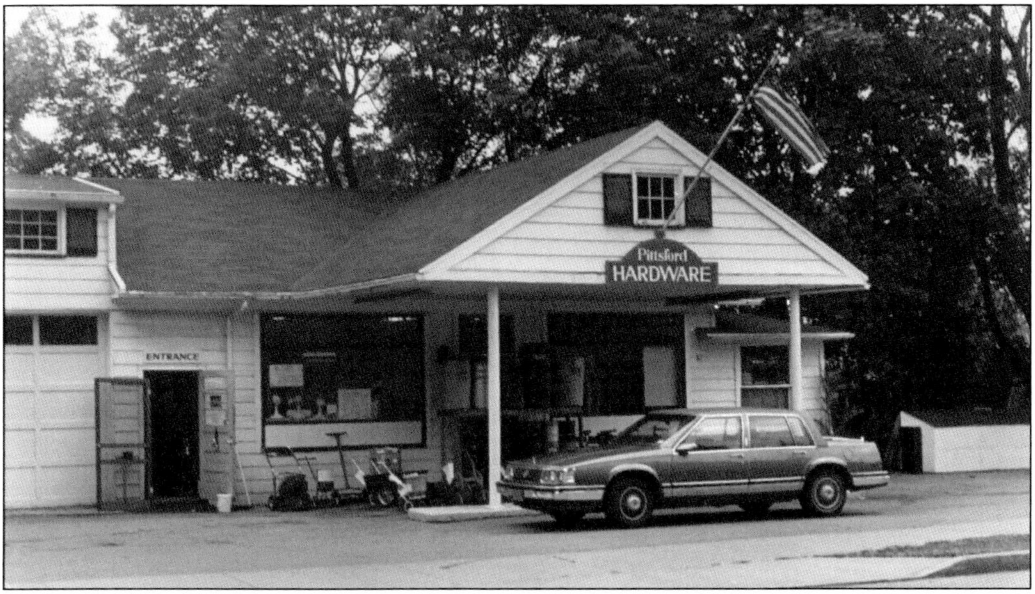

Kenneth "Rusty" Likly Jr. opened Pittsford Hardware and Bicycle at 40 State Street in the mid-1970s after a previous hardware store, operated by George Waterhouse, had closed. Employees Al Springer and Mabel Stehler assisted Rusty with the store operations. The bicycle shop moved to Schoen Place and was renamed Towpath Bike about 1985, and the hardware store closed. Suzanne's Distinctive Fashions is currently located at 40 State Street. (Courtesy of the Pittsford Town Historian.)

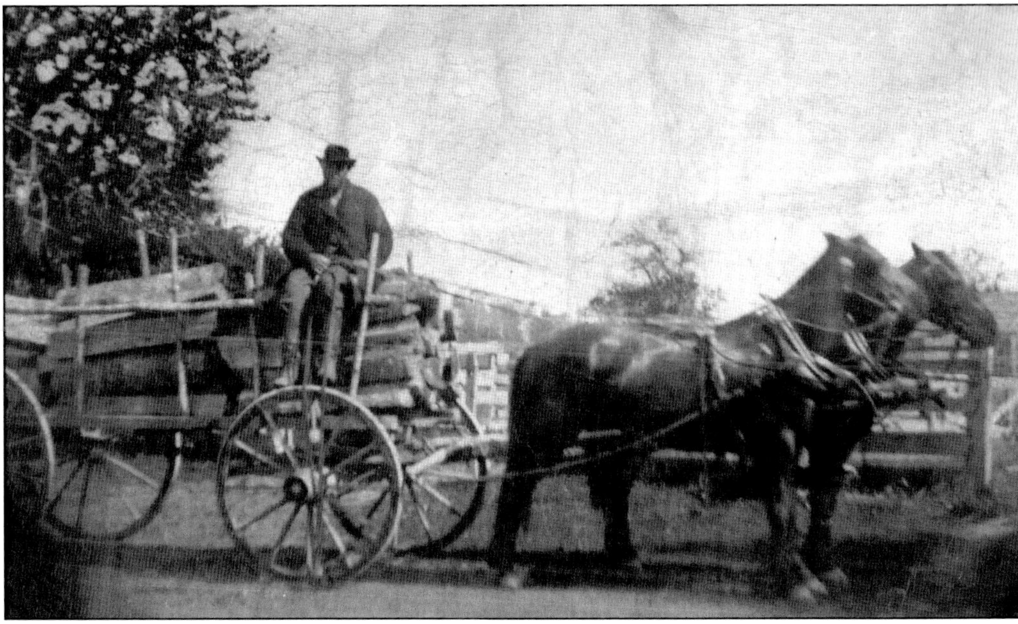

Marvin Hopkins sits atop a pile of lumber in this undated tintype. According to the 1860 census records, the Hopkins farm consisted of 206 improved acres and 137 unimproved acres. Horses, milk cows, working oxen, sheep, swine, and other cattle grazed off the Hopkins land, which also produced wheat, Indian corn, and oats. The cash value of the farm at that time was estimated at $17,150. (Courtesy of Mark Greene and John Hopkins.)

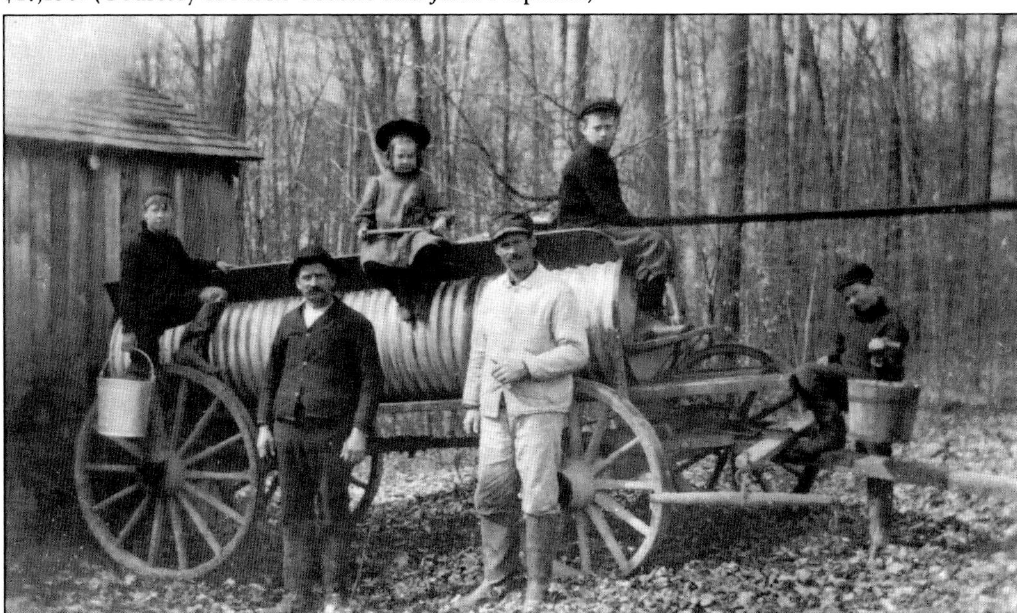

The Hopkins family is seen heading to the Hopkins woods to gather sap for maple syrup in the early 1900s. The sap was gathered and placed in the metal drum on the wagon. Jared Hopkins is shown standing to the left. The others in the photograph are unidentified. After clearing the land, many farms left a wood lot for farm use such as firewood and maple syrup production. (Courtesy of Mark Greene and John Hopkins.)

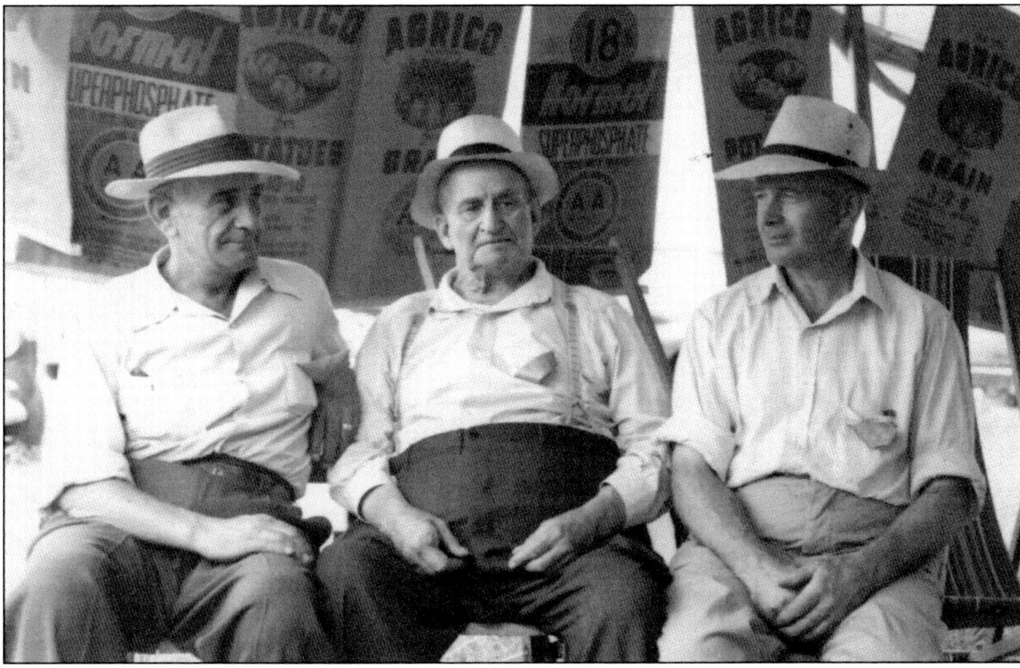

Jared Hopkins, shown here in the late 1930s, is seated between his two sons, Irving and Phelps. Jared and his wife, Lettie Maie, also had two daughters, Delora and Jane. Together, Phelps and Jared ran the Hopkins farm at 3151 Clover Street. Irving, the eldest of Jared Hopkins's four children, had a farm at 311 Mendon Center Road. Nyehurst, shown below, came to the Hopkins family through Jared's marriage to Lettie Maie Nye. Lettie's father, Alvin E. Nye, lived there. After Alvin's death in 1908, his daughter Delora served delicious home-cooked meals from the house. It sits on Clover Street, near the Calkins Road intersection and adjacent to the Hopkins homestead. (Above, courtesy of Mark Greene and John Hopkins; below, courtesy of the Pittsford Town Historian.)

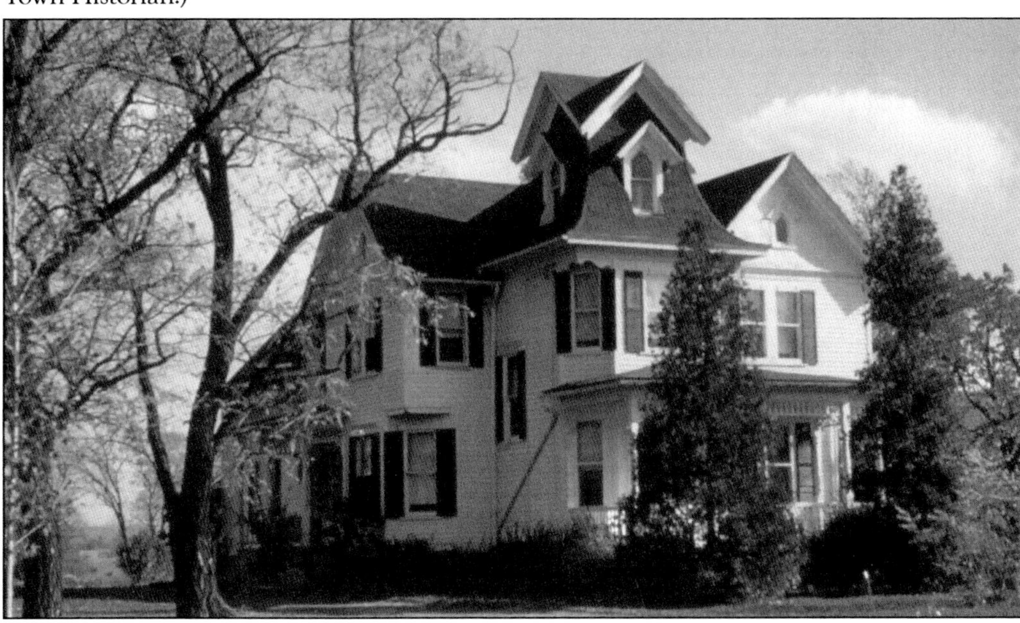

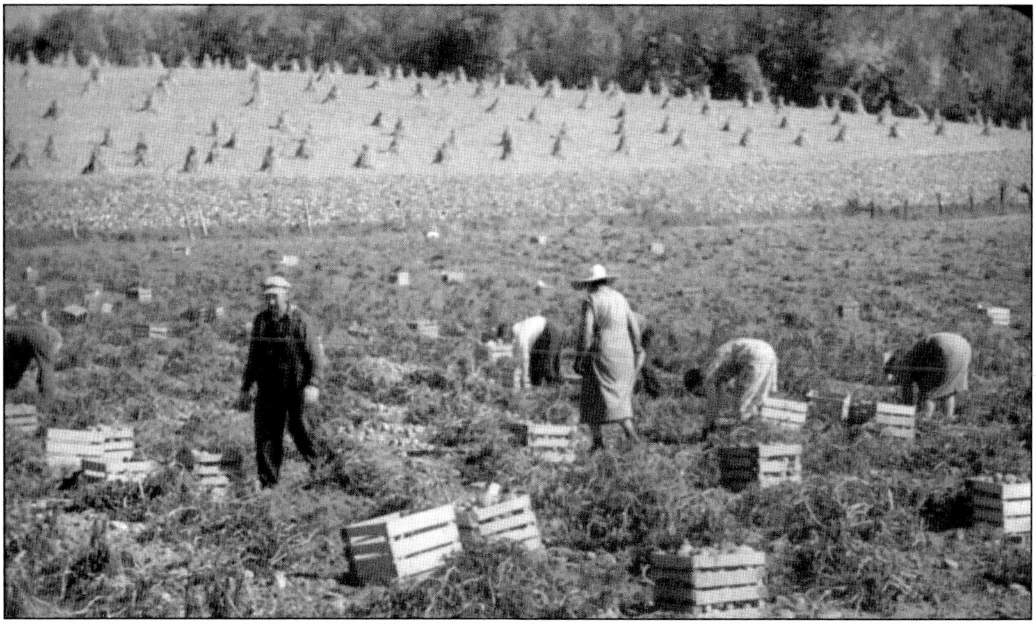

The workers here on the Hopkins farm in the late 1920s are harvesting potatoes using crates for collection. In the background, shocks of corn can be seen waiting for harvest. The Hopkins farm produced potato crops until the early 1950s. Note the women wearing dresses as they harvest the potatoes. (Courtesy of Mark Greene and John Hopkins.)

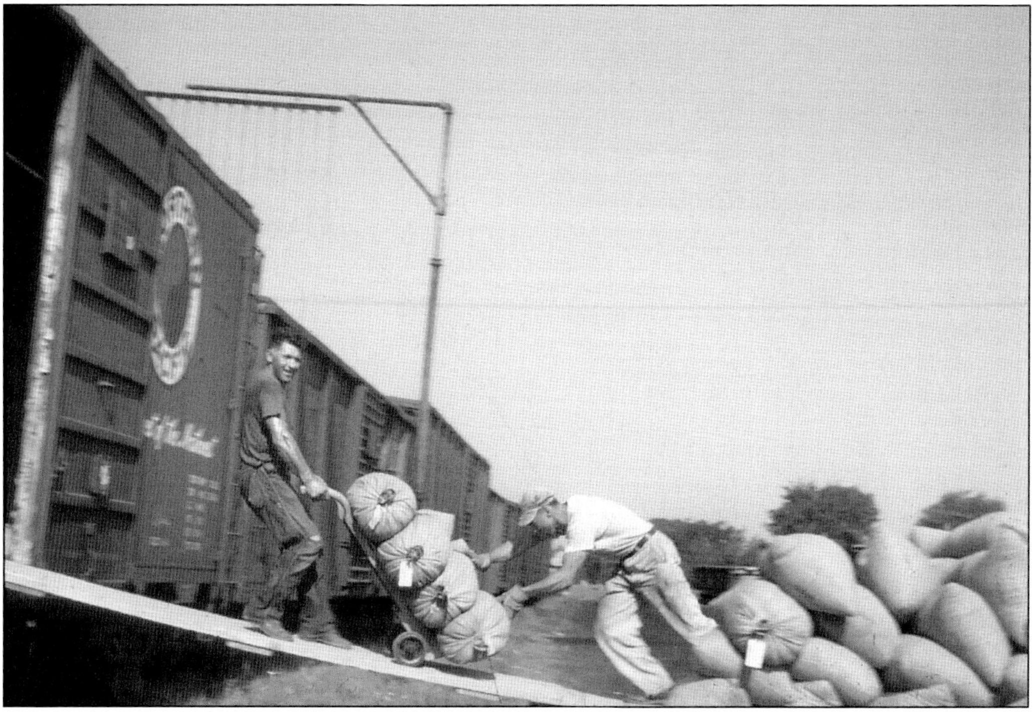

Bags full of wheat from the Hopkins farm are being loaded onto a car of the Northern Pacific Railroad in the village in 1950. Wheat has been produced on the Hopkins farm for the past two centuries. (Courtesy of Mark Greene and John Hopkins.)

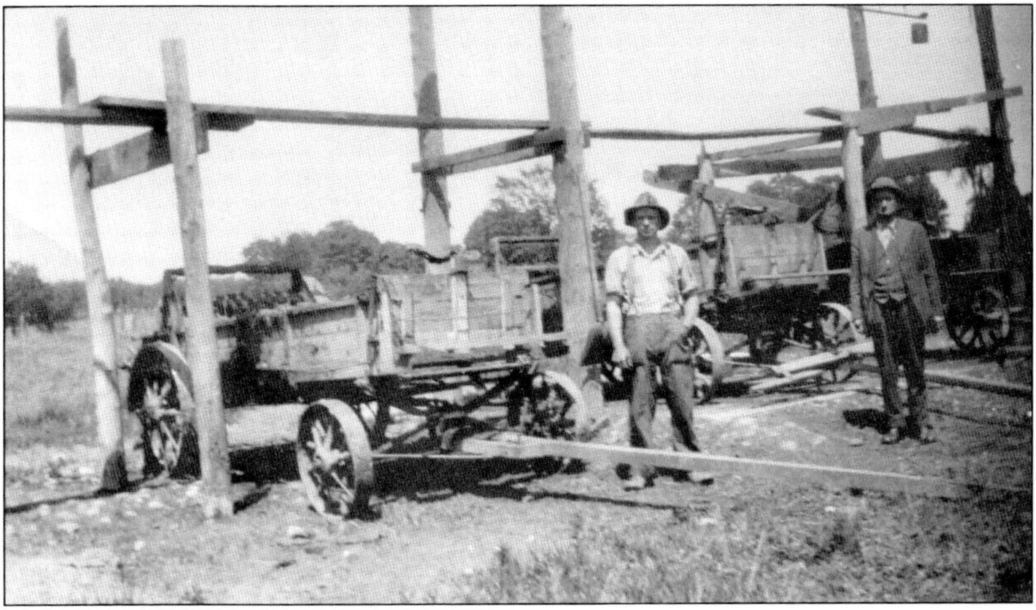

These manure spreaders at the Hopkins cow barn on Clover Street were horse-drawn. In later years, they were used with a tractor. Horses were kept on the farm until the late 1930s. (Courtesy of Mark Greene and John Hopkins.)

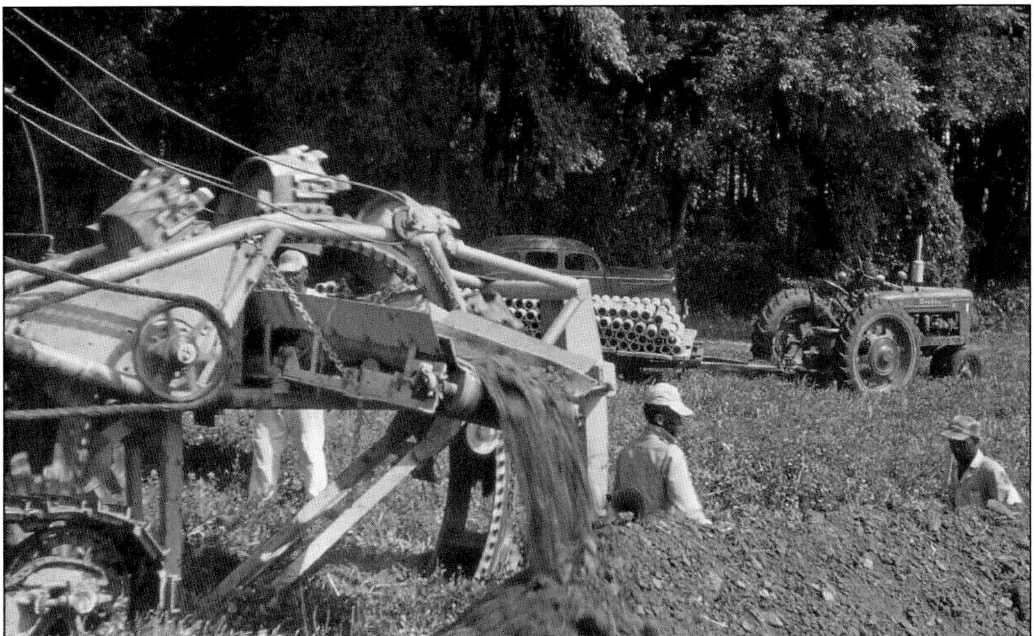

Drainage tiles were installed at the Hopkins farm beginning in 1863, when they were dug by hand. In the 1950s, ditching equipment was brought in by the contractors, shown here in the troughs. (Courtesy of Mark Greene and John Hopkins.)

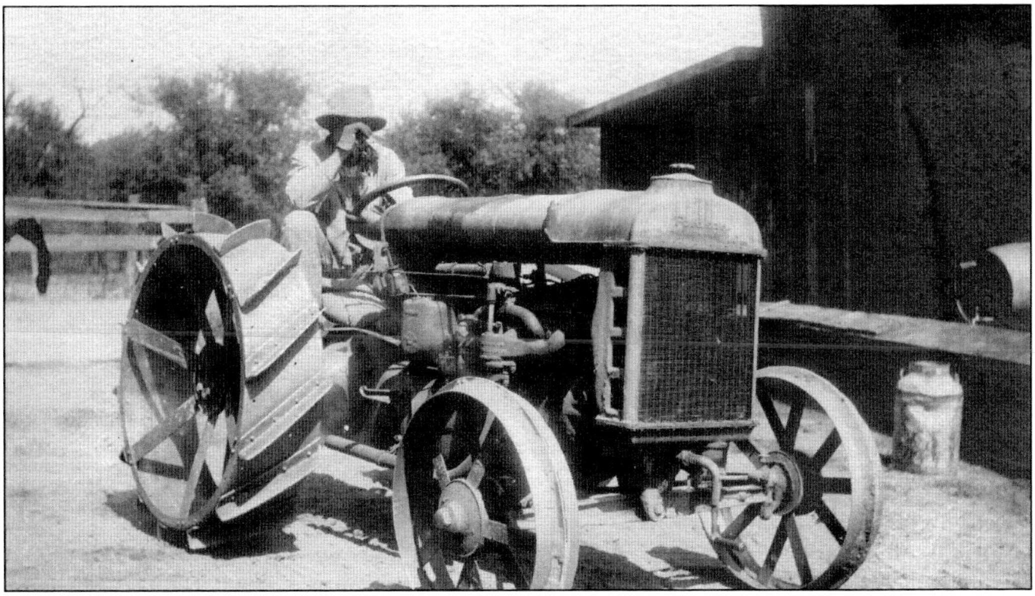

The Fordson is one of the first tractors used on the Hopkins farm. It is still family-owned and housed on location. The tractor is shown in the early 1920s behind the Hopkins homestead on Clover Street and next to the corncrib. (Courtesy of Mark Greene and John Hopkins.)

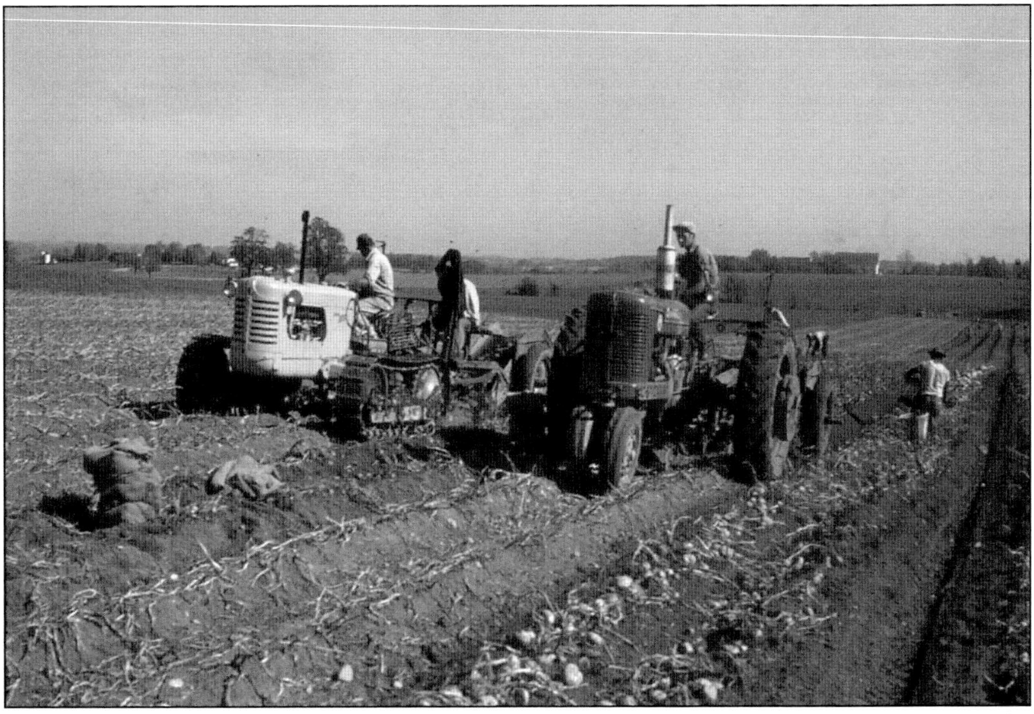

The two tractors, shown here in the 1950s on the Hopkins farm, are digging potatoes. On the left is an Oliver OC-6 agricultural crawler, produced from 1953 to 1960, which moved on tracks instead of tires. The tractor on the right is a Farmall Super M, which was produced from 1952 to 1954. Both pieces of equipment are still used on the farm. (Courtesy of Mark Greene and John Hopkins.)

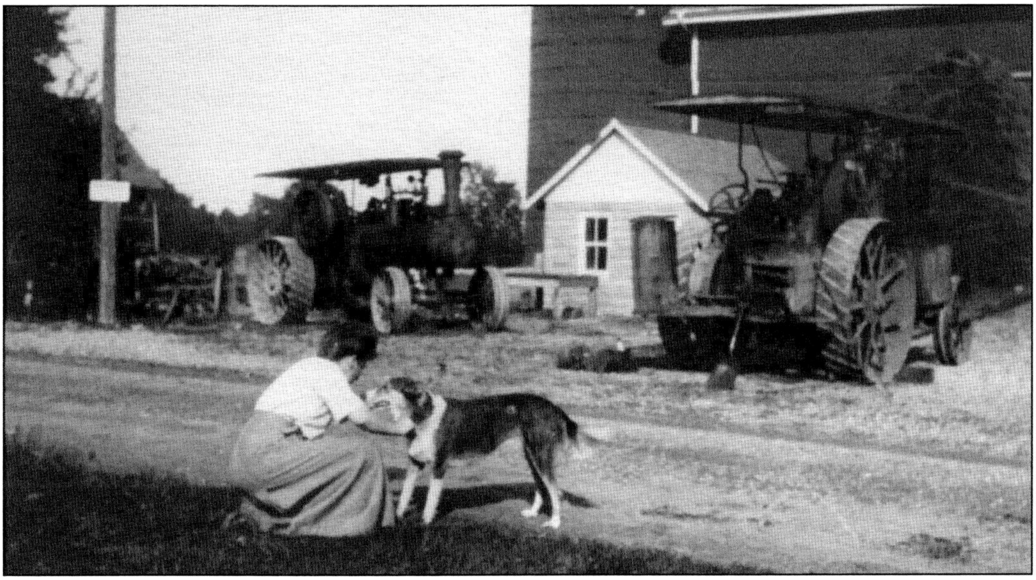

An unidentified woman and dog stand beside Clover Street, which is still a dirt road in 1910. The photograph was taken from the Hopkins homestead looking east. The milk house sits in front of the silo. Steam tractors thrash wheat in front of the cow barn where the present-day roadside stand is located. (Courtesy of Mark Greene and John Hopkins.)

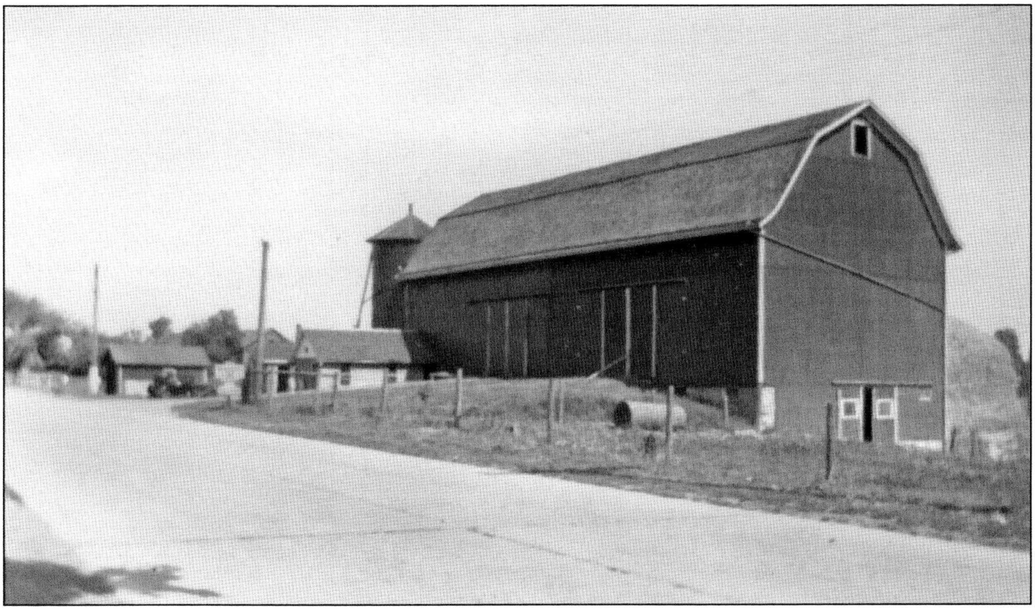

A 1930 view of the Hopkins property on Clover Street shows the cow barn and silo. The barn, which housed 60 cows, was moved to this location in 1910 and was formerly part of the Benjamin Geare farm in Long Meadow. The silo was destroyed in a windstorm in the 1950s. (Courtesy of Mark Greene and John Hopkins.)

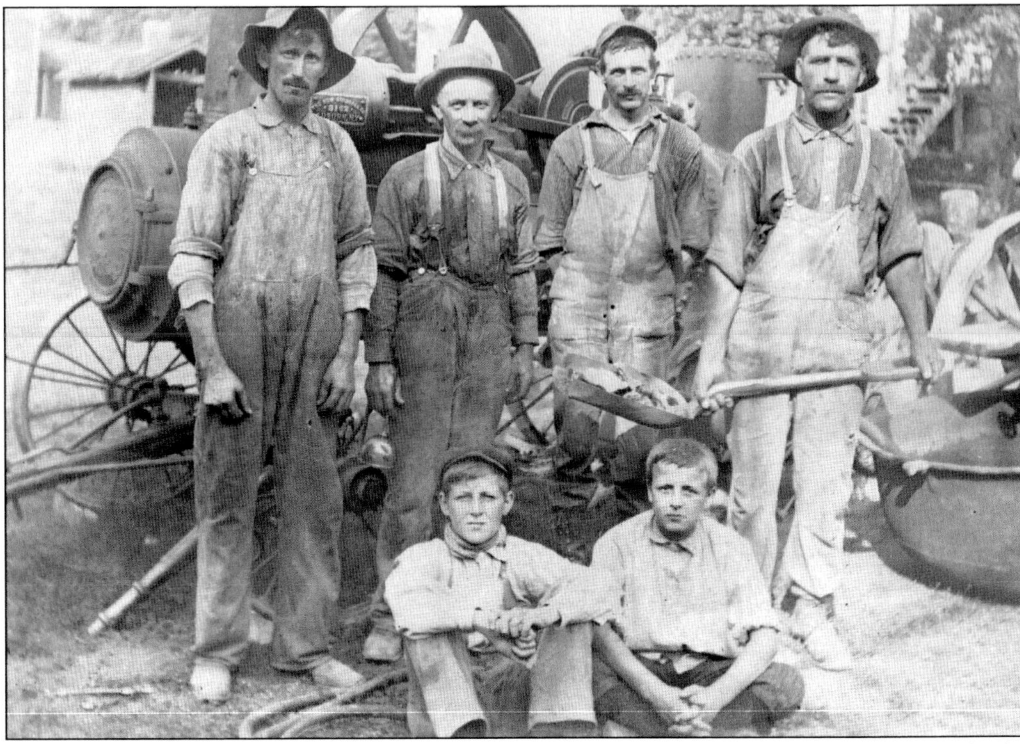

Members of the Lusk family stand in front of their New Birdsall Co. farming equipment. Charles Franklin Lusk, standing at right, holds the shovel. The two boys in front appear to be Charles's sons Charles Willard Lusk and Franklin P. Lusk. The others are unidentified. (Courtesy of Bill Lusk.)

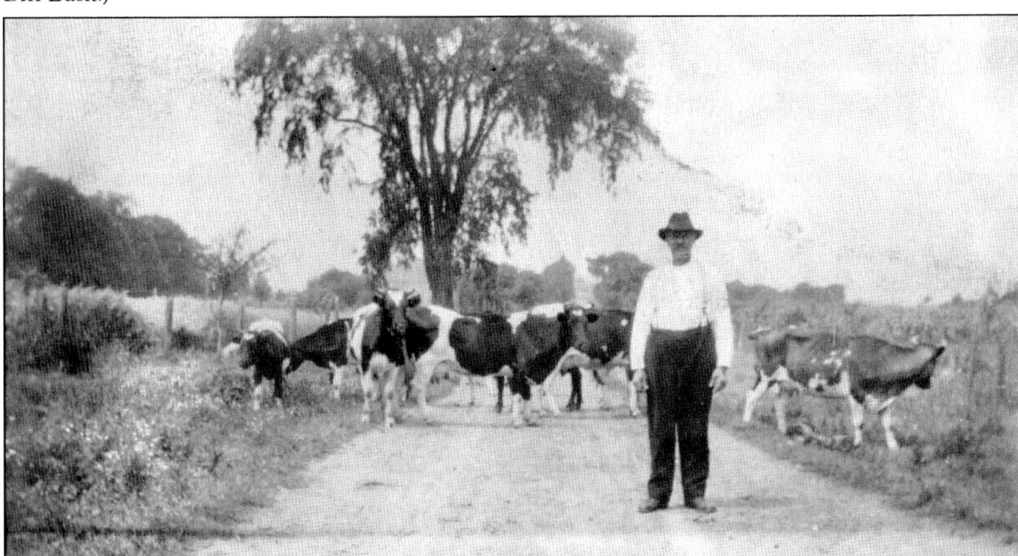

Several of William Clawson's cows are seen posing with him at his farm on Noakes Road. William, his sister Sophia, and his parents, Christian and Friederike Clawson, emigrated from Germany about 1888. He married Mary Schrader in 1898, and they had two daughters, Clara and Frances. (Courtesy of the Willard family.)

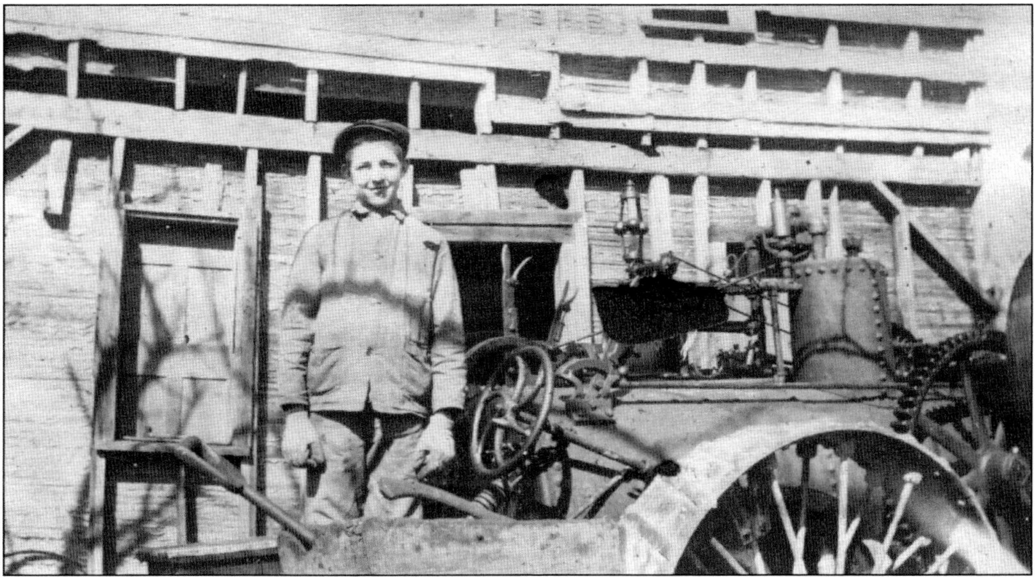

Grant Peglow stands beside the farm equipment, which likely belonged to his uncle William Clawson. The equipment appears to be a steam tractor. Grant worked as a farm laborer on the Clawson farm. Siblings Ruth and Grant Peglow, shown below, mirror each other in front of the Clawson barns. (Both, courtesy of the Willard family.)

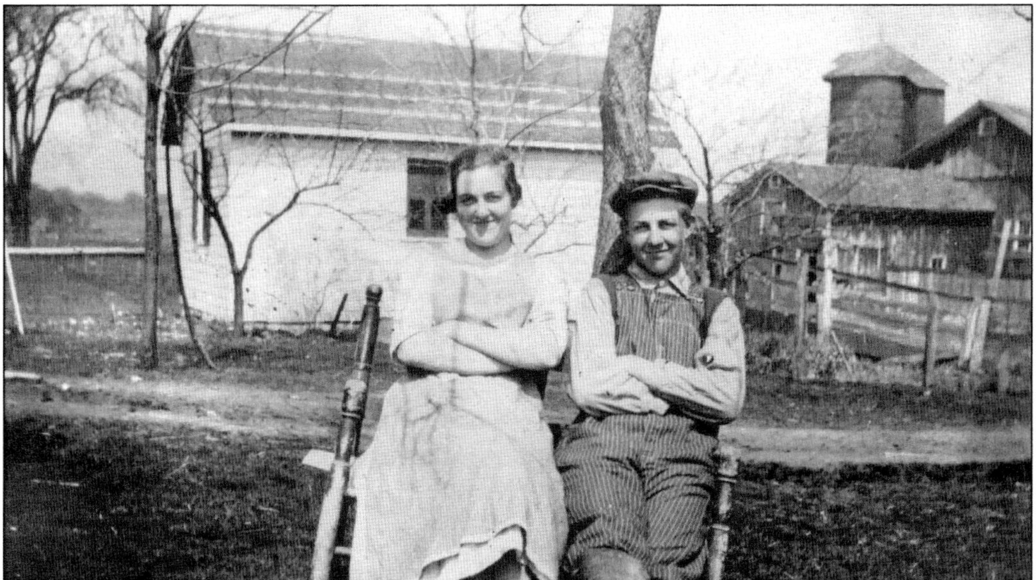

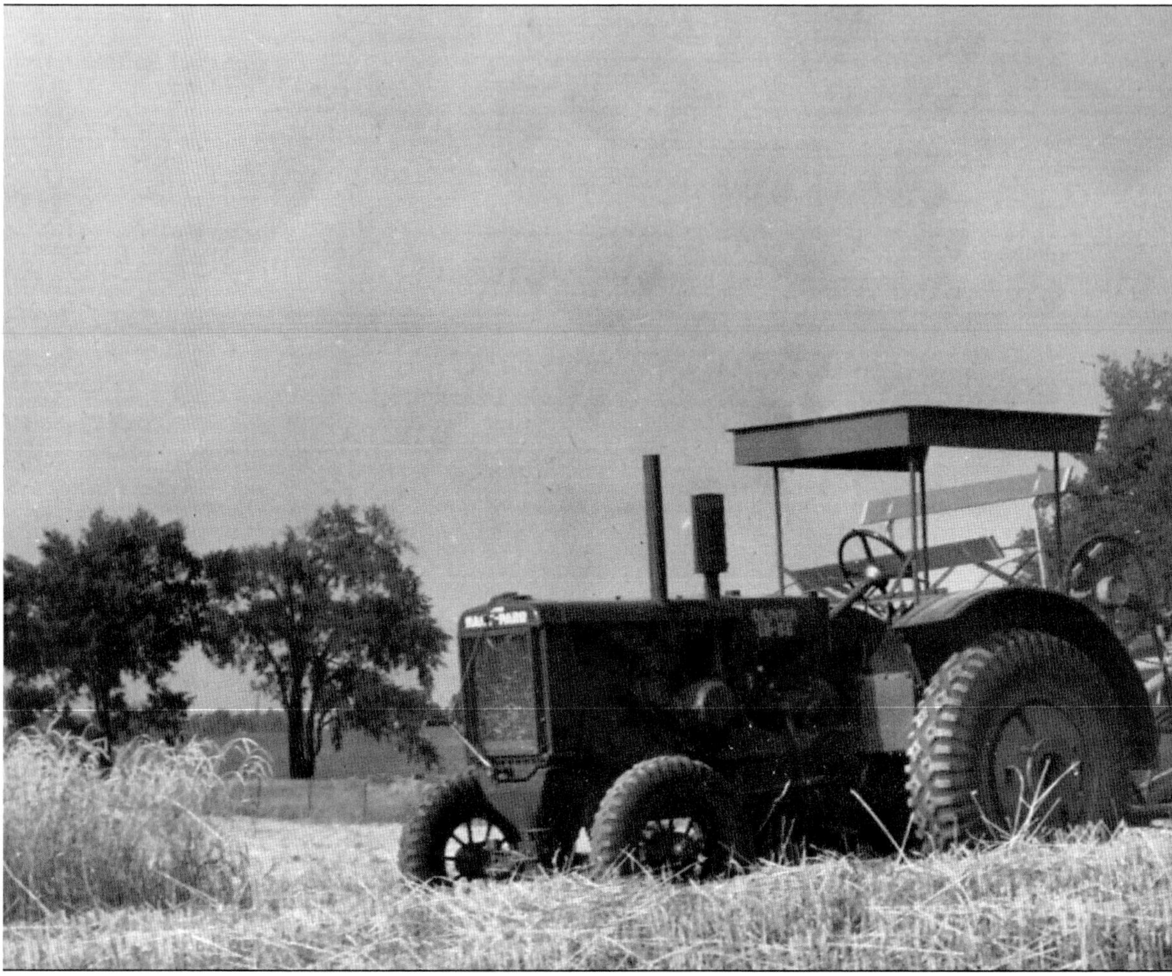

Michael Mulrooney, an agent for the Virginia-Carolina Chemical Corporation, took this photograph at the Barker farm on Mendon Center Road about 1934. Shown are, from left to right, Louis Bernard, H. Harlan Knickerbocker, Paul Knickerbocker, and Bob Bernard. A 1929 Chevrolet truck and a case combine share the spotlight with the tractor, an Oliver Hart-Parr 18-28, which was the first tractor introduced by Oliver in 1930. Charles Hart and Charles Parr, students at the

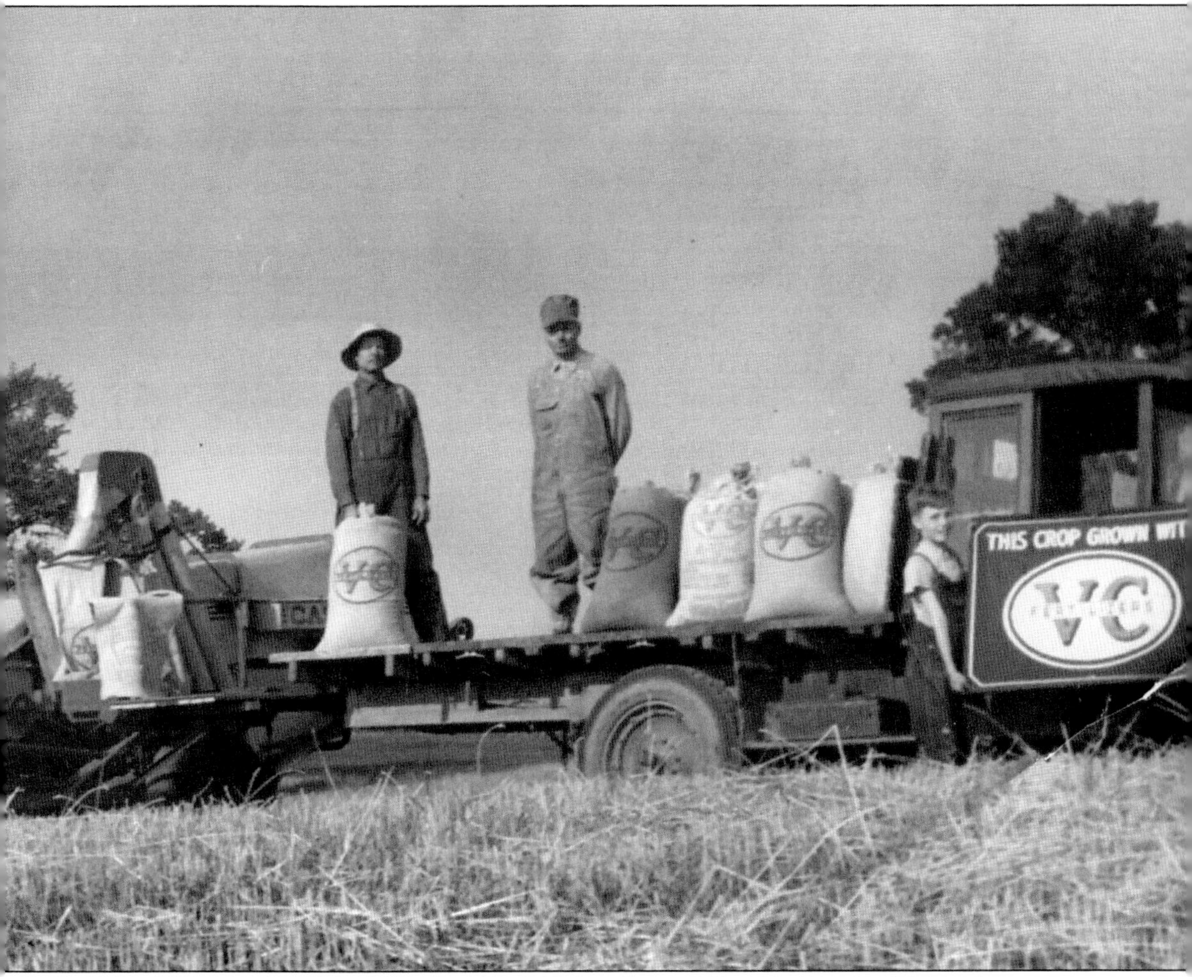

University of Wisconsin, founded Hart-Parr in 1901. In 1903, Hart-Parr became the first American manufacturer to produce gasoline tractors. The price of a Hart-Parr tractor was $1,350 in 1930. Mobil Oil purchased the Virginia-Carolina Chemical Corporation in 1963. (Courtesy of Mary Knickerbocker Menzie.)

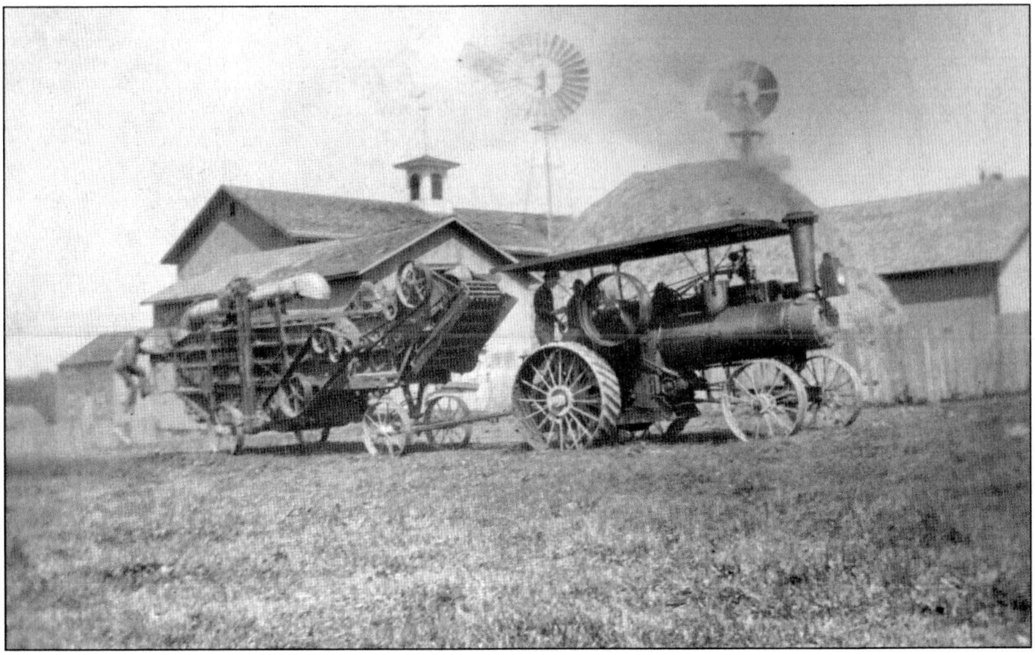

The Barker threshing rig is shown in front of the barns and windmill at 219 Mendon Center Road. William H. Barker's livestock in 1860 included horses, milk cows, sheep, and swine. He also grew wheat, Indian corn, and oats on the farm. By 1880, William had amassed 155 acres of improved land at his farm. (Courtesy of Mary Knickerbocker Menzie.)

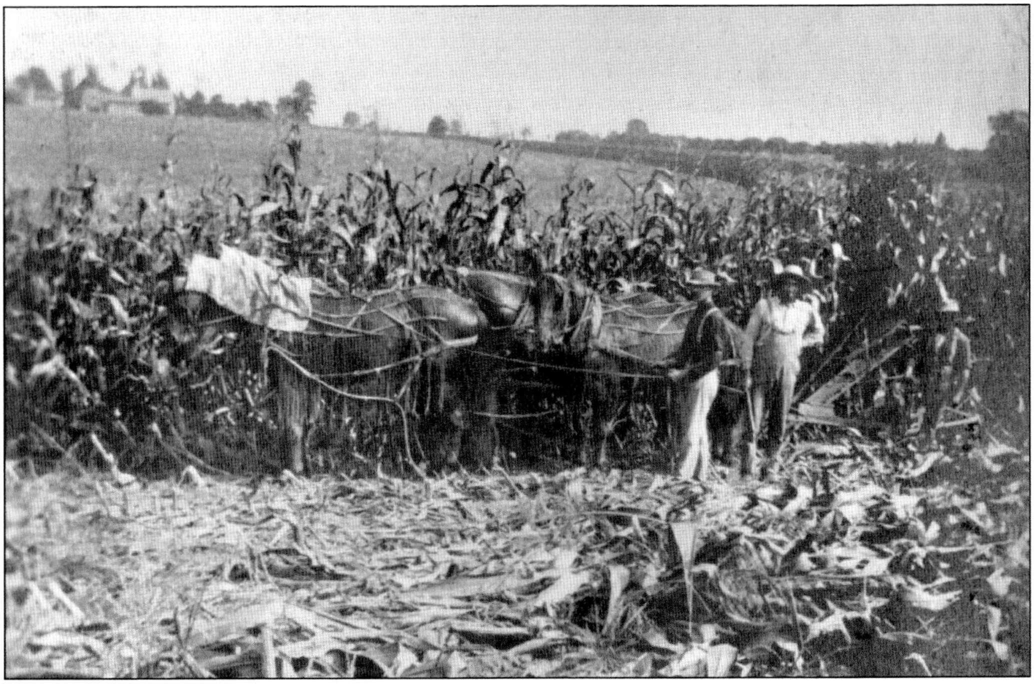

The four horses and three unidentified men standing in front of the corn stalks are barely visible; they are well camouflaged. They are working on the William H. Barker farm on Mendon Center Road. (Courtesy of Mary Knickerbocker Menzie.)

Five

TRANSPORTATION

In the very early days of Northfield, when the original families were arriving, an oxen-drawn wagon was considered the most efficient way to travel on trails and over heavily forested land. Those oxen could then be used to aid in clearing the homestead of the hardwood trees that were so prevalent in this western, virgin area of New York State.

Eventually, when landscapes were cleared and other pioneers arrived, the trails became more defined roads, and horses and other livestock could transverse the countryside. Much of the travel was completed in the winter using sleighs on frozen ground, which made traveling much smoother than going over the ruts and holes of the muddy terrain.

When the Erie Canal was completed to Pittsford in 1822, many travelers from New England and points east would pack all their worldly goods into a packet boat and shorten their travel by weeks. Gliding on the Erie from Albany to Pittsford took about six days rather than the six weeks it had taken overland.

Motorcars became the passion of some of the more adventuresome residents of the town and soon were "speeding" down village streets at five to seven miles per hour. The town fathers rapidly determined that a constable was required to enforce a speed limit. That extended even to bicycles.

Of course, the arrival of the automobile caused the demise of the wagon shop, wheelwrights, and the blacksmiths and encouraged the need for mechanical garages and gas stations. A wagon shop that was located at a busy corner of the State Road and Route 96 burned down, and the first gas and service station was eventually erected on that site.

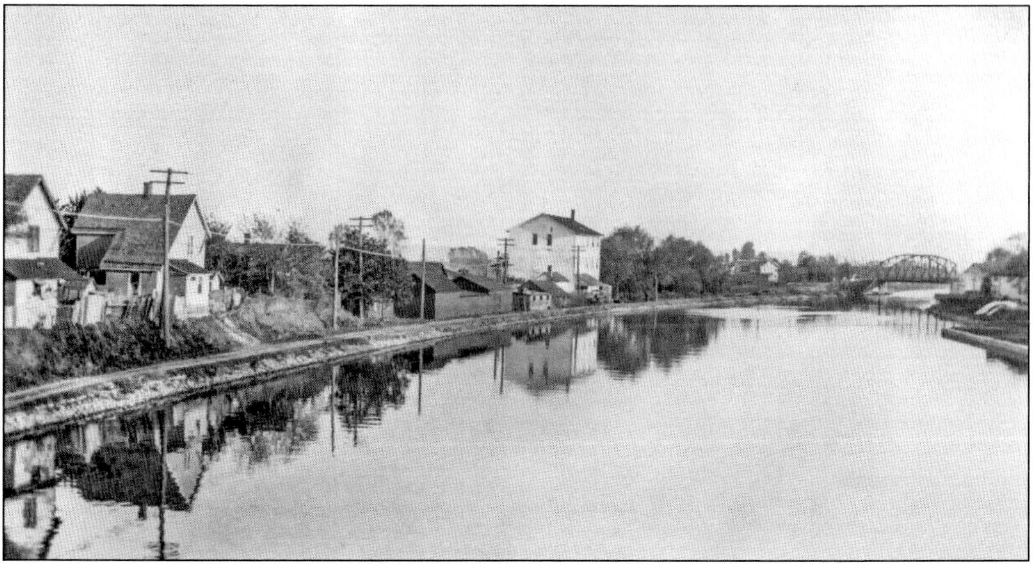

Schoen Place looks significantly different without its signature landmarks, the coal tower and grain elevator. This photograph was taken around 1915 from the North Main Street Bridge looking east. The coal tower was not constructed until the 1920s, and the grain elevator was built in 1939. (Courtesy of Lindsay Bach, D. Gordon Earl Collection.)

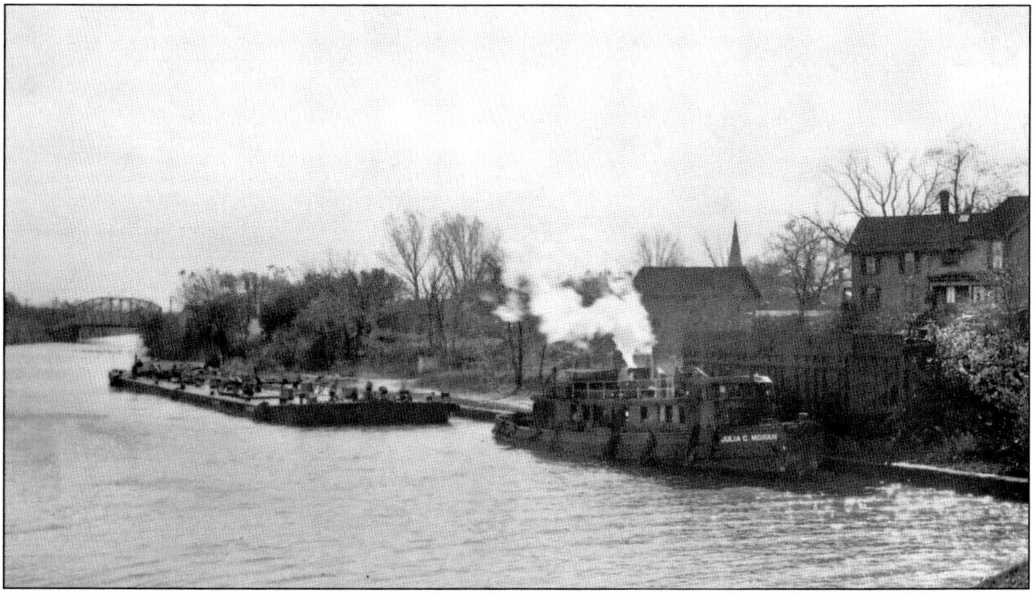

The towing vessel *Julia C. Moran* is shown here at the Zornow coal chutes, located just east of the North Main Street Bridge. The area beyond the *Julia C. Moran* is now the Port of Pittsford Park, two acres along the canal, which has recently been renovated to include a new band pavilion. (Courtesy of the Pittsford Town Historian.)

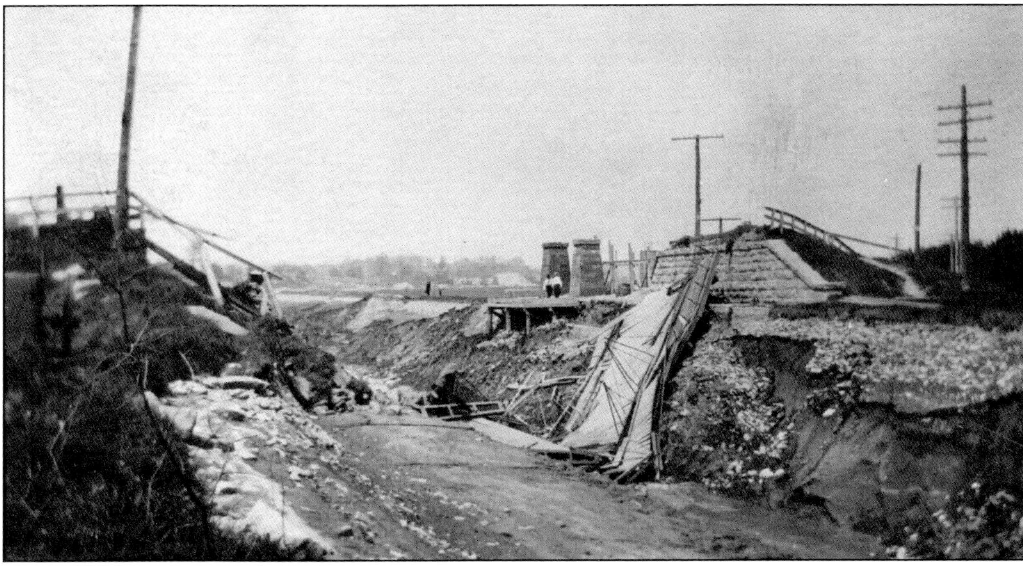

A concrete trough carrying the canal over Irondequoit Creek at Bushnell's Basin gave way on September 3, 1912, flooding area crops and damaging equipment used to enlarge the canal. No one was hurt, but 90 feet of canal were swept away, and over $250,000 of damage was done. The photograph shows just a small bit of the devastation. Enterprising automobile owners charged fees to carry groups of people to see the canal break firsthand. (Courtesy of the Pittsford Town Historian.)

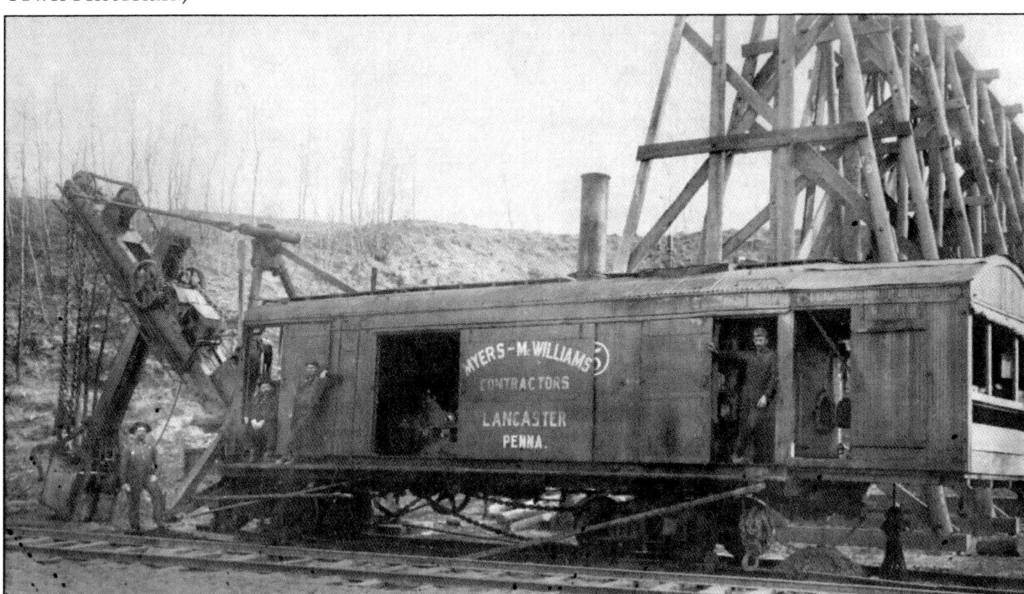

Myers & McWilliams out of Lancaster, Pennsylvania, was one of the companies contracted to work on the Barge Canal, shown here near the Great Embankment. In 1916, Myers & McWilliams celebrated the completion of their Barge Canal contract work at Bushnell's Basin by throwing a party for 400 people. The Bushnell's Basin male quartet, composed of Clinton Hegeman, Charles Kossow, John Woltman, and Fred Gerlach, with special guest baritone Harland Spiegel, performed at the celebration. (Courtesy of the Pittsford Town Historian.)

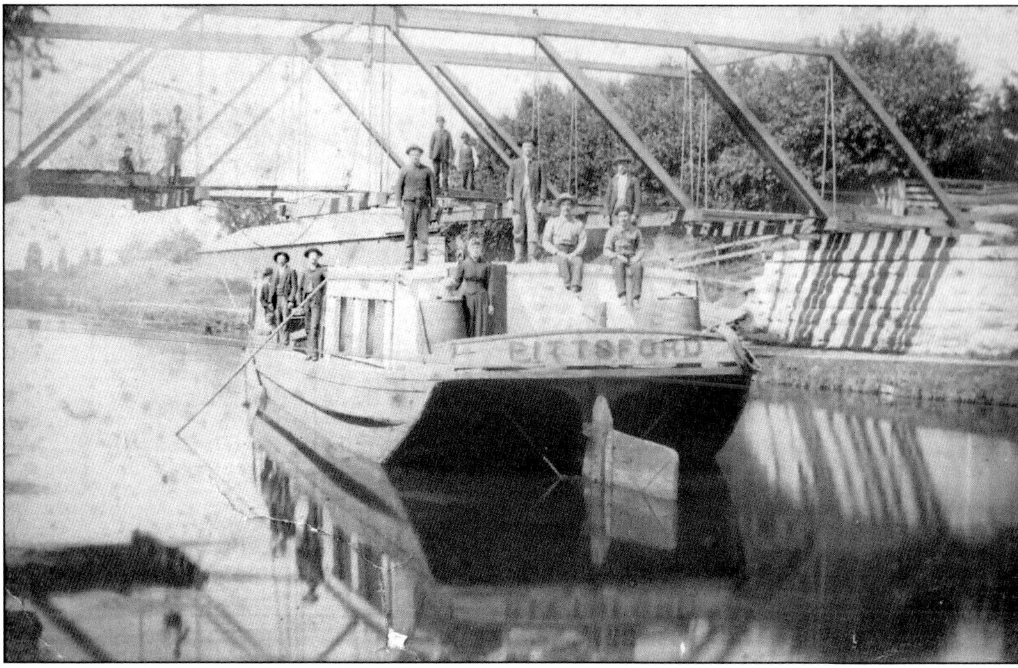

Little is known about this wonderful packet boat named *Pittsford*. A lone woman stands in the center of the photograph. Eight men are shown on the boat, and an additional four men stand on the bridge, which appears to be under repair. (Courtesy of the Pittsford Town Historian.)

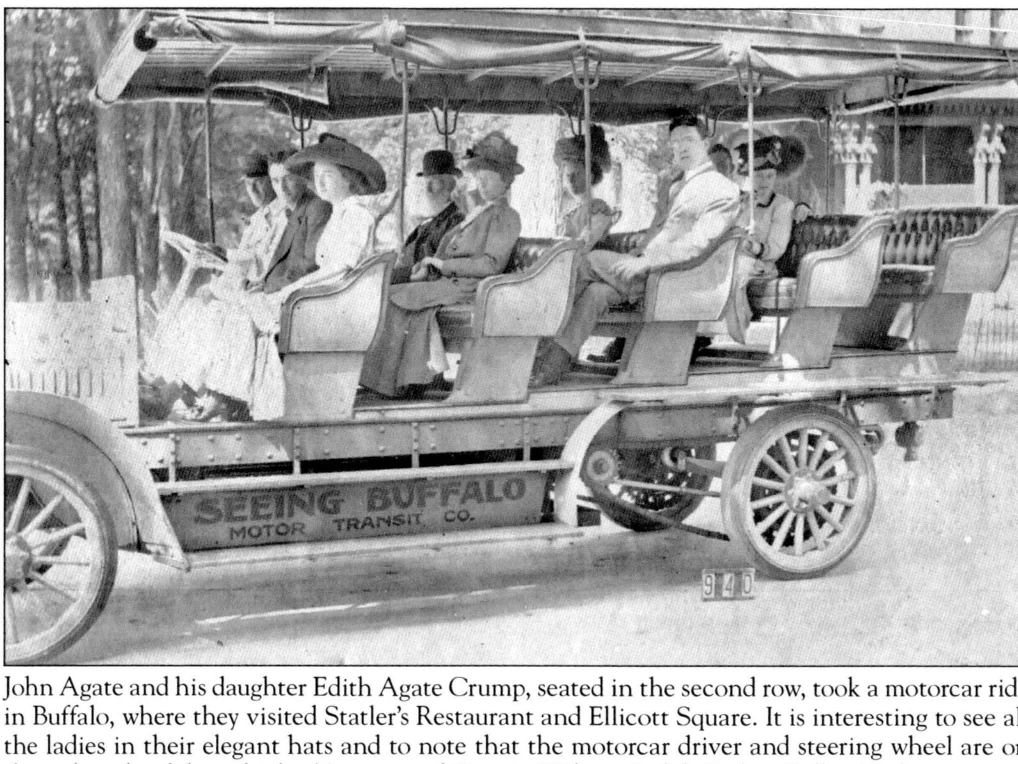

John Agate and his daughter Edith Agate Crump, seated in the second row, took a motorcar ride in Buffalo, where they visited Statler's Restaurant and Ellicott Square. It is interesting to see all the ladies in their elegant hats and to note that the motorcar driver and steering wheel are on the right side of the vehicle. (Courtesy of Connie Wilson, Ralph Parker Collection.)

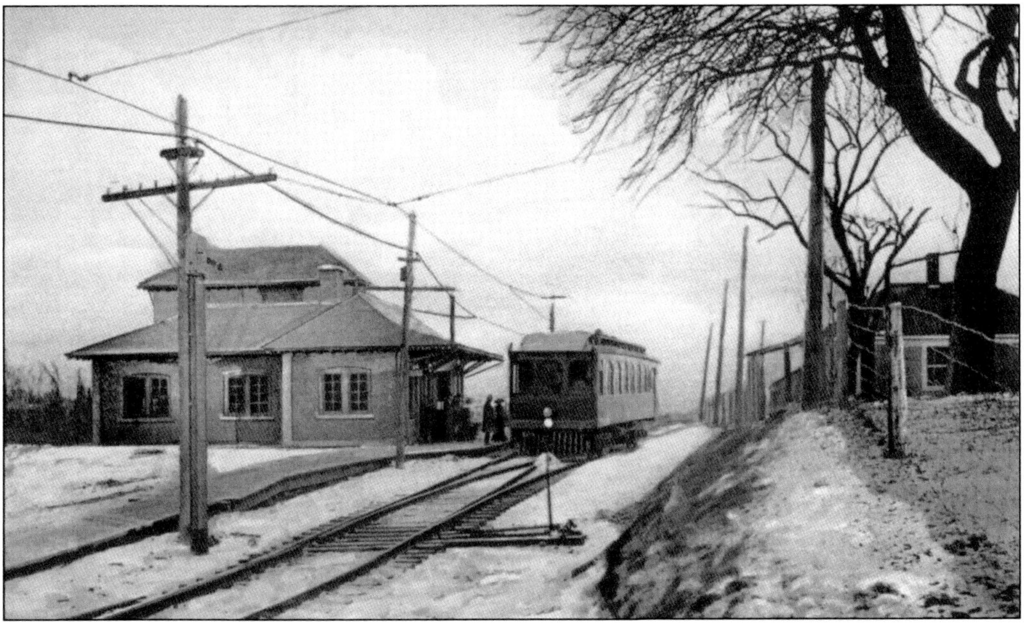

The trolley station was located at the site of the current Pittsford Pub, at 60 North Main Street. Service on the Rochester & Eastern Rapid Railway began in 1902. The line passed under the West Shore Railroad bridge, south on Main Street and east toward Bushnell's Basin. The fare was 14¢. As more people purchased automobiles, the railway business dimmed, and the last trolley run was made in 1930. (Courtesy of Mike Battle, www.flourcitypost.com.)

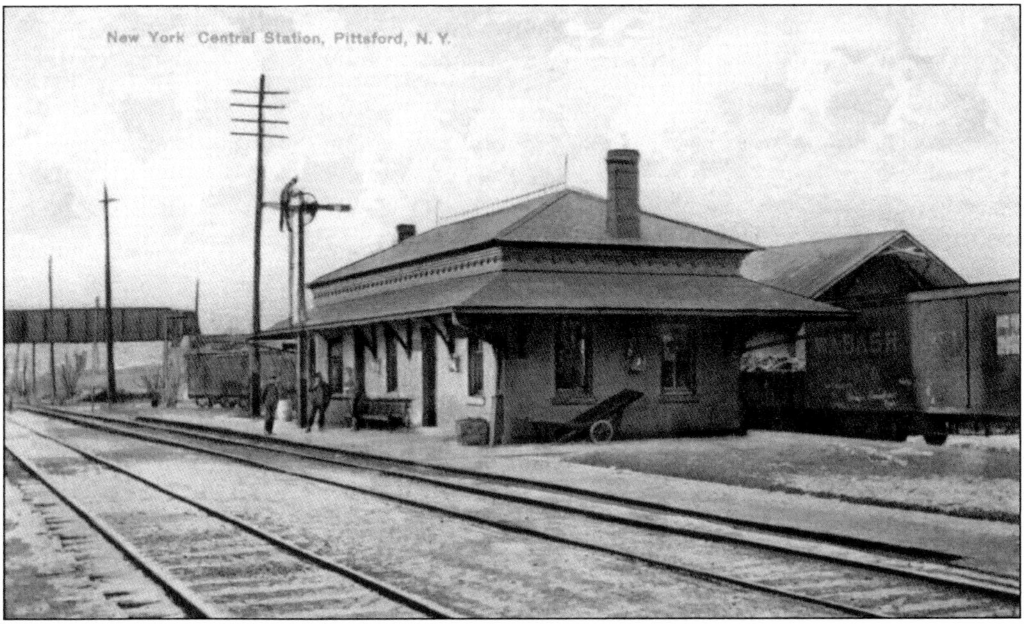

Pittsford's station house was built in 1860 by the New York Central Railroad, which owned the property at 41–43 North Main Street from that time up until 1962. The adjoining freight house was built in 1863. After passenger service was discontinued in 1959, the line became a freight spur. By 1963, the station house had been remodeled as the Depot restaurant. The complex is now Del Monte Lodge. (Courtesy of Mike Battle, www.flourcitypost.com.)

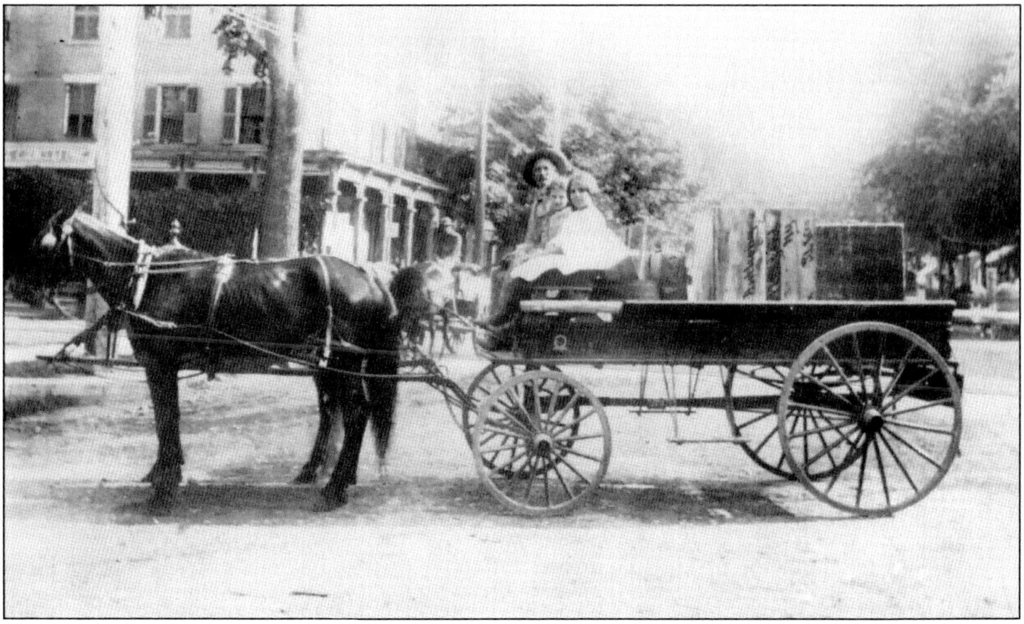

James Strickland was a carpenter before becoming a mail carrier. In 1909, James was appointed expressman in Pittsford village by the American Express Company, allowing him to deliver any express matter arriving at the railway station. He appears to be delivering packages here. James was the son of Edwin and Eliza Harmor Strickland and the husband of Elizabeth Cutting. (Courtesy of Paul M. Spiegel.)

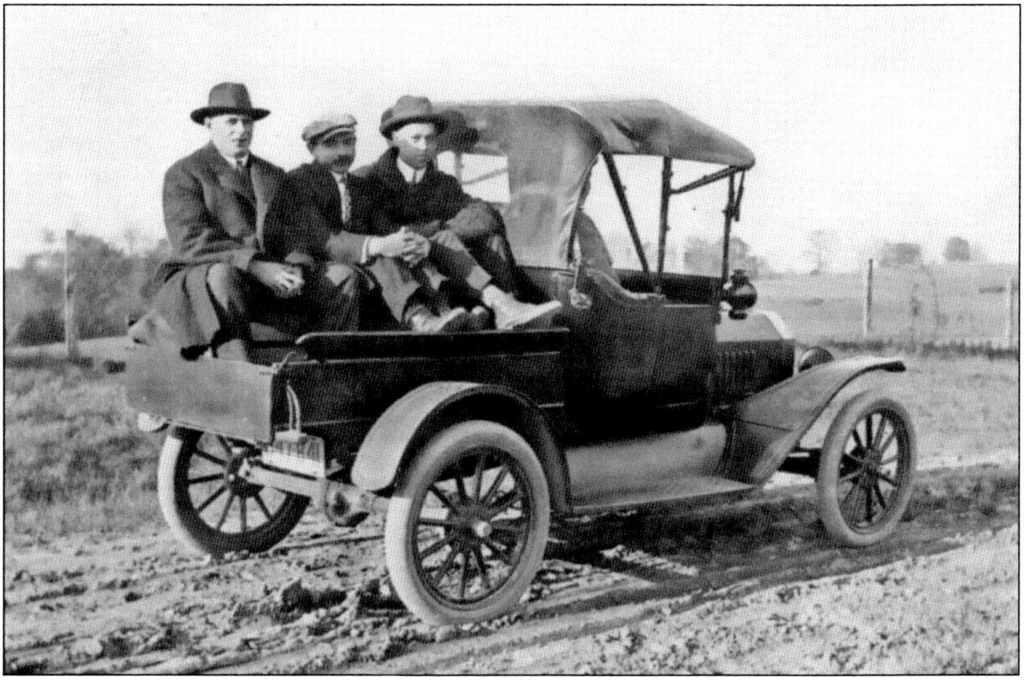

Charles Earl, his cousin Charlie Earls, and Ed Mitchell ride in Schoen's truck at Allen's Hill in 1915. Allen's Hill is near Richmond, New York, where Charlie Earls lived. (Courtesy of Lindsay Bach, D. Gordon Earl Collection.)

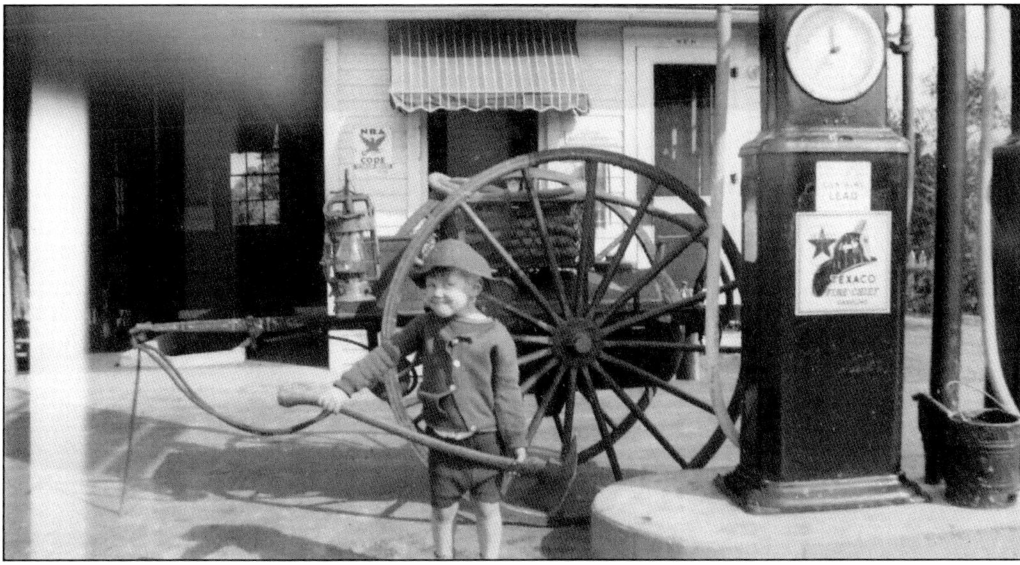

Robert Place, son of Eleanor Rand and E. William Place, is having a great time pretending to be a firefighter in this 1934 photograph. This gasoline station was the first station owned by Bill Place and was located in Bushnell's Basin where Marsh and Jefferson Roads converge. The station had six pumps, each supplying gasoline from a different company. (Courtesy of Bob Place.)

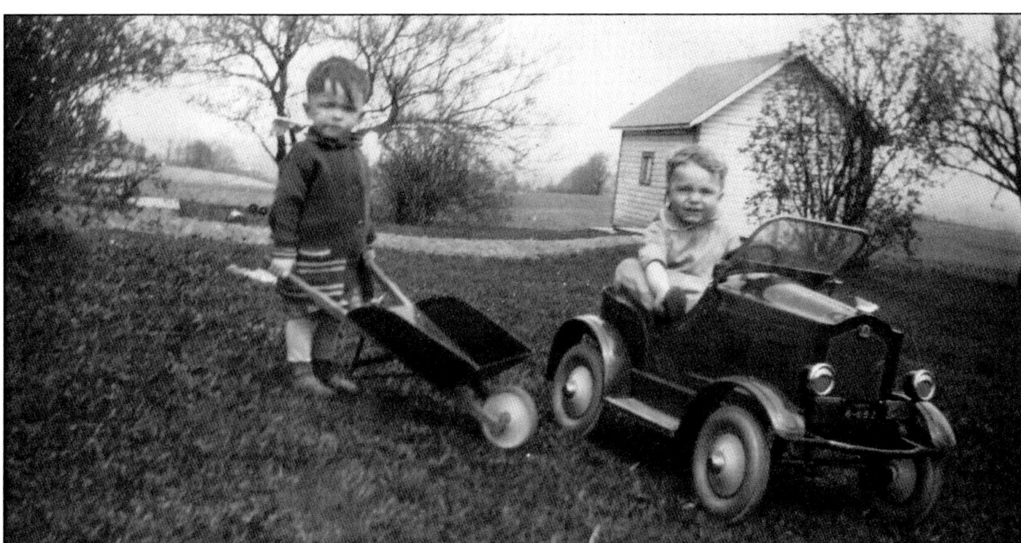

Little boys need their toys, and cousins Paul and J. Monroe Knickerbocker are no exceptions. Paul wields the wheelbarrow as Monroe prepares for a journey in his automobile. (Courtesy of Mary Knickerbocker Menzie.)

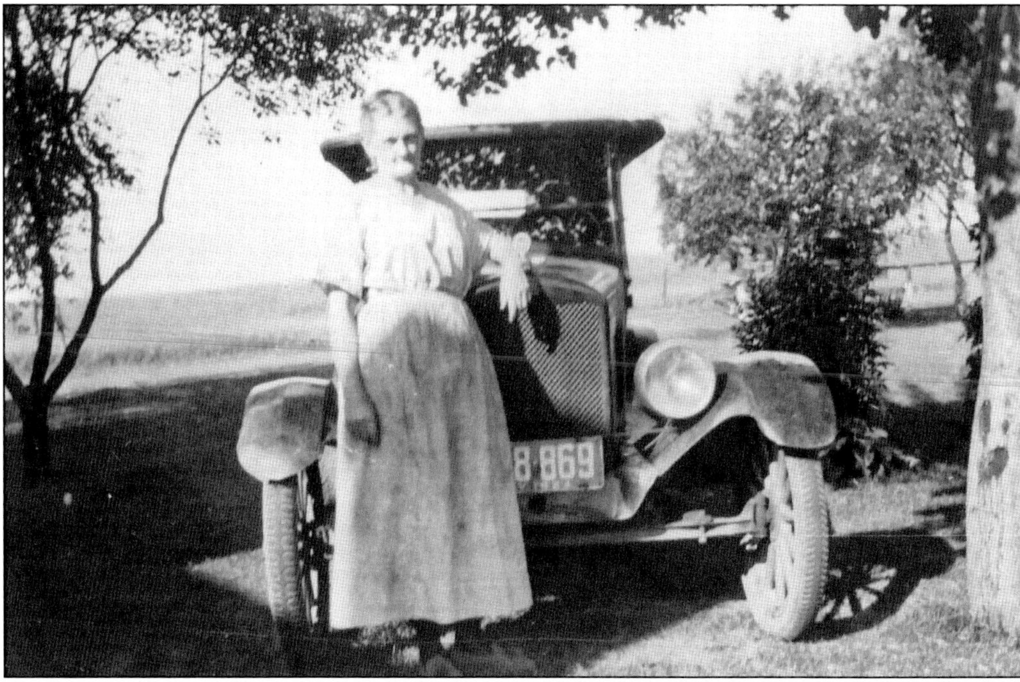

Mina Brown Hulbert proudly stands by her roadster in this undated photograph. (Courtesy of Gail Hulbert Esker and Marilyn Hulbert Nielsen.)

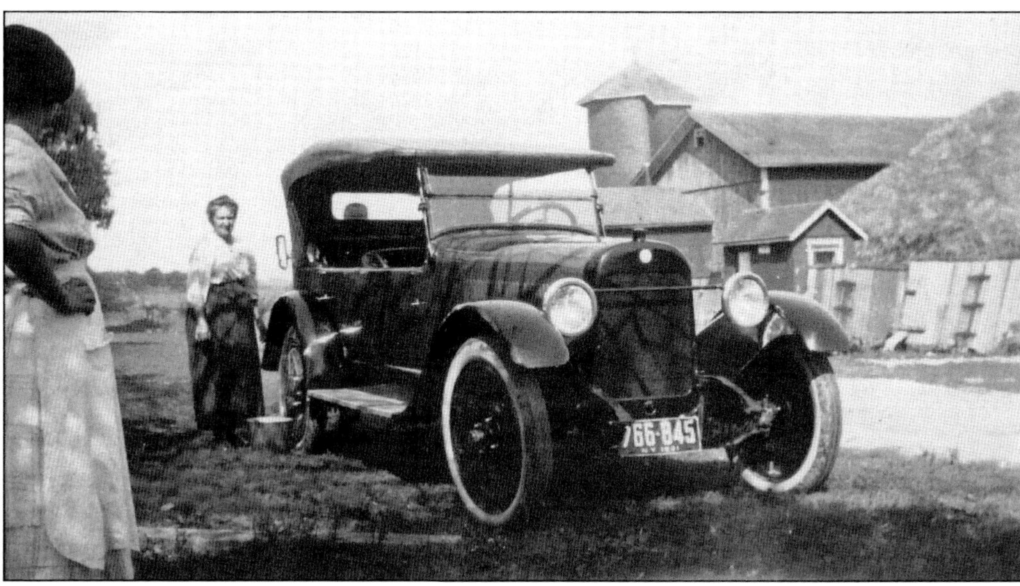

This car appears to be parked outside the William Clawson barn on Noakes Road. The woman is unidentified but may be William's wife, Mary Schrader Clawson. (Courtesy of the Willard family.)

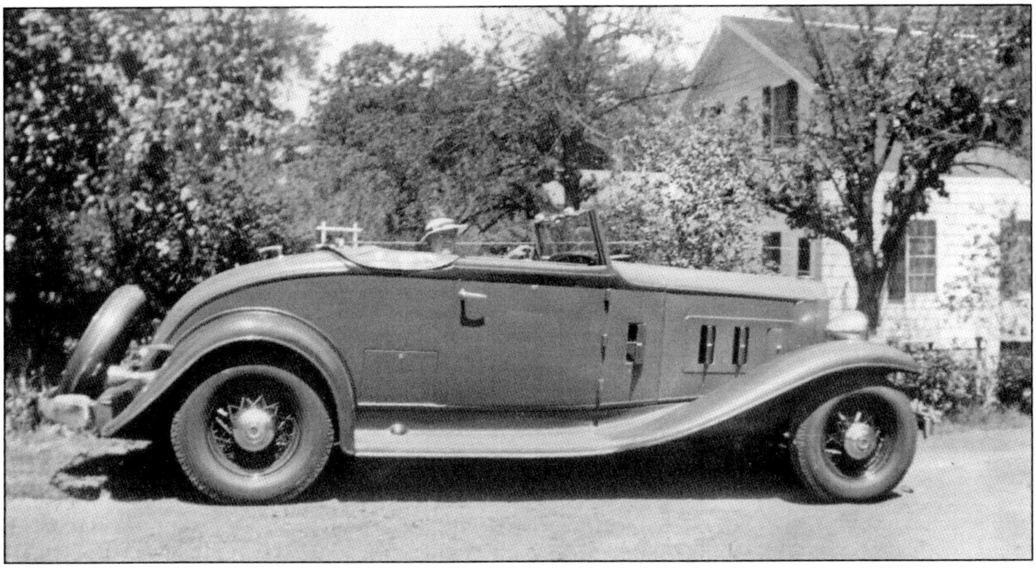

Louise Spiegel Kingsley, barely noticeable behind the wheel of her large 12-cylinder Packard, prepares to take it out for a spin. Louise was the oldest child of Thomas and Mary Walbeck Spiegel and the wife of Willis Kingsley. (Courtesy of Paul M. Spiegel.)

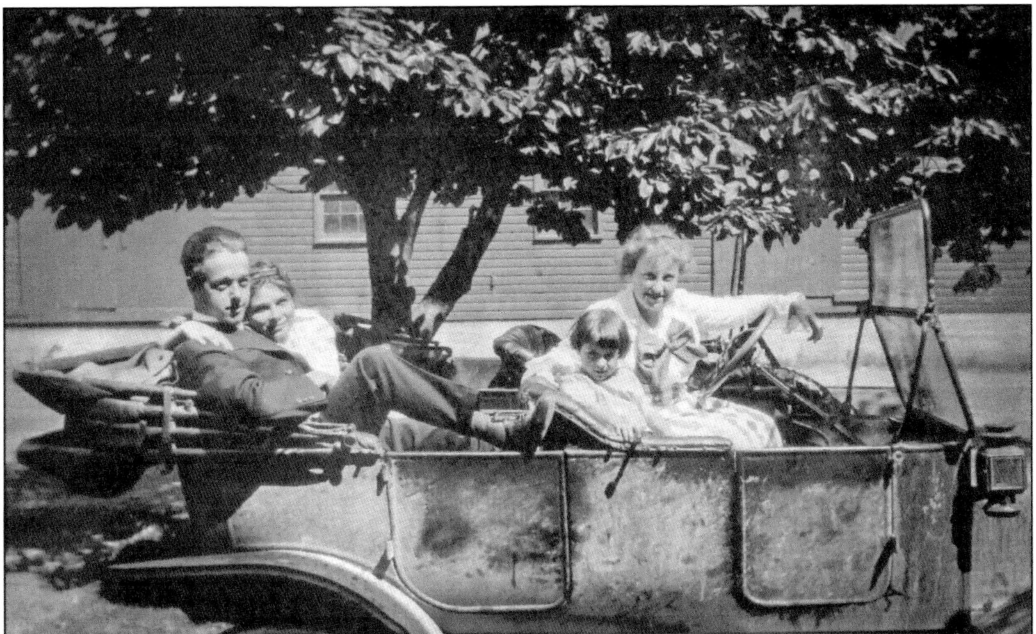

The Earl girls head out for a joy ride of their own. Edna Earl sits in back with her beau. (Courtesy of Lindsay Bach, D. Gordon Earl Collection.)

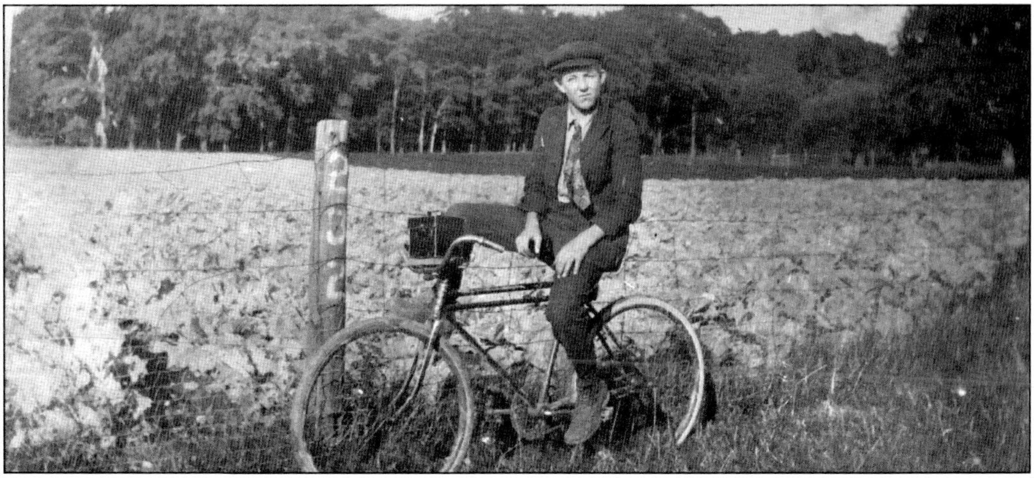

Grant Peglow appears to be on his way to school. His lunch pail is securely affixed to the front of his bike, and he is wearing his best striped pants and patterned tie. It is difficult to tell what type of crop is behind the wire fence; although, it appears to be cabbage. (Courtesy of the Willard family.)

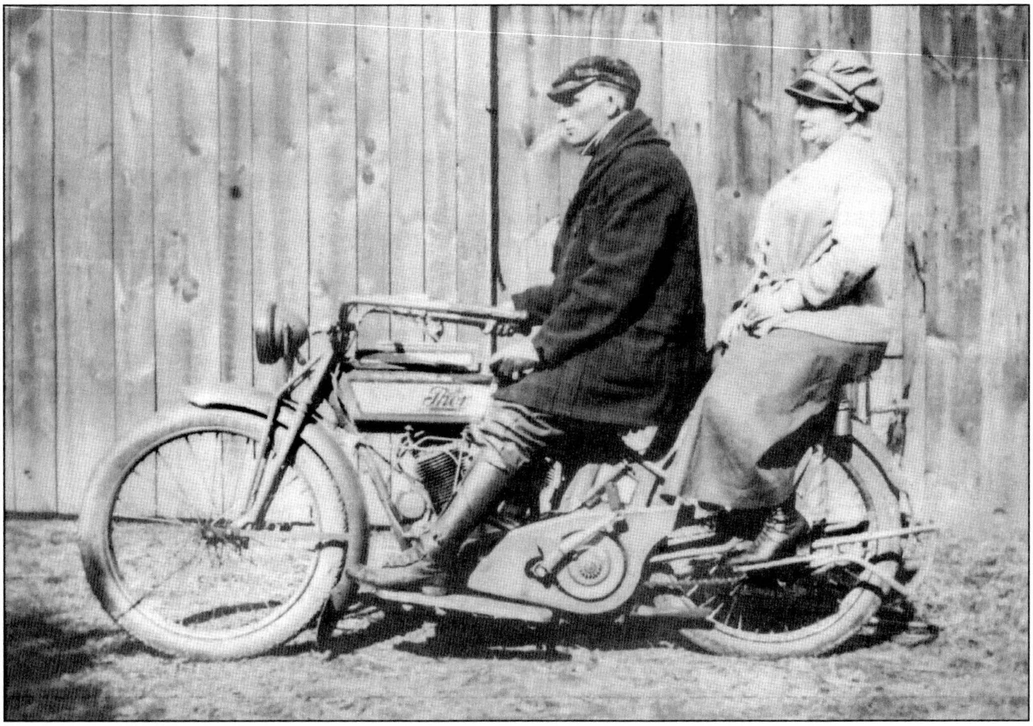

This Thor motorcycle is a beauty! It may be a Thor Twin Model U, which was produced in 1916. Thor motorcycles were produced from 1907 to 1917. The unidentified riders are wearing some nice leather gaiters. Since no acetylene gas tank is visible, the bike is equipped with electric lighting. (Courtesy of Lindsay Bach, D. Gordon Earl Collection.)

Six

Entertainment and Recreation

Most of the entertainment and recreation in Pittsford centered around the churches and their festivals, dinners, and contests in the late 19th century. Almost all the churches held summer picnics, which had racing contests and games. Many held dinners not only for members of the congregation but also for the entire town.

The Grange was established and had a very active membership. There were many forms of entertainment from that venue. Often, plays were created and produced for the enjoyment of the community and brought large crowds to the town hall where most were conducted. There were also Masonic organizations, and while their meetings were not open to the public, their dinners, festivals, and productions were. There was, and still is, a Masonic group called the Northfield Lodge, and there was a sister organization known as Northfield Order of the Eastern Star.

The Pittsford Men's Bowling League was very active and is still in existence. Almost all the able-bodied men were members of that social group. Softball and baseball teams were established in the early days of the 20th century. *Democrat & Chronicle* newspaper sponsored teams in many communities across the county.

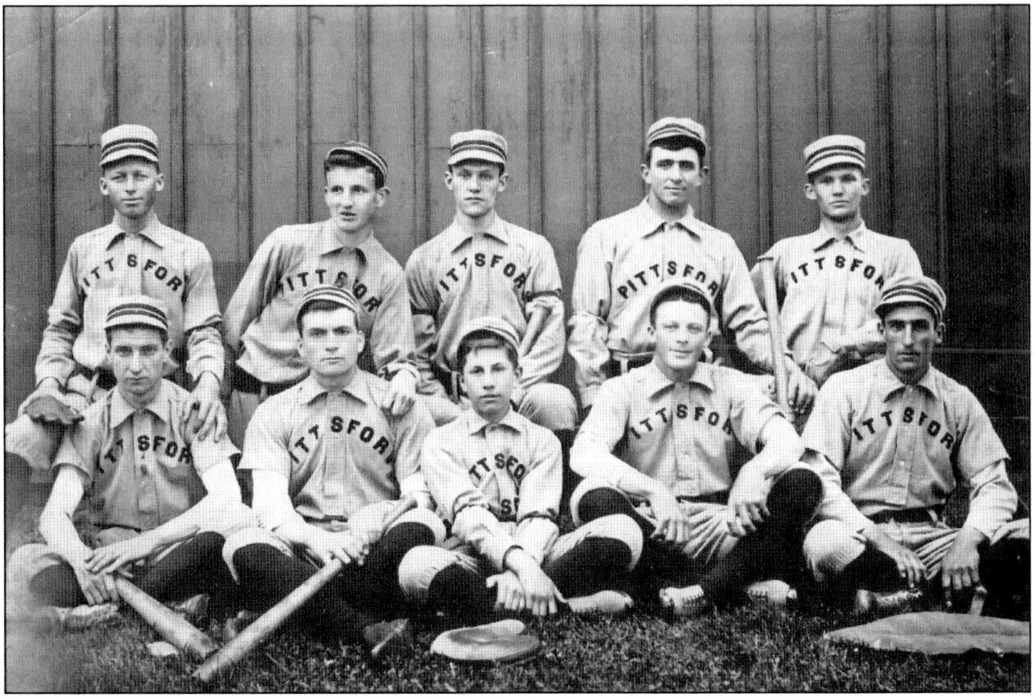

No one today recalls the record of the Pittsford men's baseball team, shown here in the 1890s. They do look quite spiffy in their uniforms, though. Pictured from left to right are (first row) Al Ives, George Miller, Fred Jones, John Ford, and Fred Farnam; (second row) Will Ford, Bert Simms, Bert Barnes, Milton Tobey, and Frank Barnes. (Courtesy of the Pittsford Town Historian.)

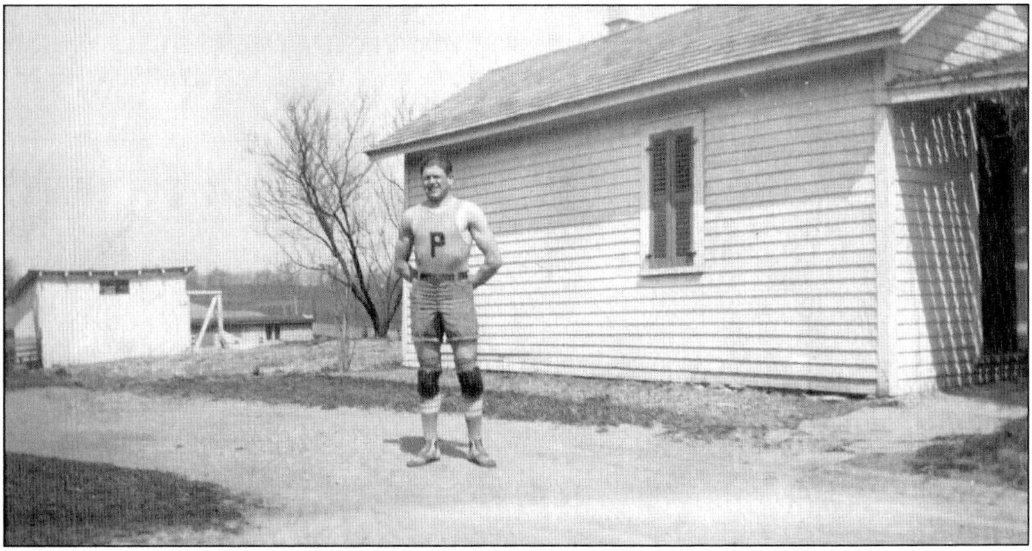

Charles Willard Lusk proudly displays his football uniform in this undated photograph. Charles, the oldest of Charles Franklin and Sarah Willard Lusk's nine children, was born New Year's Day in 1903. Charles married Hazel Minnamon in 1928. After her death, he wed Bessie Hayton Geil. Charles died in 1995 at age 92. (Courtesy of Bill Lusk.)

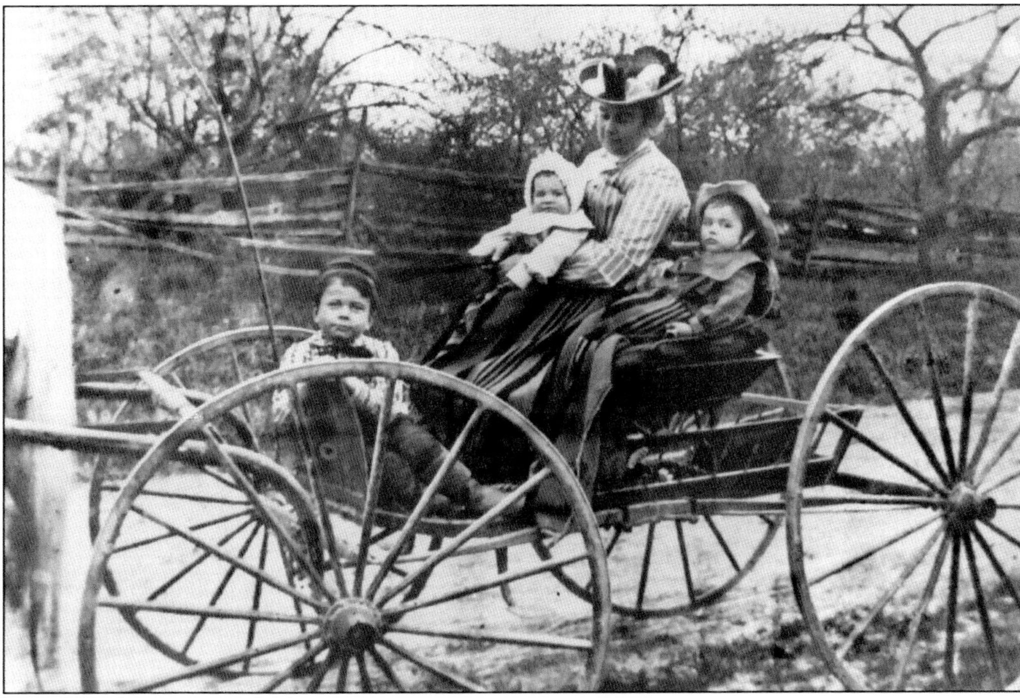

Lettie Maie Nye Hopkins takes her three youngest children for a carriage ride in 1902. From left to right are Phelps, Jane, Lettie Maie, and Delora. (Courtesy of the Engert family.)

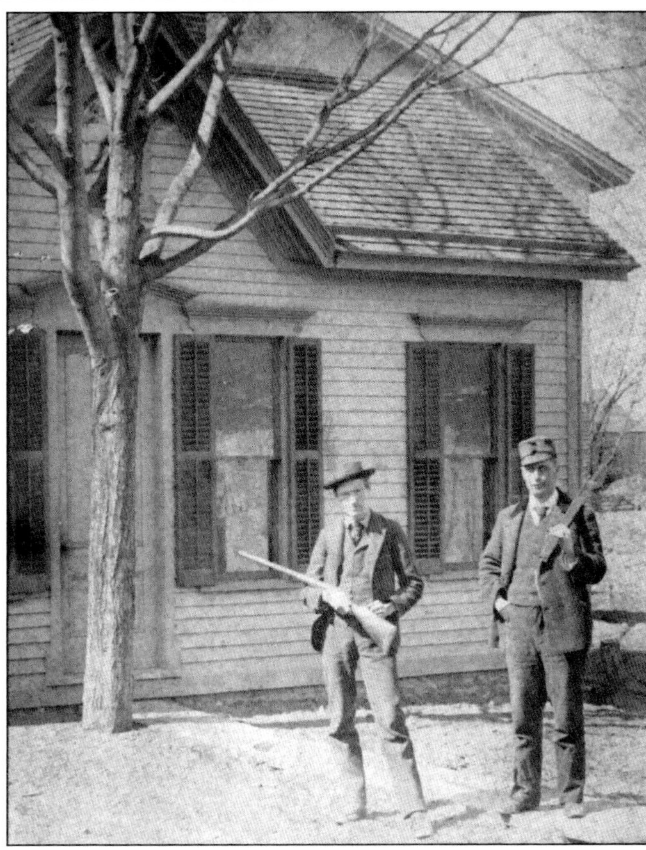

Elroy Agate, at left, and his first-cousin William J. Agate appear to be on a hunting expedition. Elroy, born in 1874, was the son of John and Mary Jane Austin Agate. William, the son of William and Helen Willard Agate, was born in 1862. The young men lived next door to each other on North Main Street and seem to have been good friends. (Courtesy of Connie Wilson, Ralph Parker Collection.)

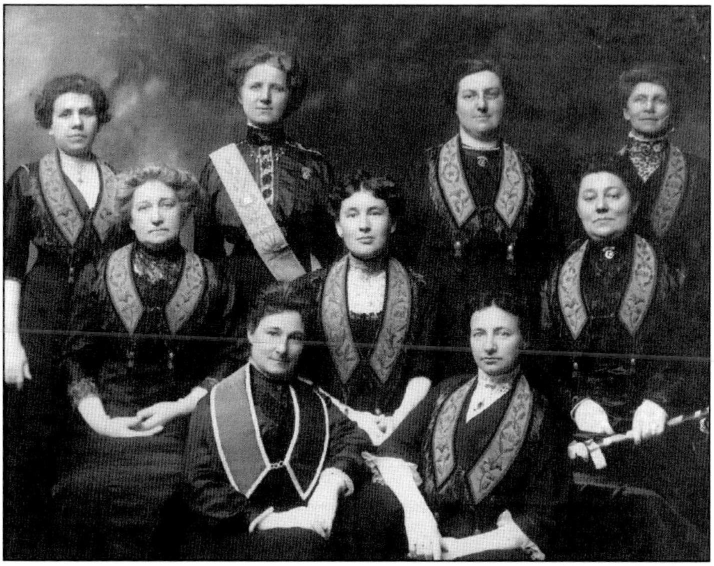

The members of the Monroe County District Deputy's Staff of Rebekahs are shown around 1915. The Rebekahs were a fraternal and service organization associated with the Independent Order of Odd Fellows. Pictured are, from left to right, (first row) Elizabeth Kelly Stone and Ida Bachman; (second row) unidentified, Lizzie Hicks, and Rose Kohler; (third row) three unidentified women and Mary LaRock. (Courtesy of the Pittsford Town Historian.)

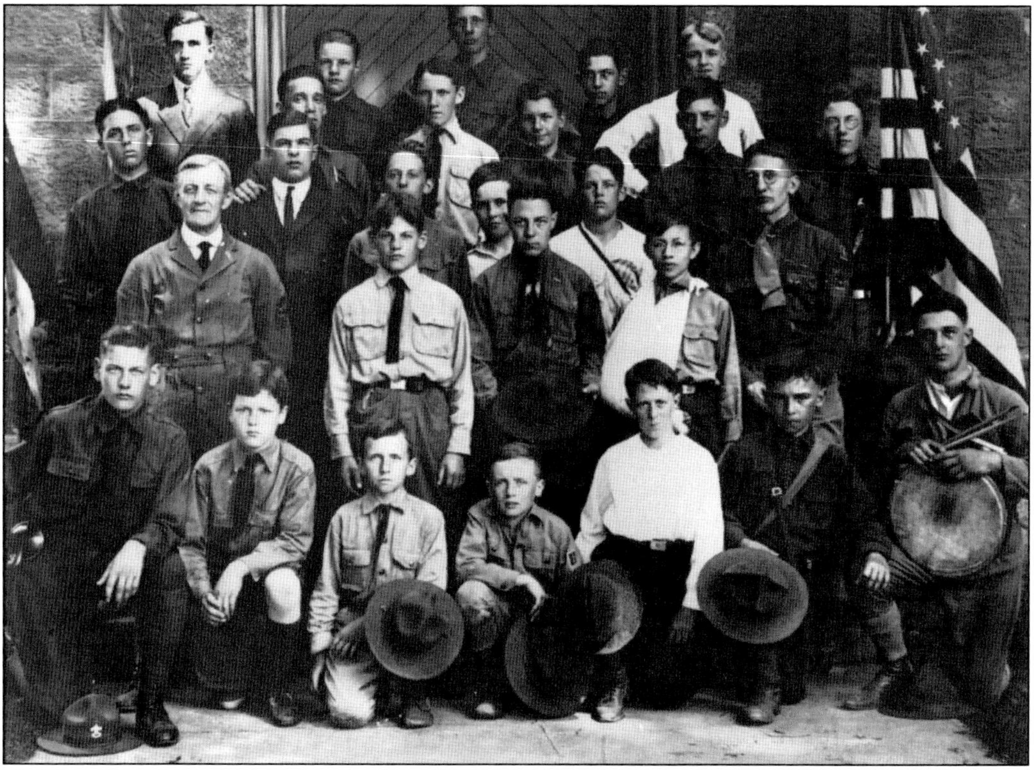

The Boy Scouts, shown around 1921, are, from left to right, (first row) Shelley D. Crump, Carol Crump, Everett Kunow, Edward Scamp, Leslie Whiting, Robert Occor, and ? Smith; (second row) Scout Master Edwin F. Smith, Elliot Crump, Willard Faulkner, Arthur Crump, and John Roach; (third row) William Chesterman, Frank Rossiter, Bradley Earls, Deryck Place, and unidentified; (fourth row) Alfred Farnam, Robert Ford, Gordon Malchow, Donnelly Gilbert, Robert Rand, Horace Rylott, Lester Schilds, Alfred Kramer, James Jewel, and Everett Cole. (Courtesy of the Engert family.)

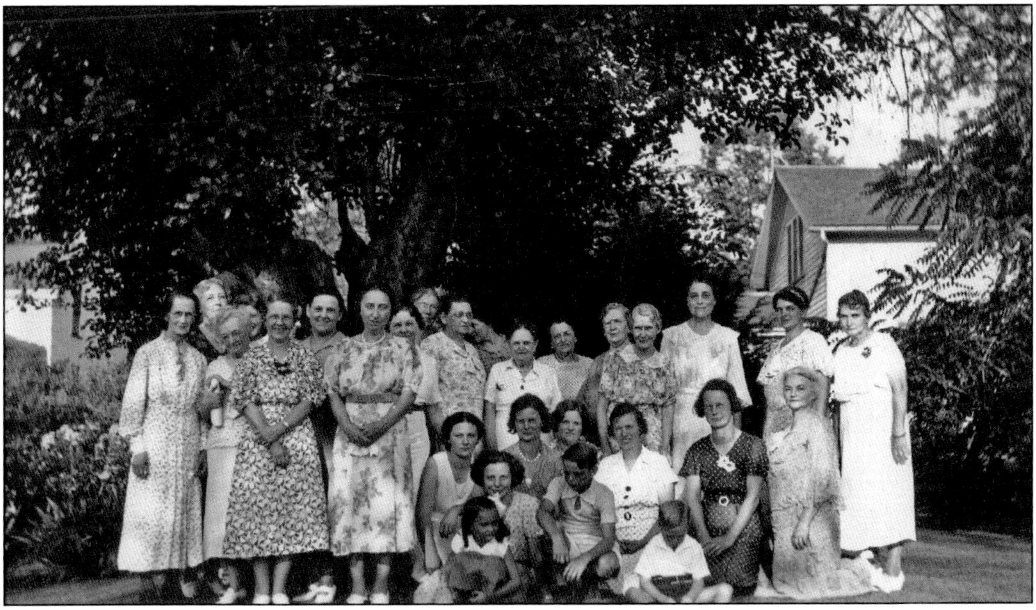

The 64th birthday of Lela Knickerbocker Whitlock was celebrated on August 16, 1937, with a surprise tea given by her friends and family. Lela, the daughter of Egbert and Mary Newton Knickerbocker, was born in 1873. She became the second wife of Andrew Whitlock in 1919. (Courtesy of Wenda Tompkins Silco.)

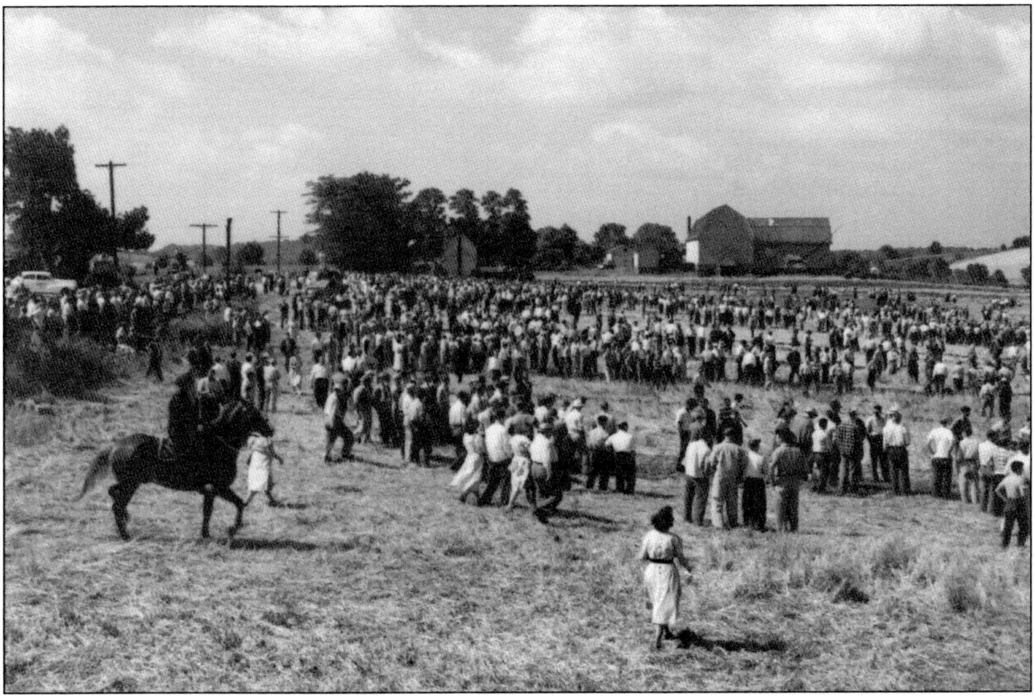

It is unclear what all these people came to see at the Hopkins farm on Clover Street in 1937. However, it must have been something very interesting to draw so many people on a beautiful cloud-filled day. The occasion may have been a harvest festival that drew people from all over the state. The mounted police even attended the event. (Courtesy of Mark Greene and John Hopkins.)

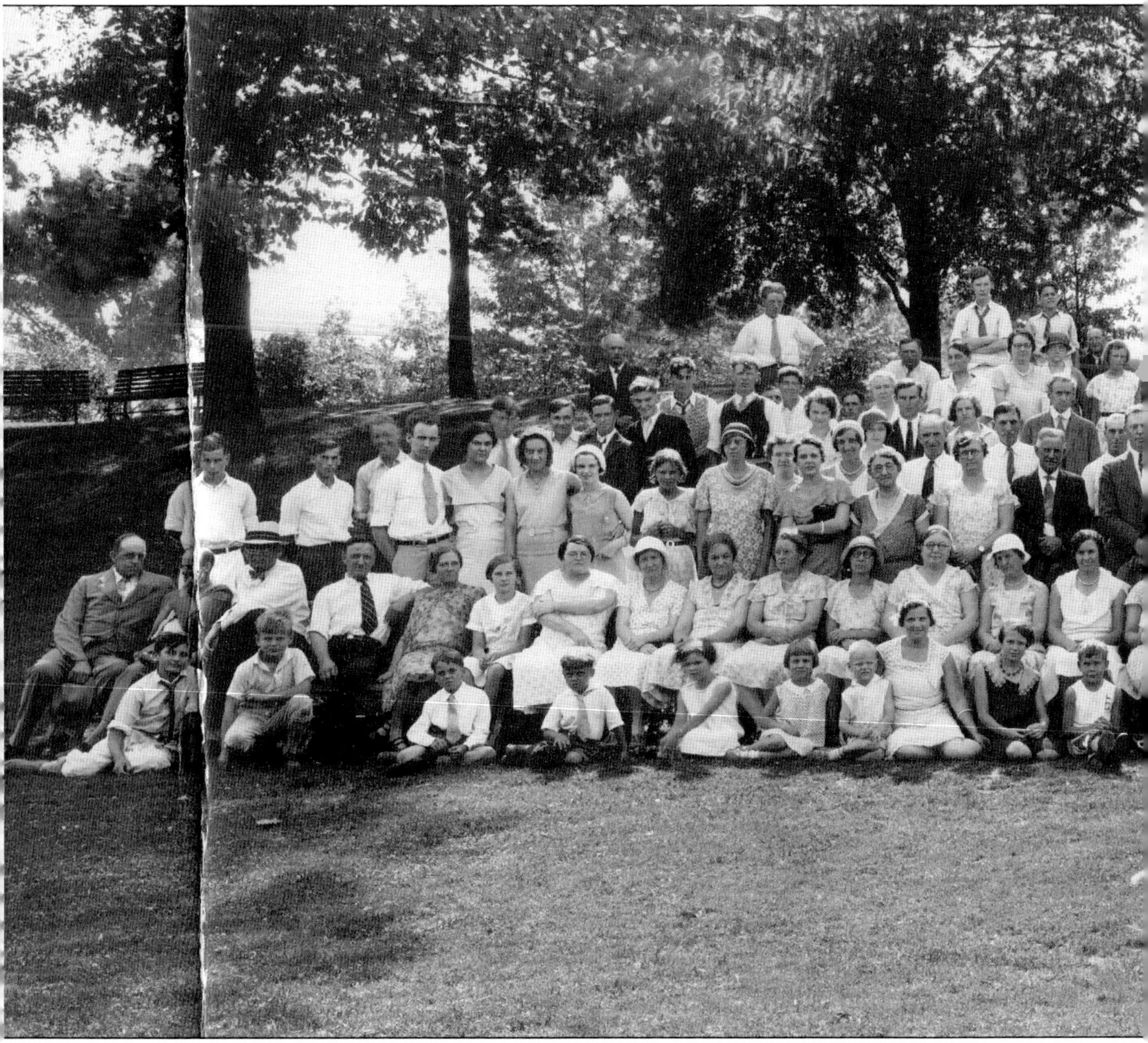

The Pittsford Grange No. 424 was active in Pittsford for much of the 20th century. Multiple newspaper articles recount the picnics, speakers, and other special events members attended in support of the Grange. Photographer Charles Rowe took this photograph of the Pittsford

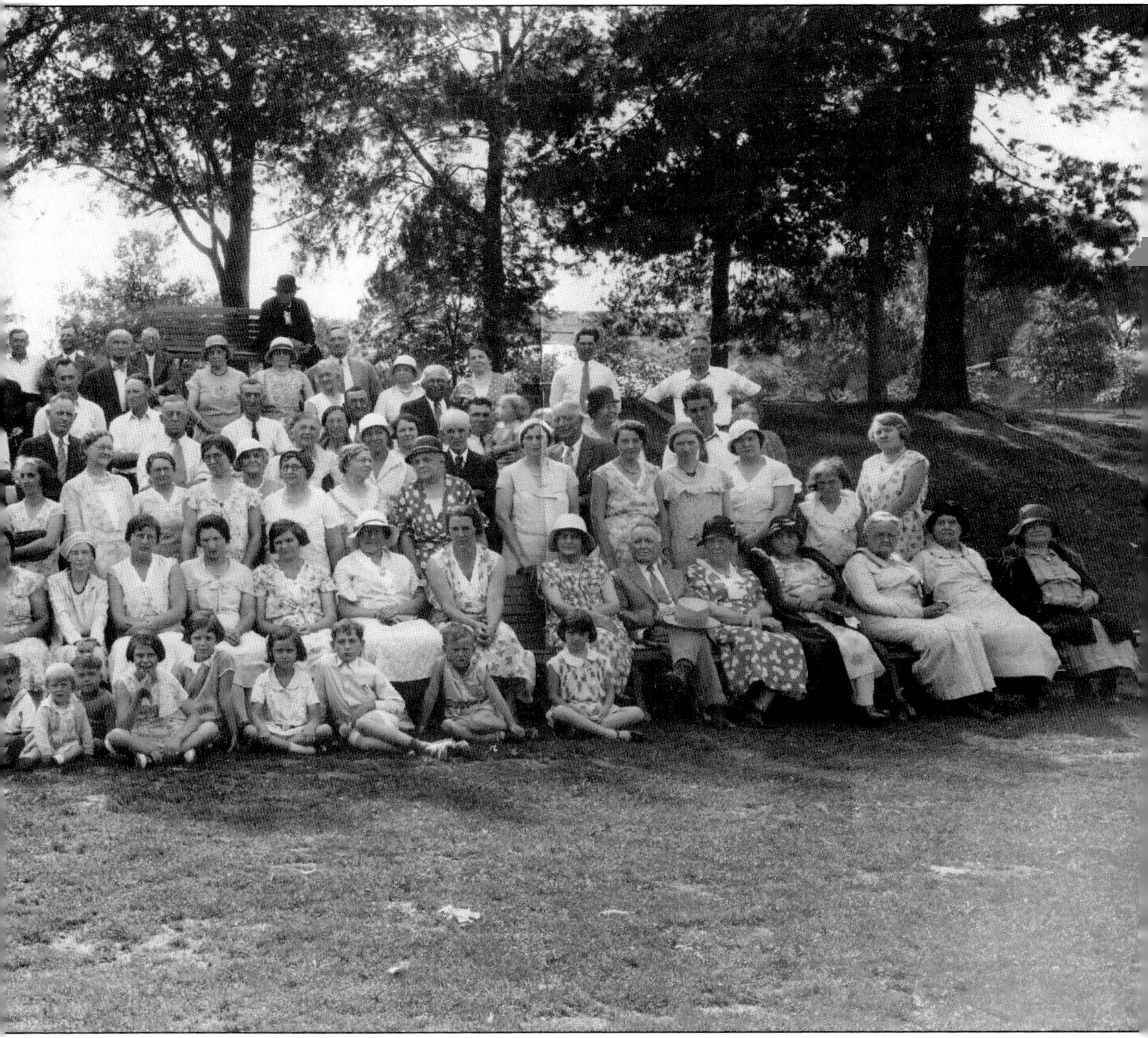

Grange members around 1930. Many of Pittsford's early families are represented here, including the Lusks, Willards, Welchs, Tobeys, Loughboroughs, Canfields, Schoens, and Ernsts. (Courtesy of the Pittsford Town Historian.)

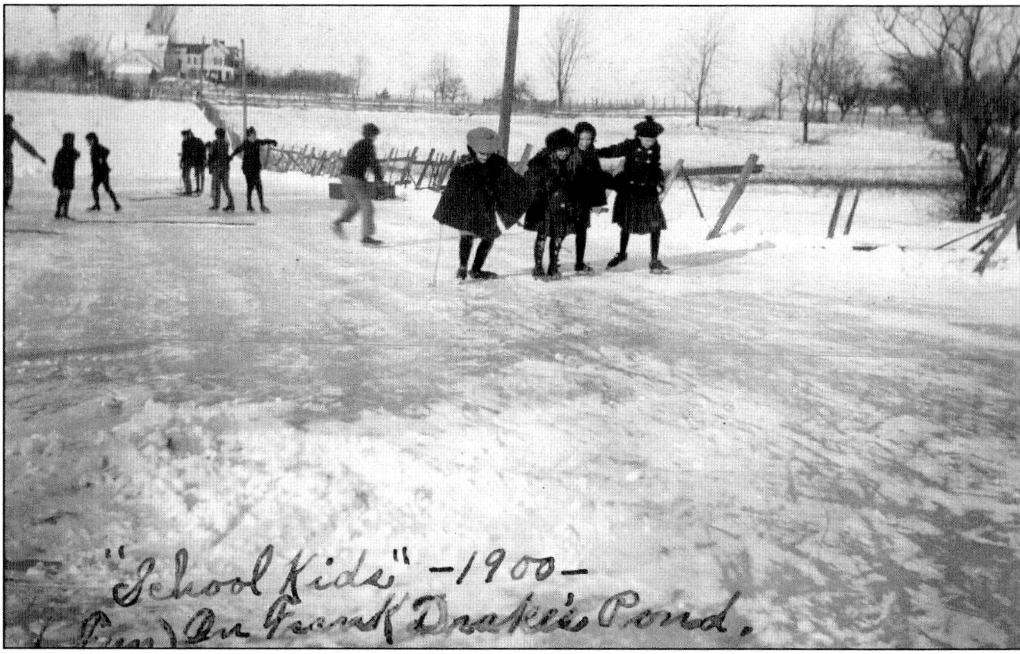

The Drake house at 73 South Main Street is a beautiful example of representative Greek Revival–style architecture, built around 1845. The children, shown here in 1900, are enjoying the other aspects of the Drake property, like skating on its pond. The large, deep lot was perfectly suited for such activities. The house in the background appears to be the Smead-Gillis residence at 30 West Jefferson Road. (Courtesy of Connie Wilson, Ralph Parker Collection.)

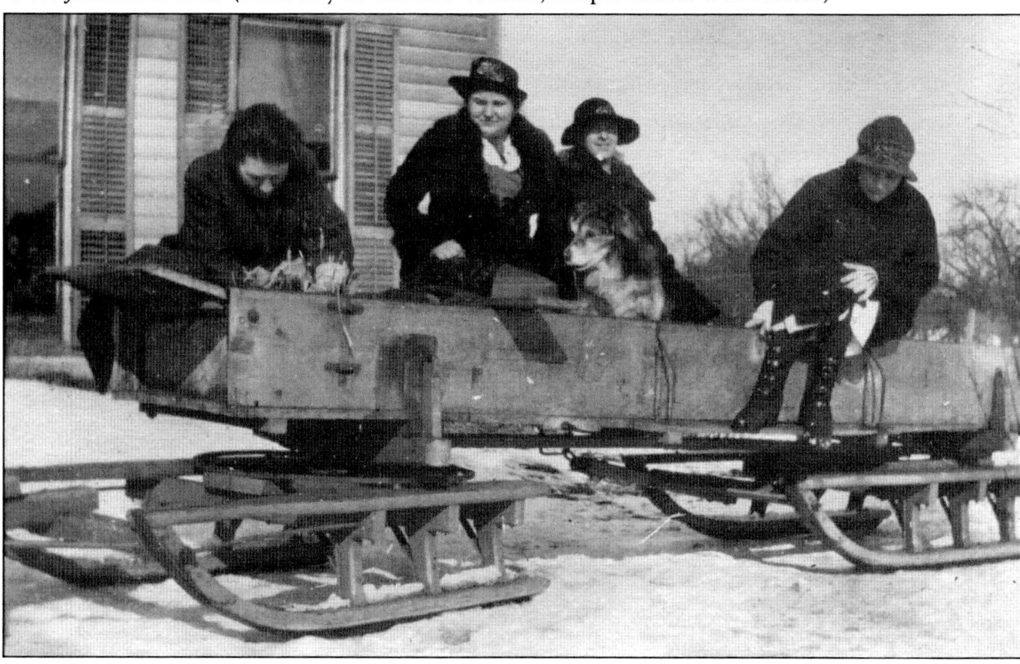

Pictured from left to right, Frances and Clara Clawson, the daughters of William and Mary Schrader Clawson, look ready for an expedition in their giant sleigh. Their neighbors, Louisa and Kate Heech, join in the fun. (Courtesy of the Willard family.)

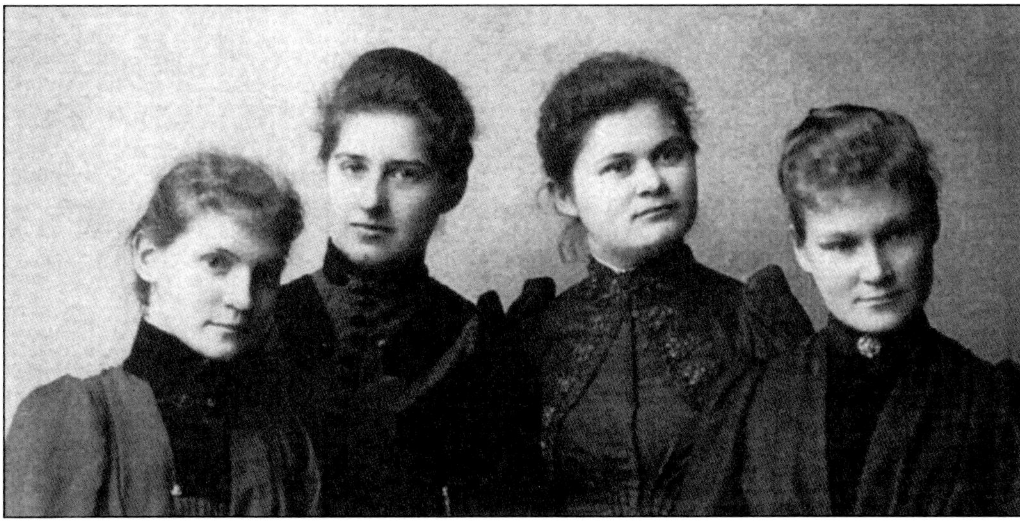

Lucia Rand and Sarah T. Sutherland pose with their friends Bessie and Clara Graves in this undated photograph. Lucia Rand, on the left, was the daughter of Daniel Curtiss Rand and his wife, Stella Wadhams Rand. Sarah T. Sutherland, second from left, was the daughter of Isaac and Gulielma Wilber Sutherland. Bessie and Clara Graves, friends visiting from Geneva, New York, were the daughters of Samuel and Elizabeth Wilson Graves. (Courtesy of Ellie Van Staagen Mitchell.)

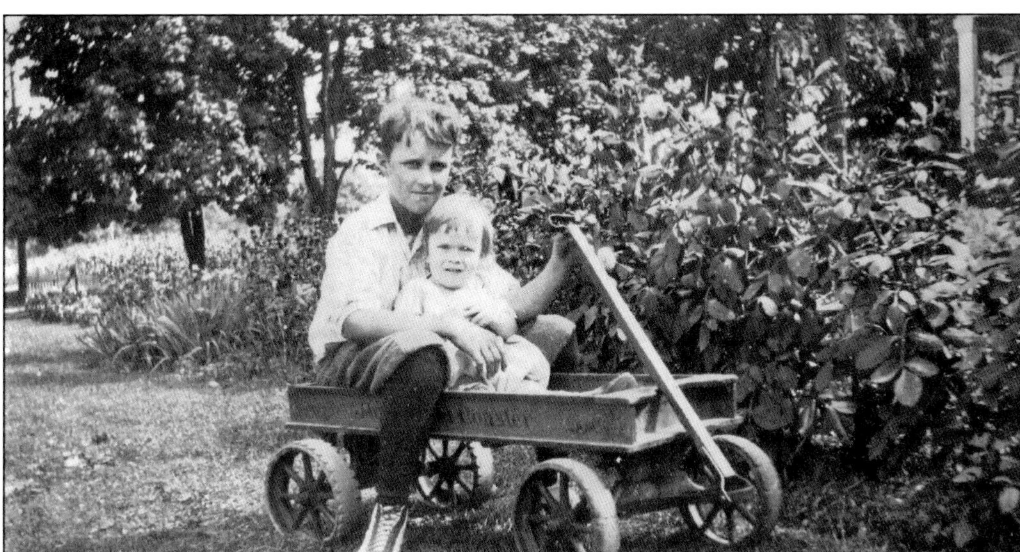

Deryck Place holds tight to his little brother Jack in this sweet photograph full of brotherly love. It is even more poignant when one learns that Deryck died in a bicycle accident a few months later on Friday, October 13, 1922, at age 13. The boys, along with older brother E. William Place, were the sons of Earl W. and Florence Minniss Place. (Courtesy of Bob Place.)

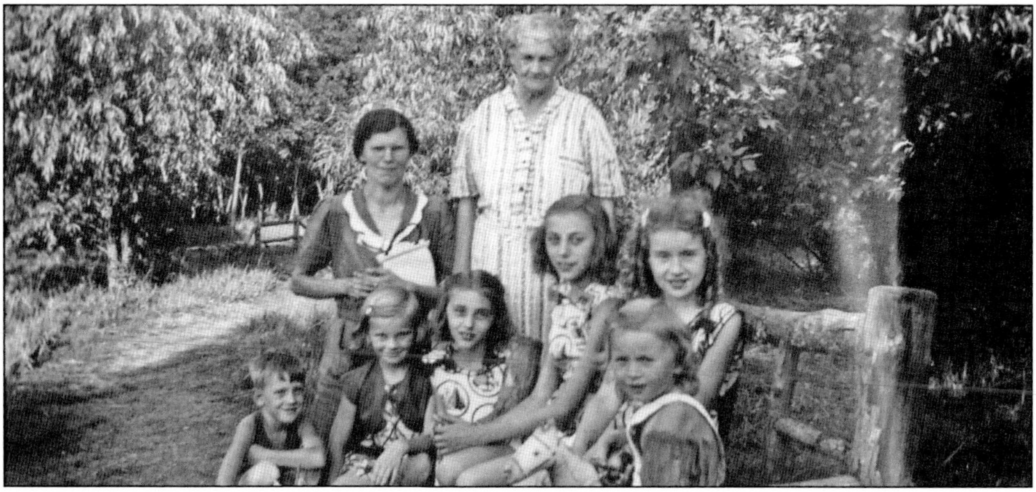

Cousins Donald and Gail Hulbert were the guests of honor at a birthday party at Mendon Ponds Park in 1940. Gail is shown front right. In the next row, from left to right, are Donald Hulbert; Gail's sister Marilyn; cousins Marjorie and Dolores Kassel; and Gail's oldest sister, Shirley. Bertha Wiegert Hulbert, Donald's mother, is in the back beside the Hulbert children's grandmother Mina Brown Hulbert. (Courtesy of Gail Hulbert Esker and Marilyn Hulbert Nielsen.)

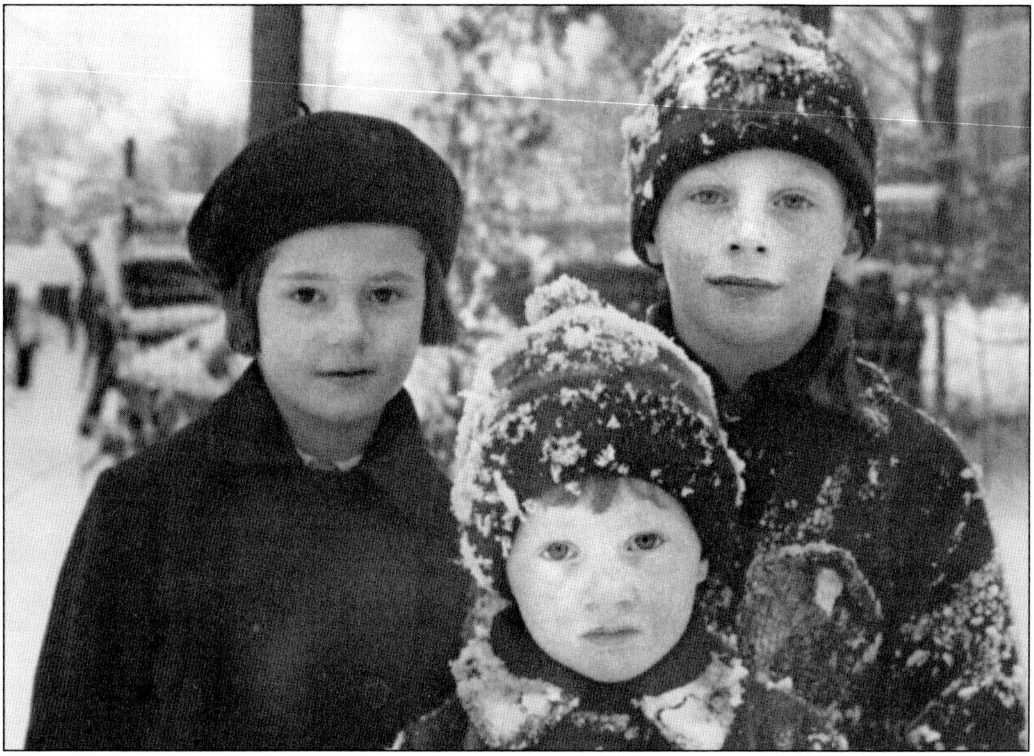

John and Stuart Bacon, sons of Howard and Elisabeth Knight Bacon, appear to have had quite the snowball fight in the backyard of their home at 46 South Main Street. Katie Allen joined them for this photograph but, judging by the pristine condition of her coat, seems to have missed the fun. Katie, the youngest child of Dr. Lloyd and Hazel Hulburd Allen, lived at 44 South Main Street. (Courtesy of the John Bacon family.)

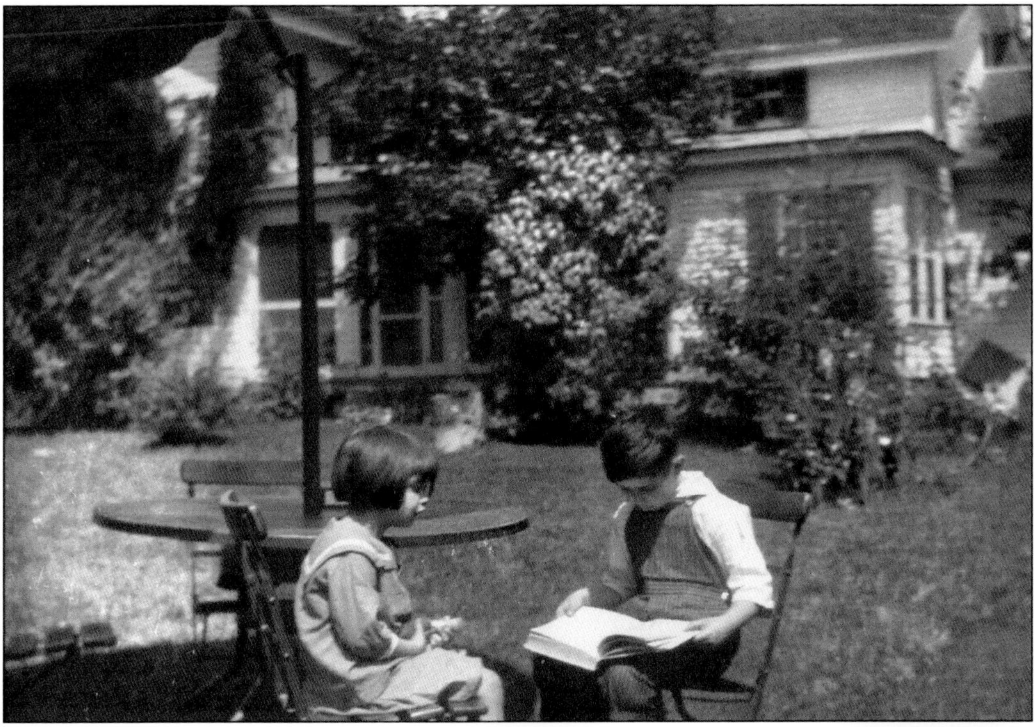

Constance "Connie" Koegler and her older brother Ansel sit outside their home at 84 South Main Street. Connie holds several rock specimens in her hand, patiently waiting for Ansel to look them up in his book. Since the photograph was staged, Connie remembers that she never did learn the names of those rocks. They were the children of Conrad and Olive Arey Koegler. Conrad died in 1925 at age 37, and Olive had to support the family. To make ends meet, she opened the Garden Gate Teahouse that summer in her home. All the fashionable ladies came to tea and were served delectable desserts in the front room. After Connie's marriage to Robert Wilson, they moved into the house and raised their daughters there. The Koegler family has owned the house since 1918. The front of the house with the Garden Gate Teahouse sign in a prominent location is shown below. (Both, courtesy of Connie Wilson.)

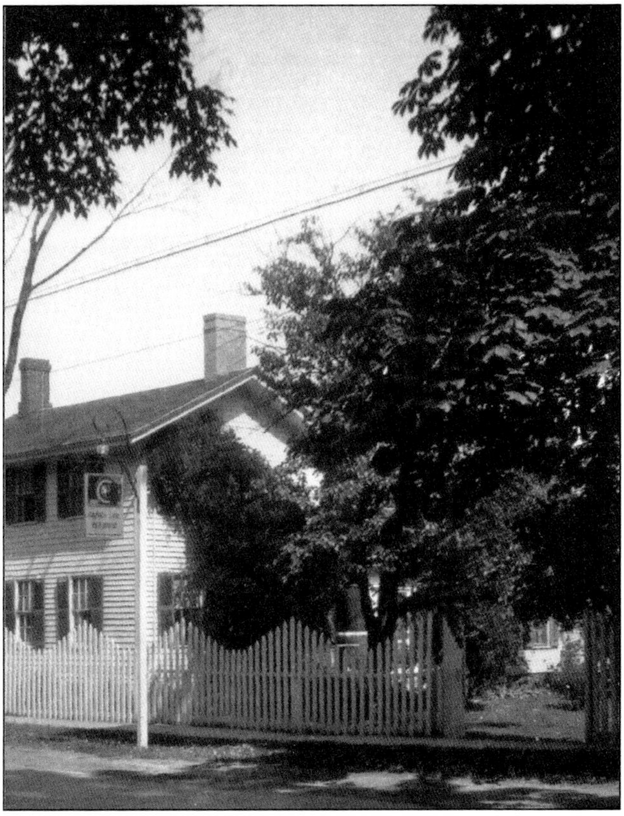

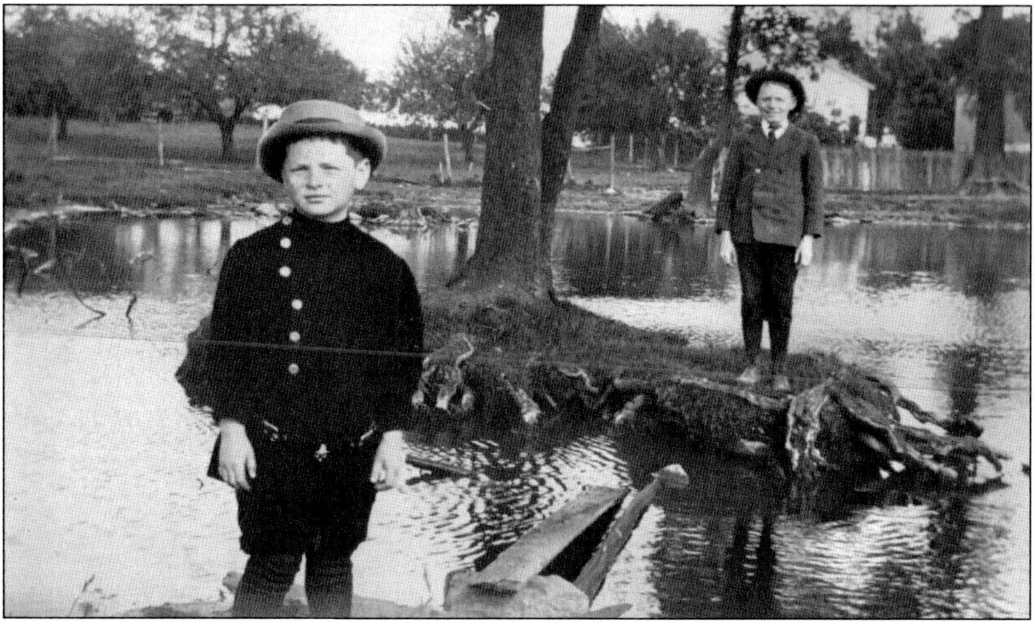

Whitney and Harlan Knickerbocker rigged up an impromptu dock with a boulder and a piece of wood in order to get to the island in the pond. The boys must have loved visiting their grandparents William H. and Clarinda Eckler Barker at their farm at 219 Mendon Center Road. It appears there were many fun activities there to keep two little boys entertained. (Courtesy of Mary Knickerbocker Menzie.)

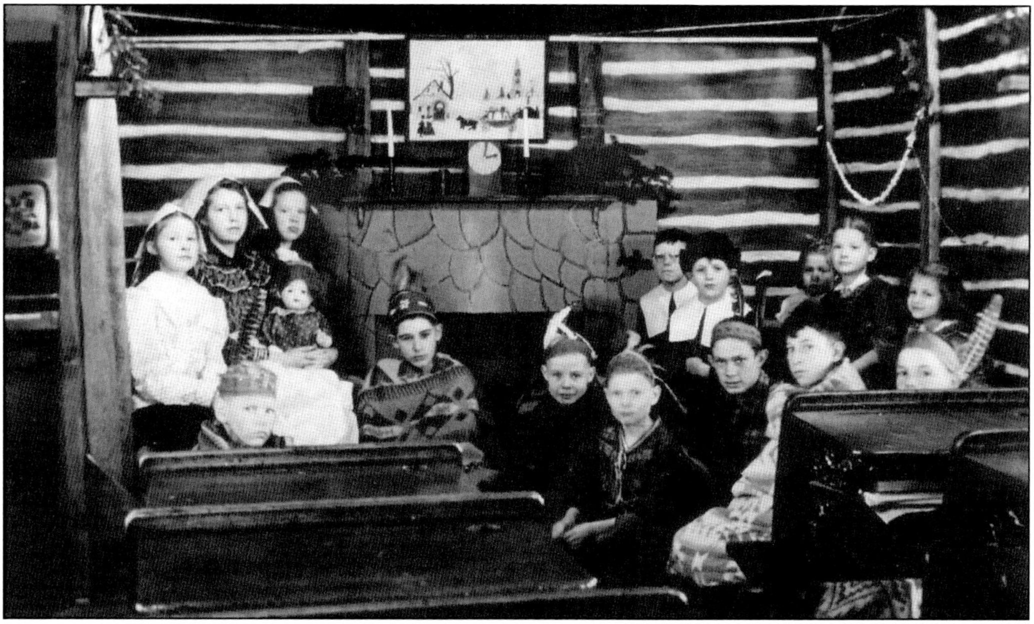

Pittsford celebrated its sesquicentennial on October 7–8, 1939. The festivities included parade floats and exhibits. These children participated dressed as pilgrims and Indians. Mildred Kruger, June Silco, Gene Schuyler, Bruce Tobey, and Marian Kruger played the pilgrims. Phil Osterling, Walt Kruger, Ben Schuyler, Glenn Silco, and Dudley Schuyler portrayed the Indians. Priscilla Jones and Shirley Plain were also present. (Courtesy of the Pittsford Town Historian.)

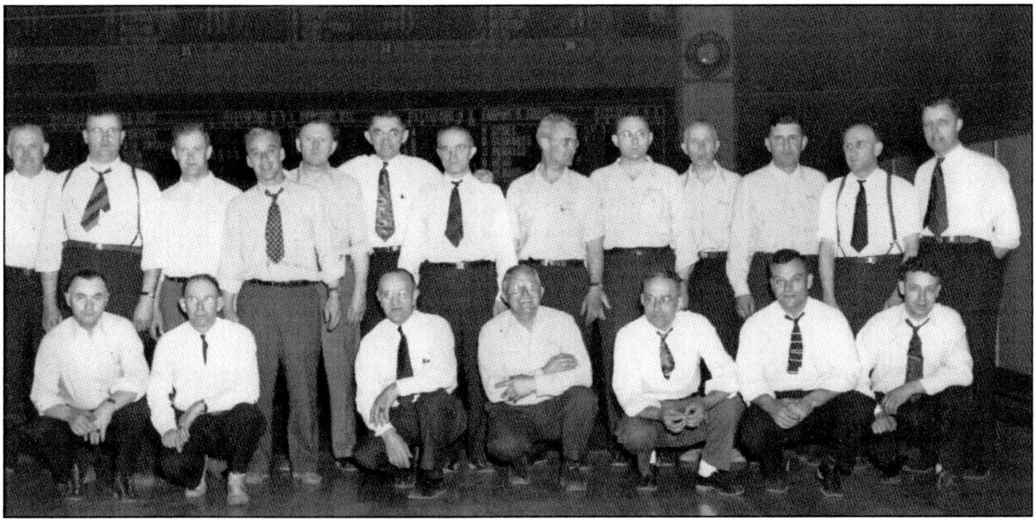

Pictured at the 1946 World Championship ABC 43rd Annual Tournament in Buffalo, New York, are, from left to right, (first row) E. Barnard, W. Lines, Carl Schieterle, Chuck Bonhurst, Marv Geisler, C. Perrigo Jr., and unidentified; (second row) Ray Steve, Harold Tobey, Cortland Newcomb, Bob Ford, M. Hinterleiter, Clarence Zornow, Dutch Earls, Bill Place, Frank Worboys, Frank Heisler, John Rand, D. Schwartz, and Al Pfromer. (Courtesy of Bob Place.)

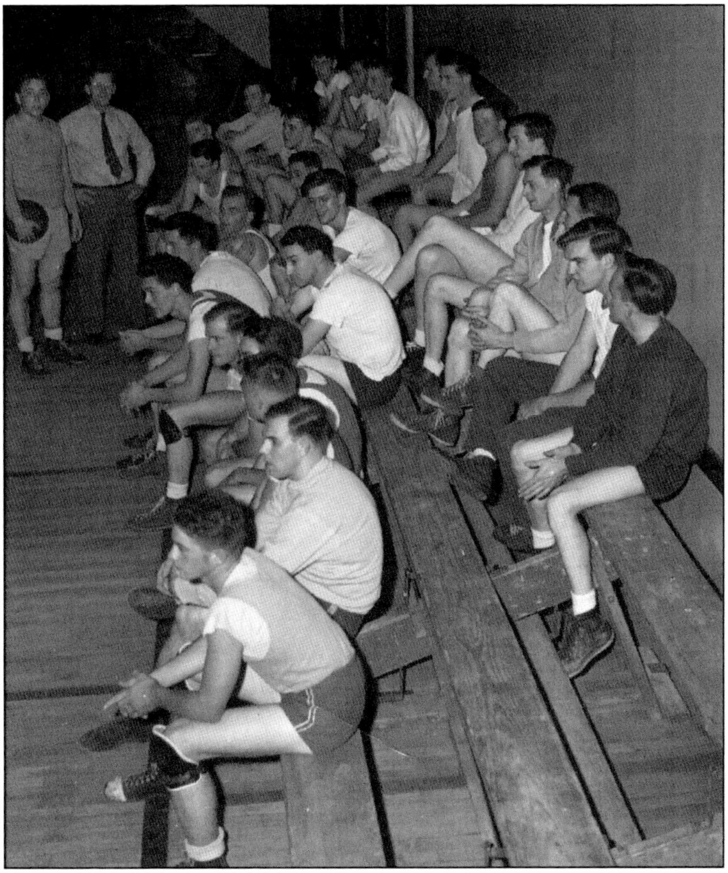

Warming the bench at Pittsford High School are, from top to bottom of the picture, (left row) Paul Spiegel, unidentified, "Treak" Matthews, unidentified, Bruce Milliman, Bill Crichton, two unidentified, Bucky Prutzman, and unidentified; (middle row) unidentified, Roger Burden, Bud Silco, and Don Hoeltke; (right row) Don Hegeman, two unidentified, John Emery, Bob Sweeney, ? Connaughton, Bob Grover, Jack Hutchinson, unidentified, Jim Smith, and Jim Burdett. Tom Burden and Joe King stand at left. (Courtesy of the Burdett family.)

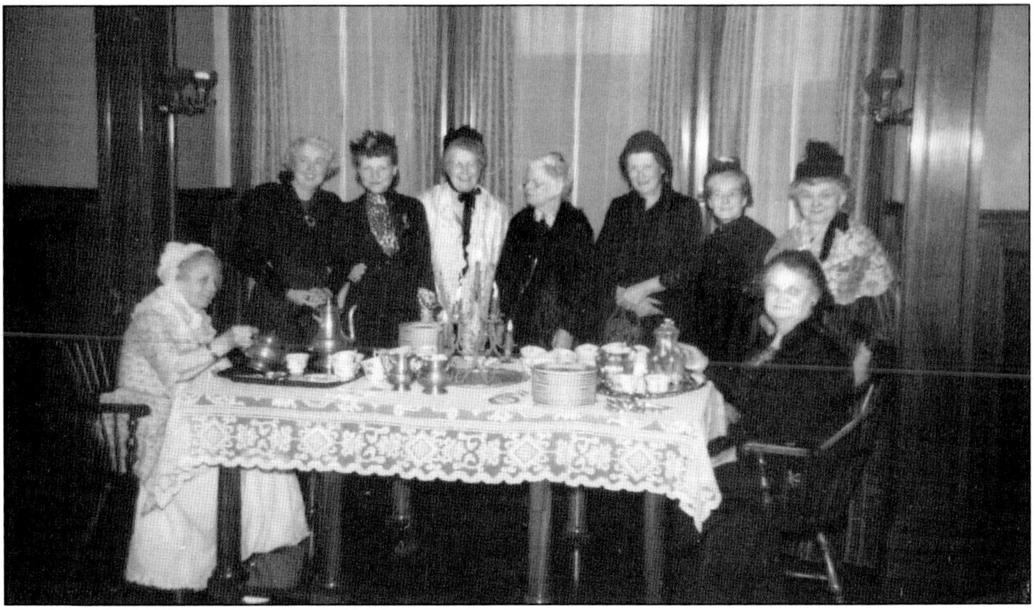

A Christmas tea was held on December 6, 1950, at the Pittsford Library, which, at that time, was located in the Wiltsie Memorial Building at 21 North Main Street. The ladies, dressed in festive finery, are, from left to right, Emma Greenfield, Mary Ballarian, Alma Jackson, Myrta Danser Canfield, Stella Rand Paul, Elisabeth Knight Bacon, Martha Morrison, Bessie Battams, and Alice Lincoln Lusk. (Courtesy of the Pittsford Town Historian.)

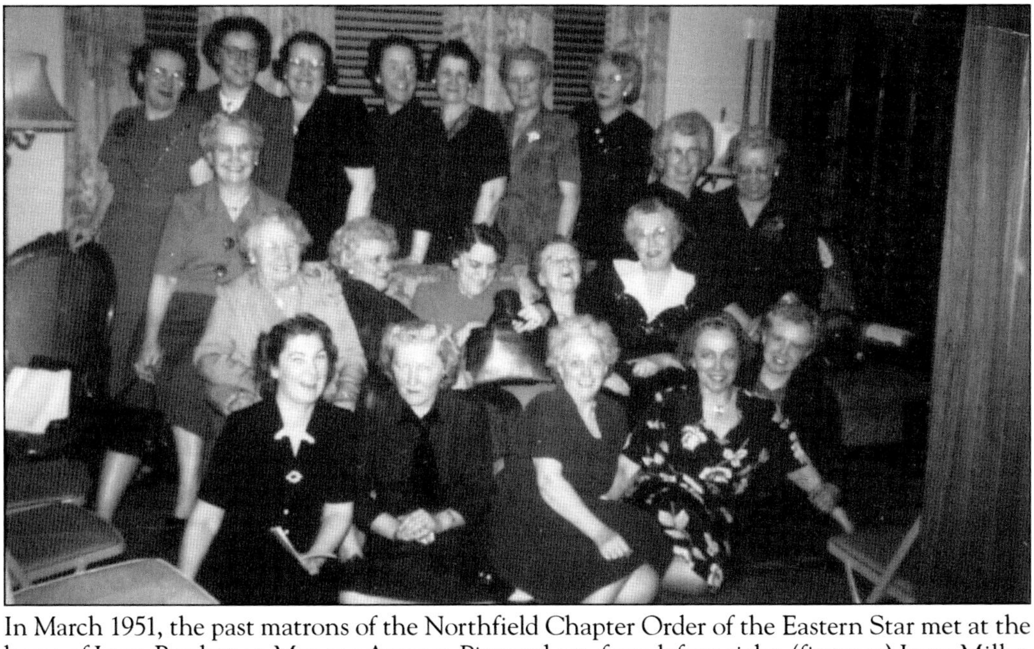

In March 1951, the past matrons of the Northfield Chapter Order of the Eastern Star met at the home of Irene Burdett on Monroe Avenue. Pictured are, from left to right, (first row) Irene Miller, unidentified, Irene Burdett, Elsie Forman Ross, and Dorothy Bahringer; (second row) Pauline Lowry, Blanche Snyder Rowland, two unidentified, Carrie Knickerbocker Cleveland, and Sarah Bahringer Gilmore; (third row) Helen Feasel Maxfield, unidentified, Edith McConnell, Maude Holt, Mary Shearer, Laura Rylott, and two unidentified women. (Courtesy of the Burdett family.)

Seven

Pittsford in the 20th Century

Pittsford became a center of Western New York frontier life. The community grew rapidly and its wealth and sophistication are evidenced by its many superb examples of Federal-period architecture as well as Colonial revival and Queen Anne styles. Pittsford can claim credit for the first school, first library, and first regular church as well as the first doctor and lawyer to practice in Monroe County.

Grocery stores, a department store, restaurants, as well as a pickle factory, a dairy farm, a railroad, gas stations, and garages were all within easy distances. However, there was no movie theater or bowling alley or recreation center for the young or young at heart. Pittsford was content to let other towns and villages handle those establishments.

Pittsford remained the predominately agrarian community with farms on large acres of land until the late 19th century, when it became the location of country estates. This heralded the beginning of suburban development. Long Meadow, a housing development in the western end of the town was the first such place in the county. The area had been a large meadow and had been the pasture for the show horses and ponies of the Hawley family until two developers began to custom build houses on large lots. It was located near the trolley stop so that those heads of households could leave automobiles at home and ride the public transportation into Rochester. Pittsford continued to be a desirable area and the community is proud of its rich historical heritage. In order to retain some of the architectural excellence and original character of the village, builders are encouraged to maintain traditional design. In many cases, fine old buildings have been restored to house commercial enterprises. The town has become the bedroom community for the larger city of Rochester, and commuters, now in high-speed cars, hurry along the expressways on their way to offices and commerce elsewhere.

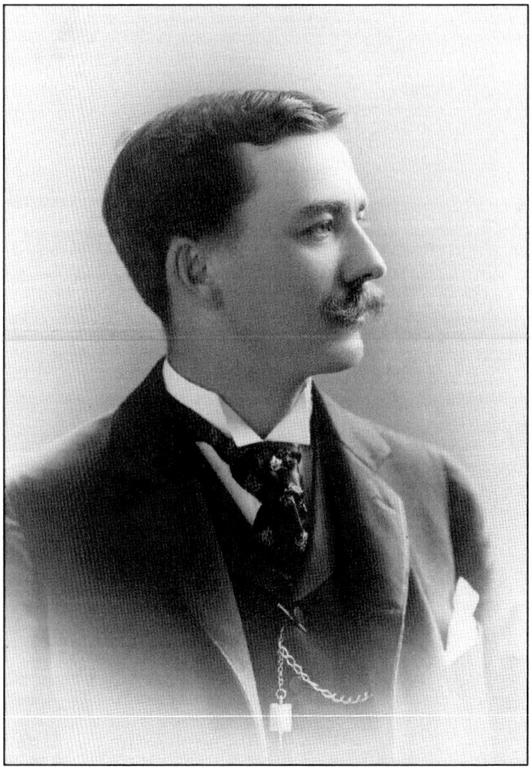

The son of James Martin Wiltsie and his wife, Emily Ward Hastings, Charles Hastings Wiltsie was born in Pittsford in 1859. This photograph was taken on October 5, 1893, the day he wed Harriet Potter Hart. Charles was an attorney who served as president of the Rochester Historical Society in the 1920s. He died in Rochester in 1935 and was interred at Mount Hope Cemetery. (Courtesy of the Perinton Historical Society, Karl Jost Collection.)

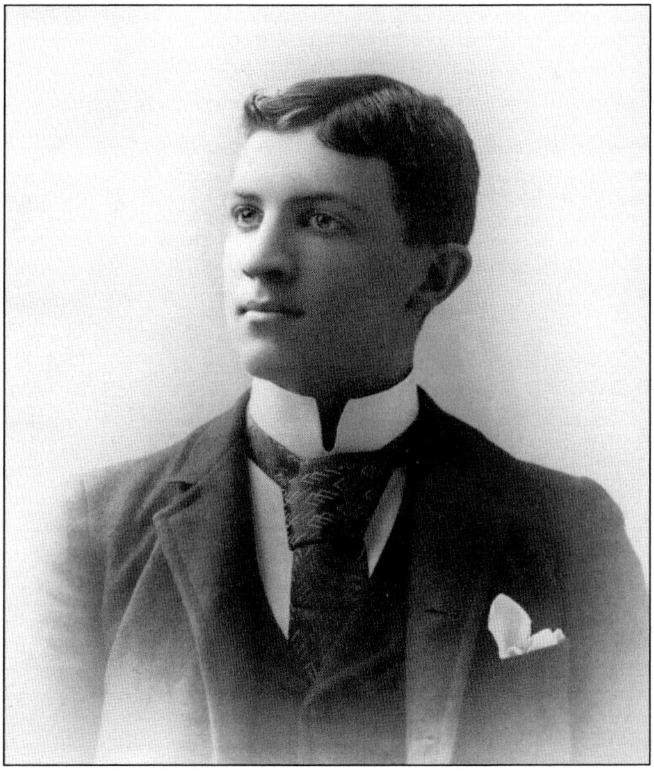

Arthur S. Light, born in 1871, was the youngest of Harvey and Mary Helen Shepard Light's five sons. His formative years were spent in Pittsford and Michigan; he assisted his father with the family's Eureka Steam Heating Company. Arthur wed Maude Merritt, and they had three daughters, Lina, Grace, and Frances. (Courtesy of Glenn Berggren.)

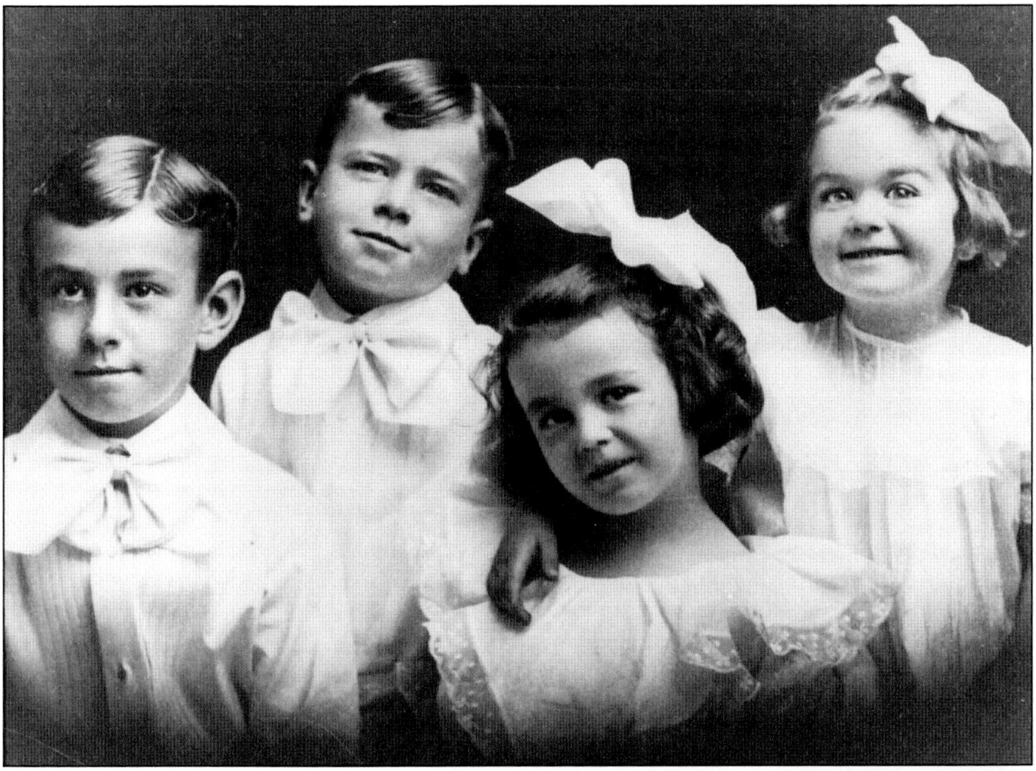

The four children of Jared and Lettie Maie Nye Hopkins are shown in this adorable photograph taken about 1905. The children are, from left to right, Irving, Phelps, Delora, and Jane. (Courtesy of the Engert family.)

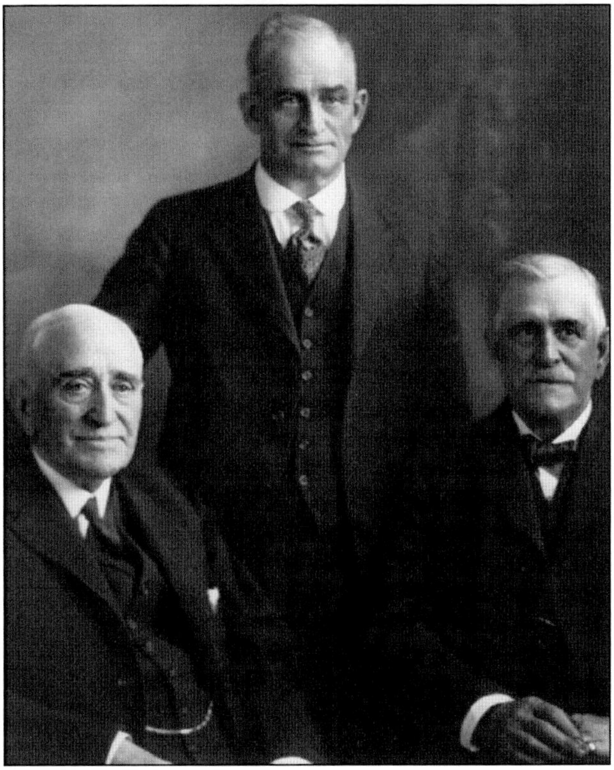

Brothers James, Jared, and George Hopkins came together for this undated photograph. They are three of the eight children of Marvin and Jane Phelps Hopkins. (Courtesy of the Engert family.)

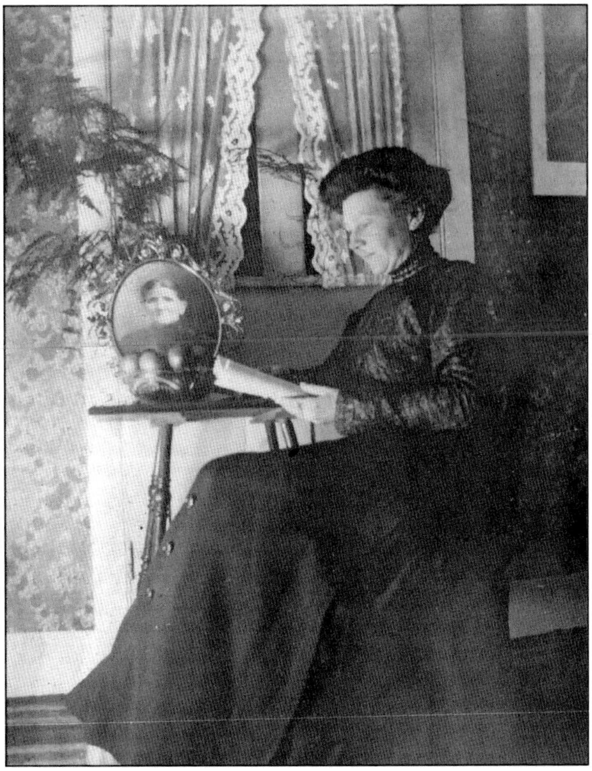

Kate Heech sits in front of a photograph of a woman who is likely her mother, Mary Ludwig Heech. Kate's mother died in 1912. Kate was the youngest of Mary and George Heech's three children. She and her siblings Louisa and John lived with their parents on Noakes Road near the Clawson farm. George Heech supported his family by farming. (Courtesy of the Willard family.)

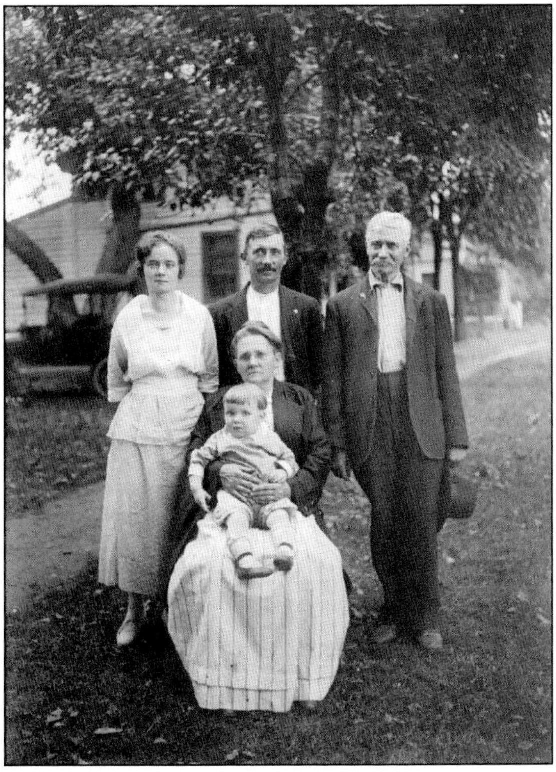

The Scamp family gathered together around 1920 for this four-generation family portrait. Roxana Hulbert Scamp, seated in the center, holds her great-grandson Elbert Davis. Standing are, from left to right, Verna Scamp Davis, George Scamp, and William Scamp. William and Roxana had six children, of whom George was the eldest. Verna is George's daughter and Elbert's mother. (Courtesy of Gail Hulbert Esker and Marilyn Hulbert Nielsen.)

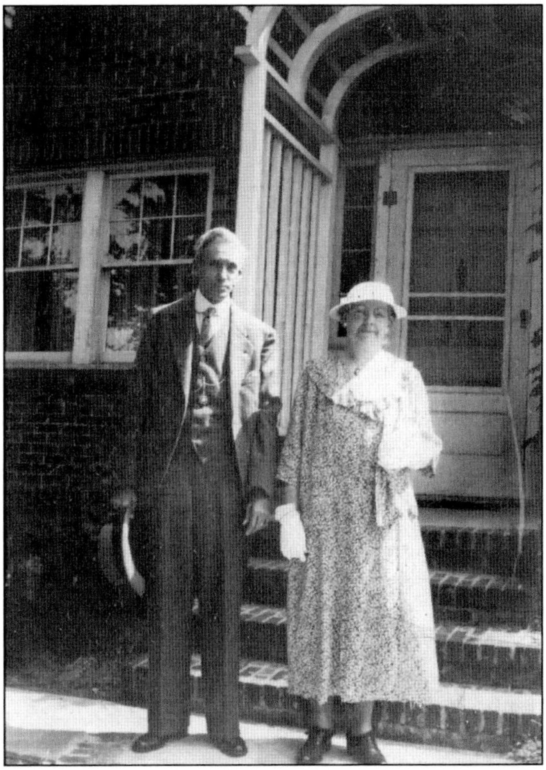

Marion Adelia Bushman was the daughter of Charles and Myrta Danser Bushman. Seven weeks after her birth in 1909, Marion's father died of liver cancer at age 51. In 1916, Myrta married Stewart Canfield whose first wife, Grace Snyder, had died in 1915. Myrta and Stewart celebrated 27 years of marriage before his death in 1944. Stewart and Myrta are pictured in the photograph above. Marion wed Albert Bruce Corby in 1934. She died in 2001, aged 91. Little Marion Bushman is shown below. (Both, courtesy of the Pittsford Town Historian.)

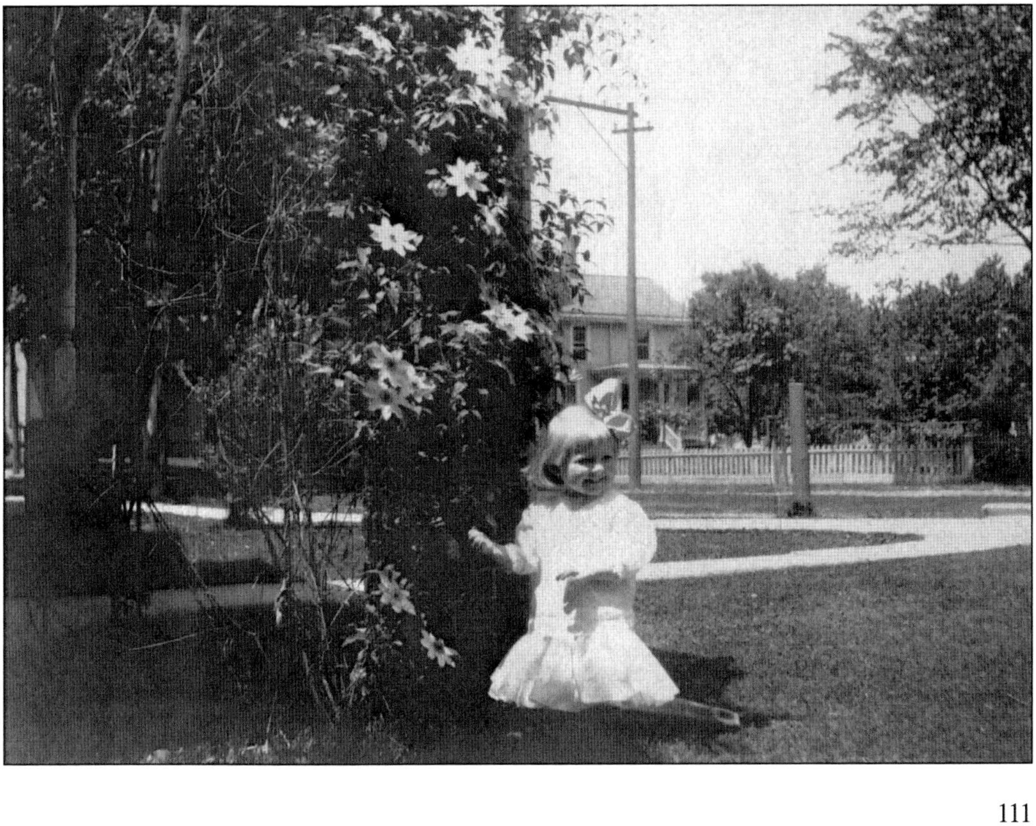

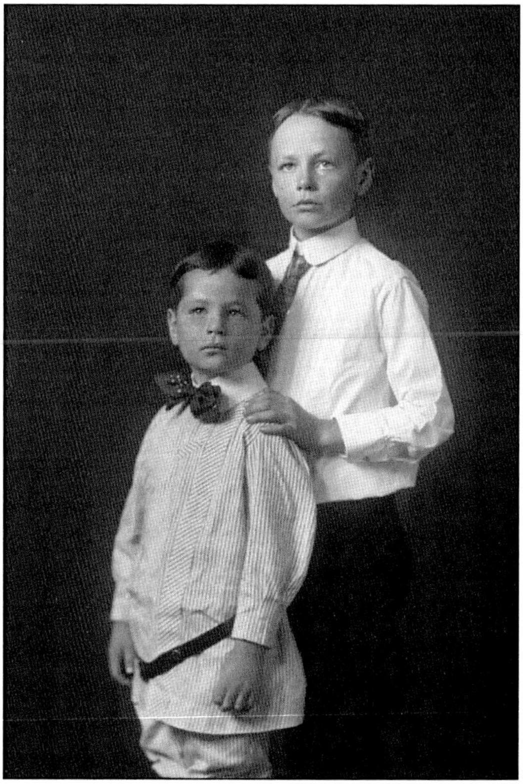

Whitney Monroe Knickerbocker and his older brother Henry Harlan were the sons of Harry and Mary Barker Knickerbocker. Whitney was born in 1904 and Harlan in 1899. They grew up on the family farm on Knickerbocker Road. Whitney wed Gertrude Welch in 1926. They had two children, James Monroe and Nancy. In 1925, Harlan married Esther Kehl, and they had two children, Paul and Mary. (Courtesy of Mary Knickerbocker Menzie.)

The Earl, Earls, and Belcher families took a trip to Allen's Hill. Charlie Earls, seated in front center, holds his daughter Paulina. Charles Earl's son Gordon is standing in the back with the tall hat, with his sister Edna at his side. Young Elmer Earl is aiming the gun in this photograph taken about 1915. (Courtesy of Lindsay Bach, D. Gordon Earl Collection.)

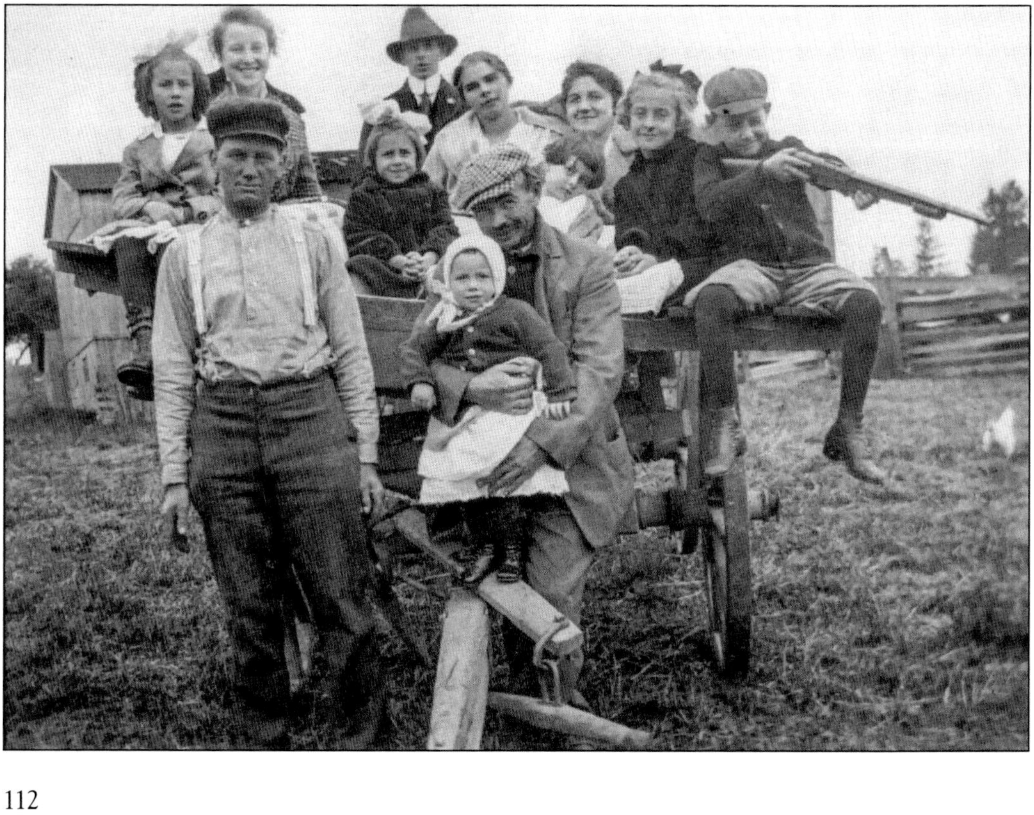

Strong women stand united in a decades-long friendship. Pictured are, from left to right, Lena Ketcham Thomas, the co-owner of the Thomas store in the Parker Building; Marian Snyder Plumb, the bookkeeper and clerk for the Thomas store; Elta Ketcham Becker, Lena's sister; and Nellie Longyear Stewart. (Courtesy of Mary Knickerbocker Menzie.)

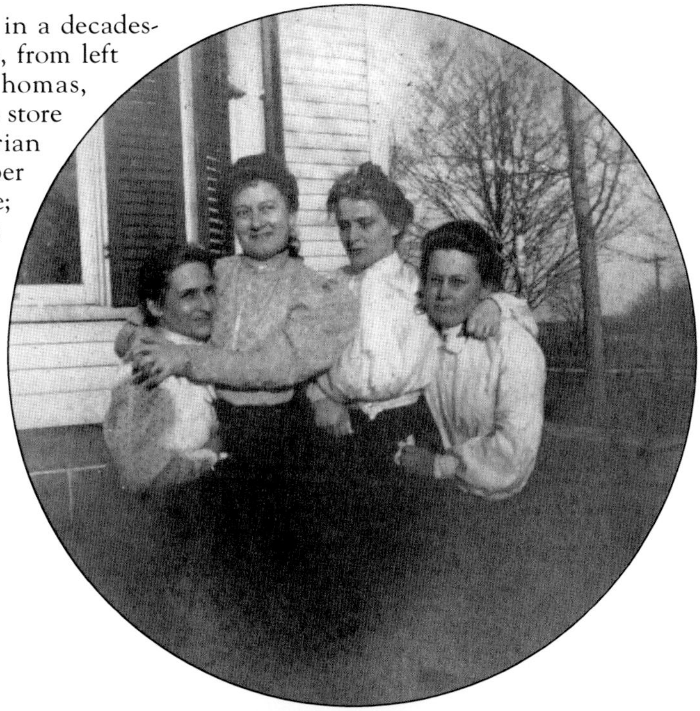

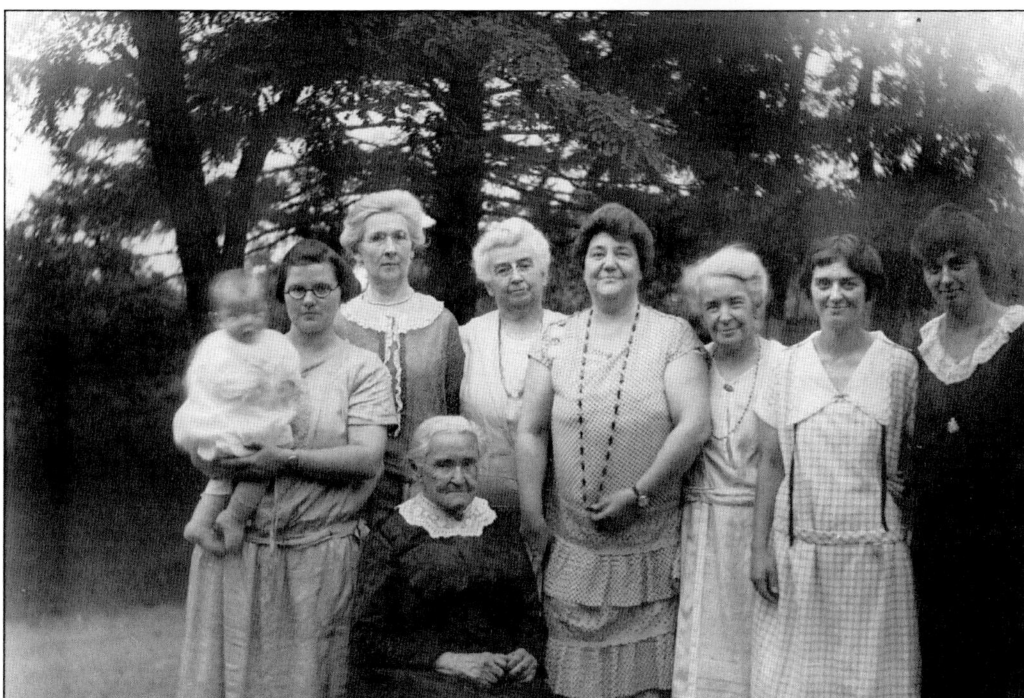

The women of the Hopkins and Nye families are shown here in 1924. Standing behind Josephine Fowler Cronkhite, from left to right, are Mabel Schoen Hopkins, holding her son John Hopkins; Mame Frazer Nye; Lettie Maie Nye Hopkins; Cora Nye; Delora Nye; Jane Hopkins Roach; and Delora Hopkins Engert. (Courtesy of Mark Greene and John Hopkins.)

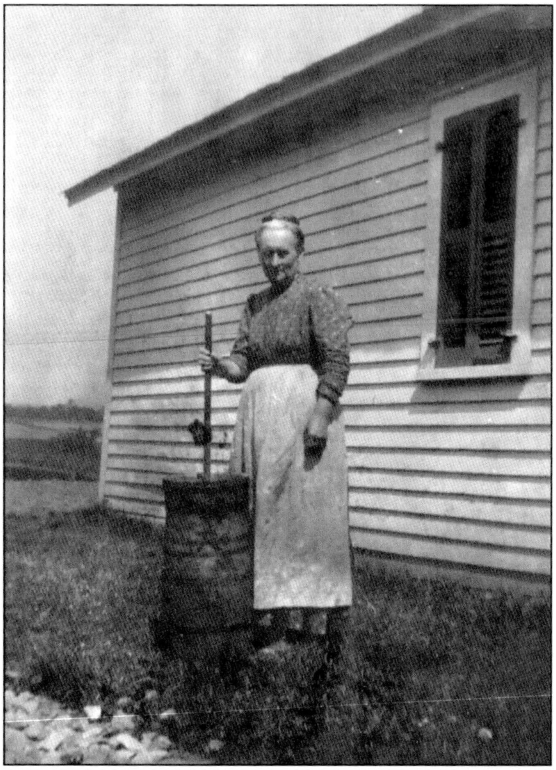

Addie Lunette Peets was born in 1852, the daughter of Lemuel and Adelia Peets. She grew up in Henrietta, New York, and wed Franklin B. Lusk in 1874. They had three sons, Henry Stephen, Charles Franklin, and Lemuel Heman Lusk. Addie died in 1939 at age 87 and was interred at Pittsford Cemetery. She is pictured here with her butter churn. (Courtesy of Bill Lusk.)

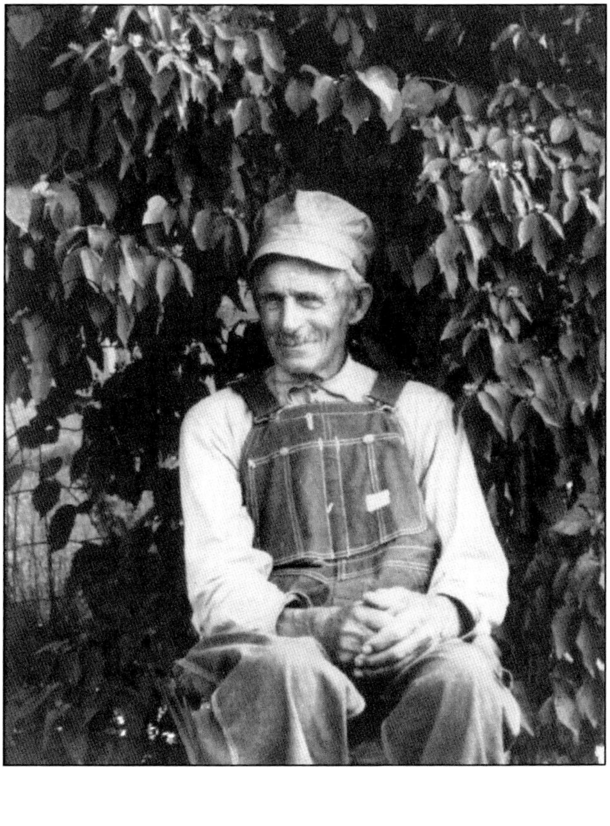

Charles Franklin Lusk, the middle child of Franklin B. and Addie Peets Lusk's three childen, was born in 1877. He and his wife, Sarah Willard Lusk, had nine children whom he supported as a farmer. Charles F. Lusk died in 1951, aged 73, and was buried at Pittsford Cemetery. (Courtesy of Bill Lusk.)

Arthur Henry Lusk, the sixth of Charles and Sarah Willard Lusk's nine children, was born in 1916. His siblings included two sets of twins, Franklin and Frances, born in 1904, and Irving and Elmer, born in 1919. Arthur wed Eileen Trahan, and they had four children: John, William, Judith, and Michael. John died soon after birth. Arthur supported his family by working as a crane operator. (Courtesy of Bill Lusk.)

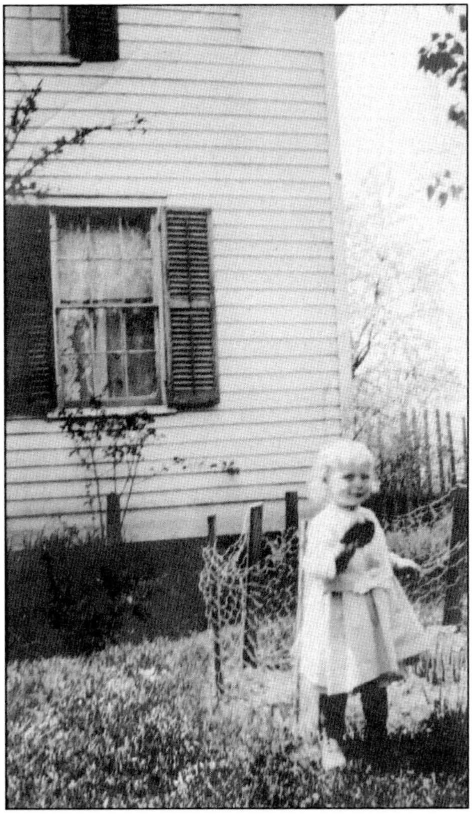

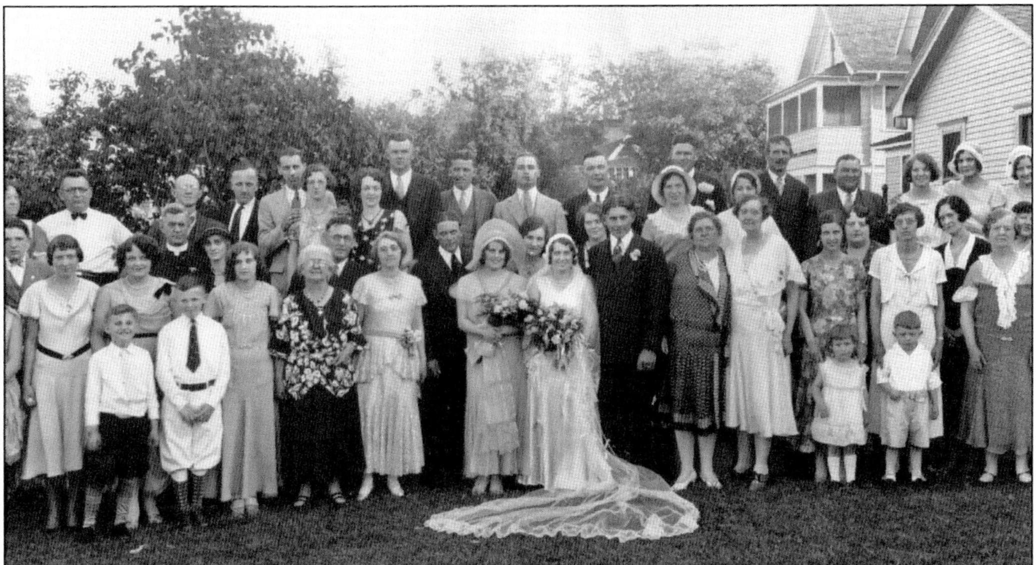

The wedding of George Kenneth Lusk to Velda L. Davidson was celebrated on June 2, 1931, with a large contingent of friends and family present. The bride and groom are standing in the center, surrounded by members of the following families: Powell, Davidson, Smith, Kates, Fritz, Minnamon, Schmidt, Van Avery, Miller, Evans, Yack, Tyler, and Stappenbeck. (Courtesy of Bill Lusk.)

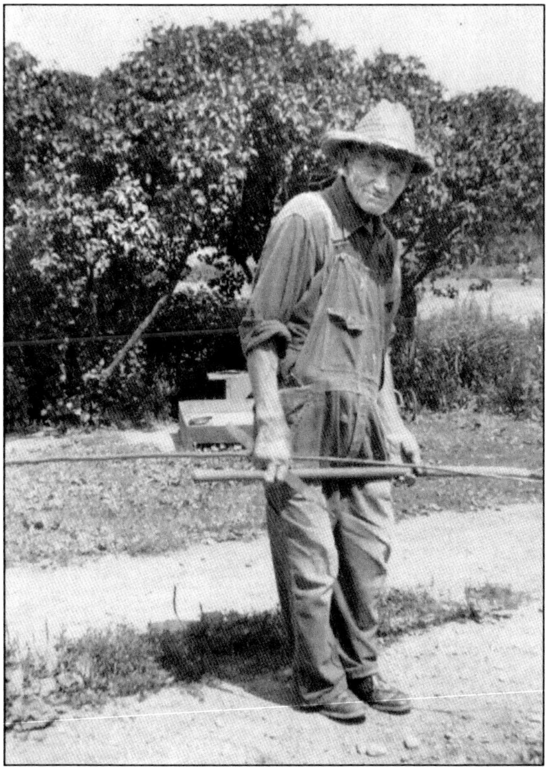

Charles Steffenhagen was born in Germany but immigrated to the United States in the late 1880s. He married Marie Witt, and they had three children, Elsie, Alfred, and Elizabeth. Marie died shortly after Elizabeth's birth, and Charles worked as a stone mason to support his family. He died in 1941. (Courtesy of Gail Hulbert Esker and Marilyn Hulbert Nielsen.)

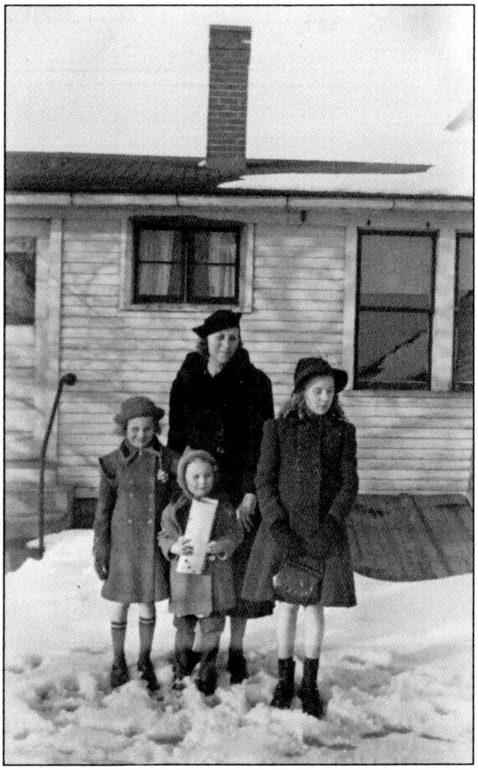

Elizabeth Steffenhagen Hulbert stands behind her three girls, Marilyn, Gail, and Shirley Hulbert. Elizabeth's husband Raymond Hulbert, a World War I veteran, had passed away in 1937. Elizabeth died in 1946, just a few years after this photograph was taken. She was the daughter of Charles and Marie Witt Steffenhagen. (Courtesy of Gail Hulbert Esker and Marilyn Hulbert Nielsen.)

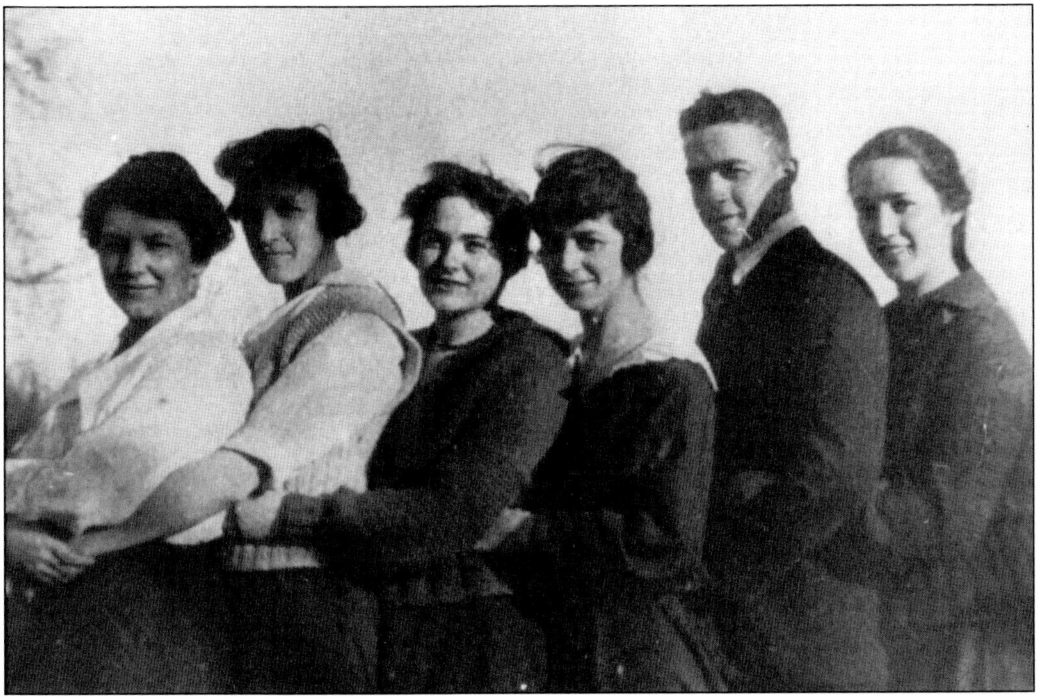

Six of Albert and Anna Kane Kates's seven children gathered for a family photograph in 1918. The Kates family lived at 20 Rand Place. Shown in birth order are, from left to right, Bertha Kates Sweeney, Anne, Cecelia, Gertrude, Bernard, and Marguerite Kates. Theresa, the second oldest Kates child, died of heart trouble in 1904. (Courtesy of Molly Malchow Szumilaski.)

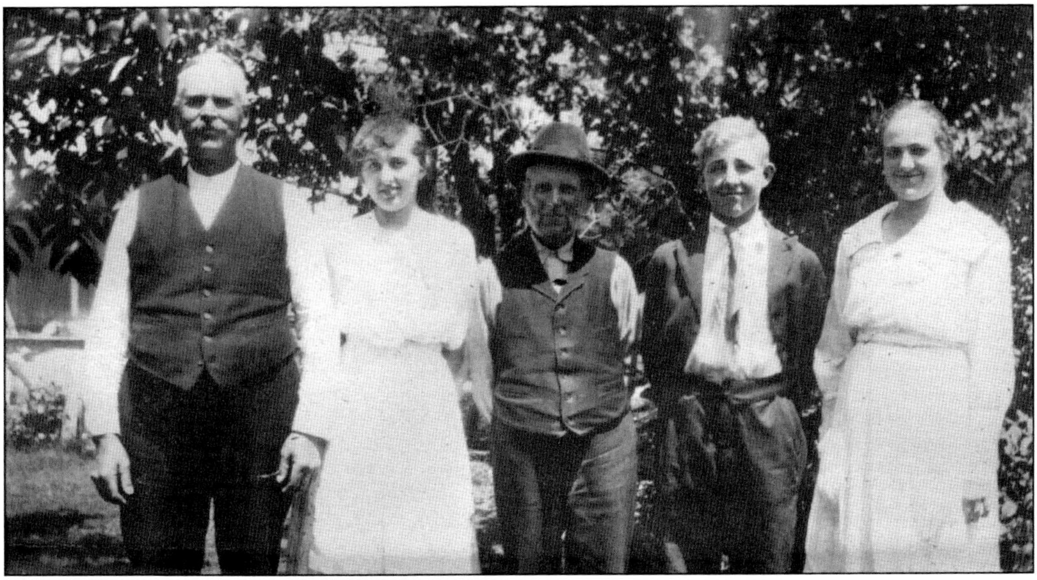

Helen, Grant, and Ruth Peglow were the children of Charles and Sophia Clawson Peglow. Charles died in 1912, and the children were orphaned four years later by the death of their mother, Sophia. Grant went to live with his maternal uncle, William Clawson, and the girls resided with John Peglow. Shown above in 1919, from left to right, are William Clawson, Helen Peglow, maternal grandfather Christian Clawson, Grant, and Ruth Peglow. (Courtesy of the Willard family.)

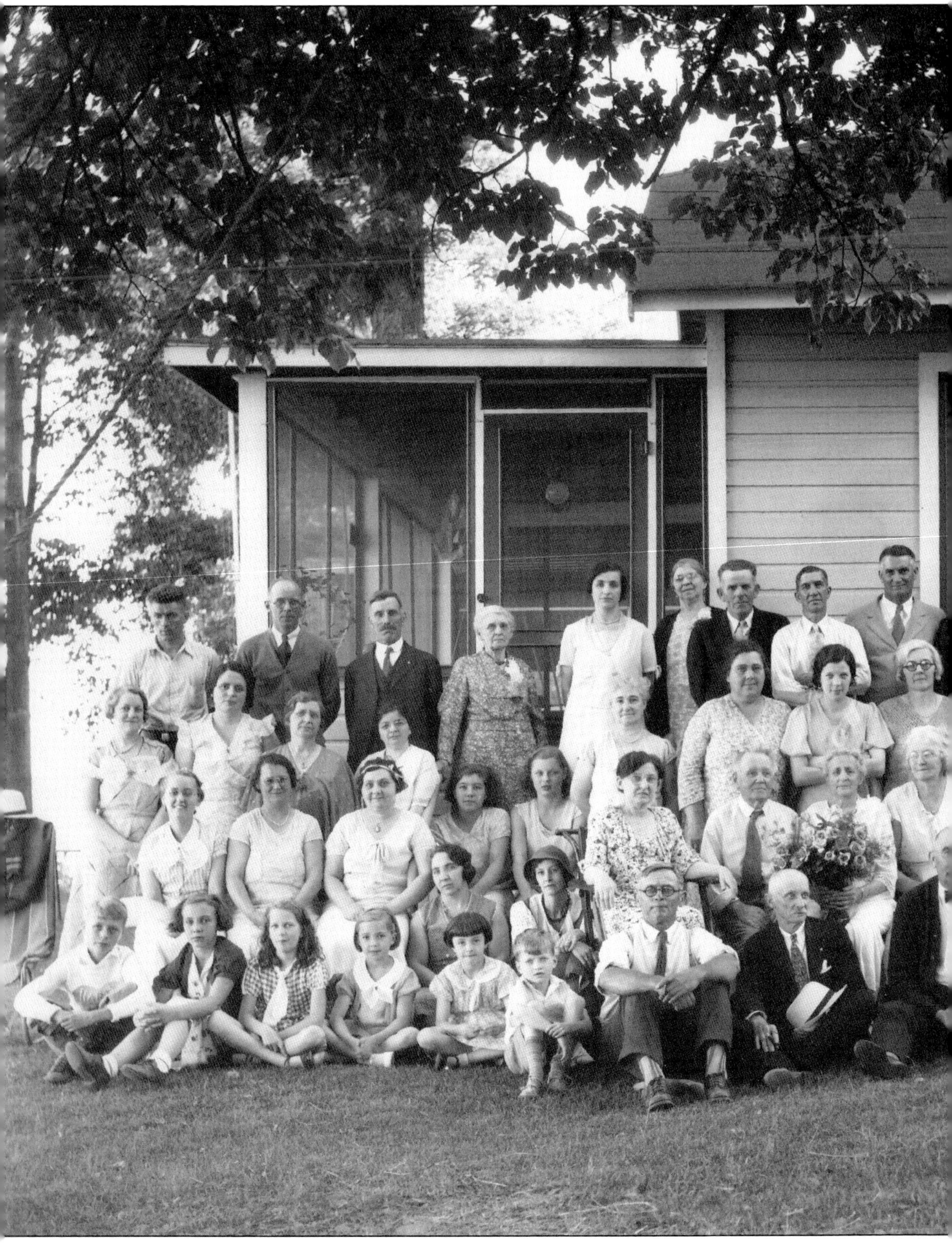

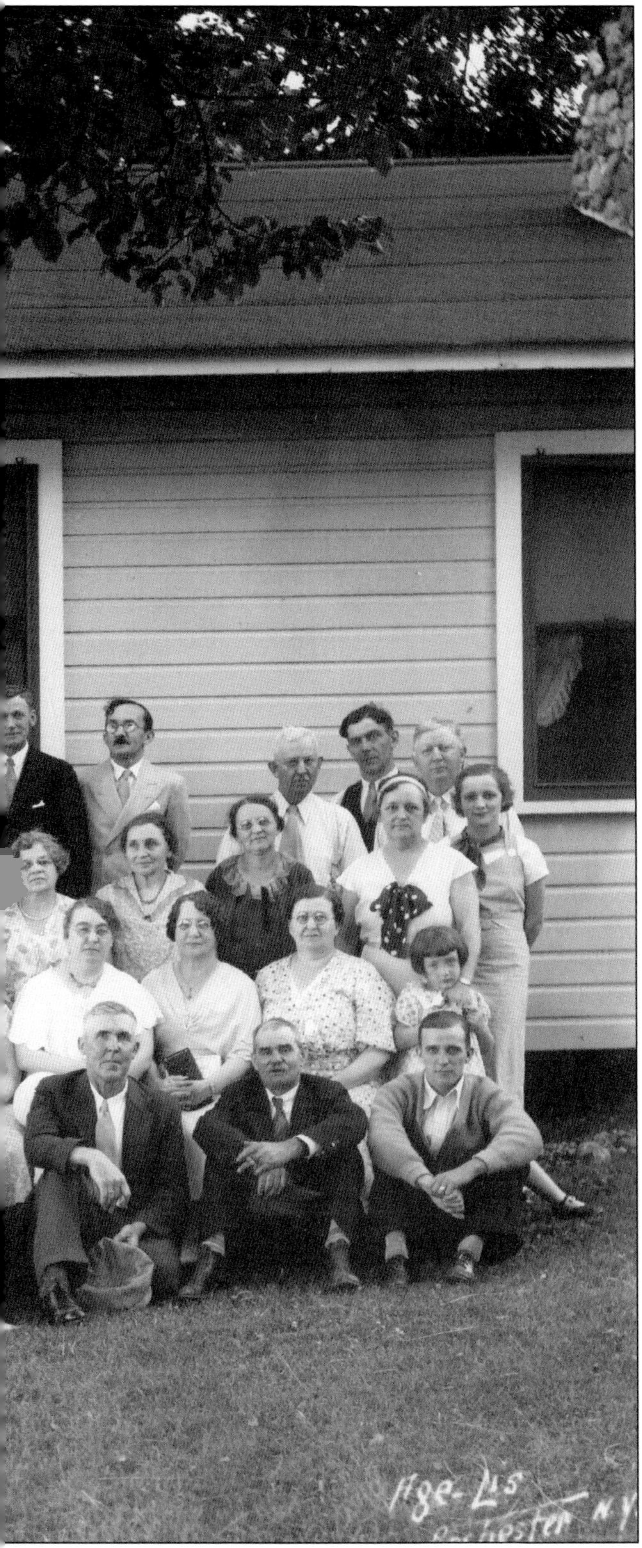

July 4, 1923, marked the 50th wedding anniversary of Eva Gillam and Charles B. Emmons. To celebrate this golden milestone, the Emmons family held a party for 25 people at Tyler's Inn at the Phoenix Building. Dinner was followed by a reception at their home at 10 North Main Street, which appears to be the location of this photograph. Eva is seated in the center of the second row holding a lovely bouquet. Charles is to her right. Mr. and Mrs. Emmons were highly regarded citizens of Pittsford, and were quite active in the community. Their son, Gillie, died in childhood, and daughter, Nellie, died of typhoid fever just days after beginning college at Geneseo. Eva and Charles celebrated 64 years of marriage before his death in 1937. Eva died in 1939. (Courtesy of the Pittsford Town Historian.)

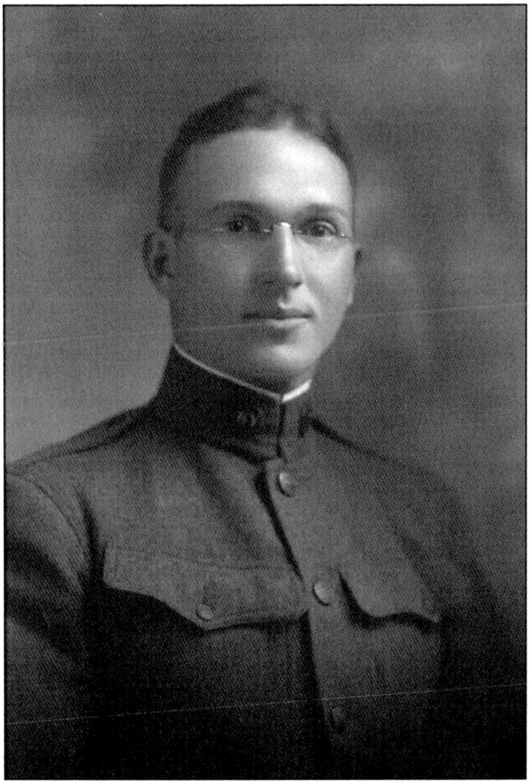

Howard Bacon, son of John Buckley and Frederica Rogers Bacon, had a long military career and served in both world wars before retiring at the rank of lieutenant colonel in 1954. Following his military service, Howard owned an insurance company. He and his wife, Elisabeth Knight Bacon, raised their sons, John and Stuart, at the family home located at 46 South Main Street. (Courtesy of the John Bacon family.)

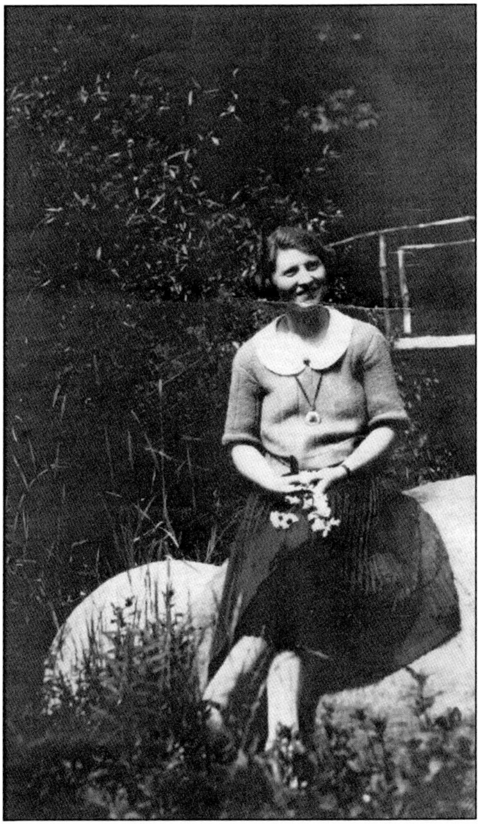

Isabella Hicks was born August 19, 1900. Her father, George A. Hicks, served for a time as the Pittsford Town supervisor. Lizzie Hicks, Isabella's mother, was active in many local organizations. Isabella's early marriage to Walter Evans produced a daughter, Lois Jean, who died at age four. Isabella then married Edward Hart in the 1920s. After serving as town historian from 1959 to 1979, Isabella Hicks Hart died in 1987. (Courtesy of the Pittsford Town Historian.)

E. William Place, son of Earl W. and Florence Minniss Place, is shown in this 1924 University of Rochester yearbook photograph. He graduated in 1925 and went on to own six gas stations in Monroe County. (Courtesy of Bob Place.)

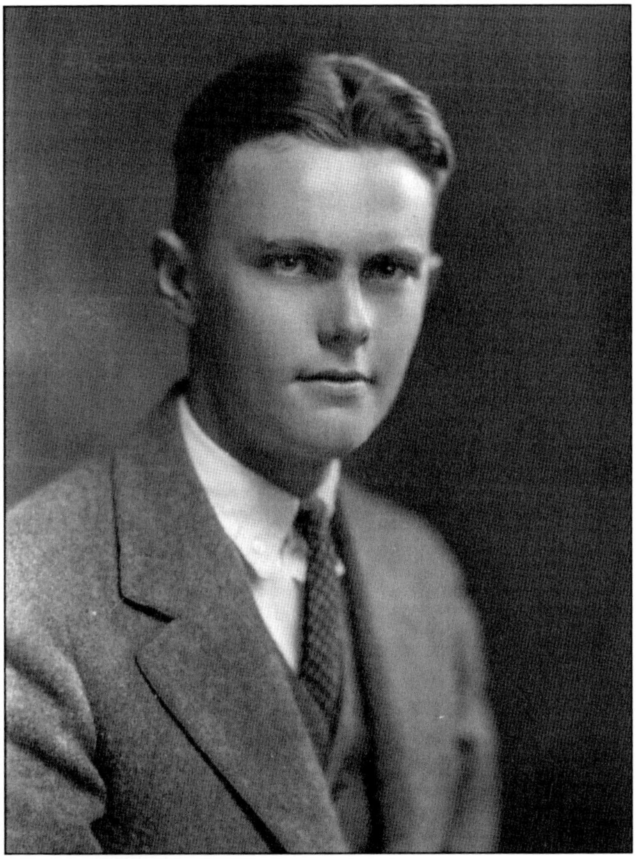

Sarah "Sally," Patricia, and Ann, the young daughters of Swayne and Ruth Thompson Goodenough, are shown in this portrait taken in the mid-1930s. Sally wed Peter Merrill, Patricia married Robert Place, and Ann married John Dinse. Patricia was associated for many years with Historic Pittsford, the local preservation and historical society. (Courtesy of Bob Place.)

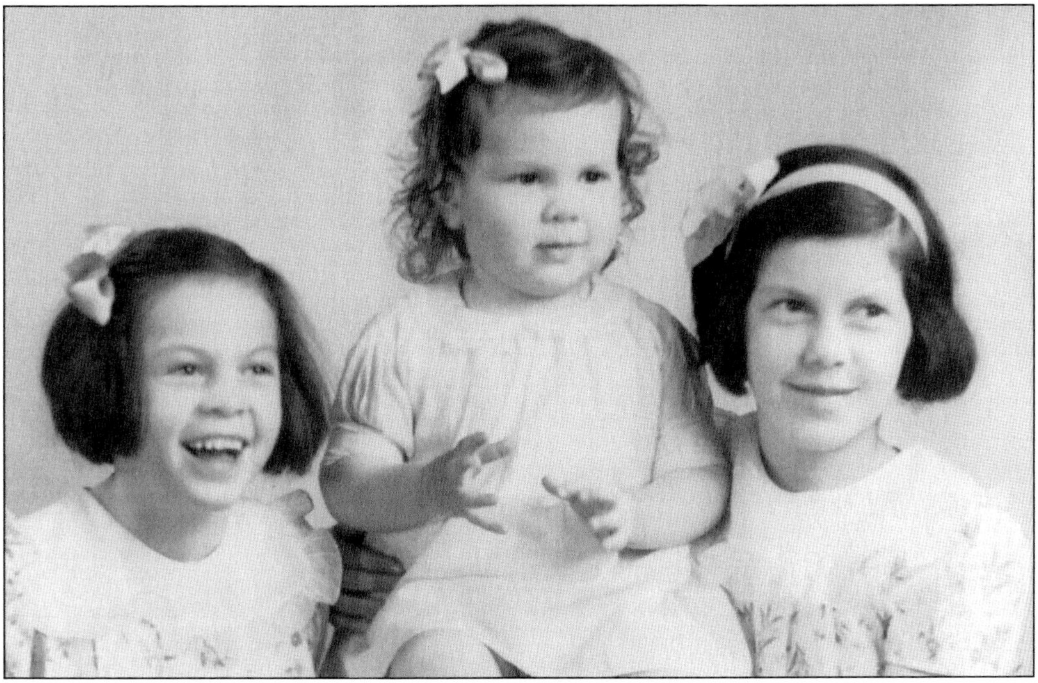

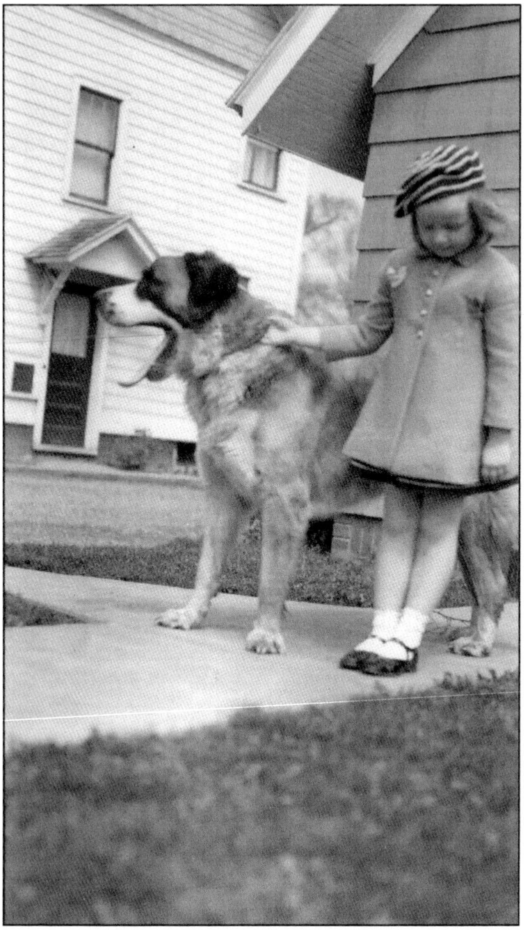

Kay Utz, daughter of George and Florence Lusk Utz, seems intent upon looking at her pretty shoes and is not at all distracted by the large dog standing beside her. The Saint Bernard, Judy, was the beloved pet of the E. William Place family for many years. This photograph was taken at the corner of Jefferson Road and Eastview Terrace. (Courtesy of Jonatha "Shotsie" Rand.)

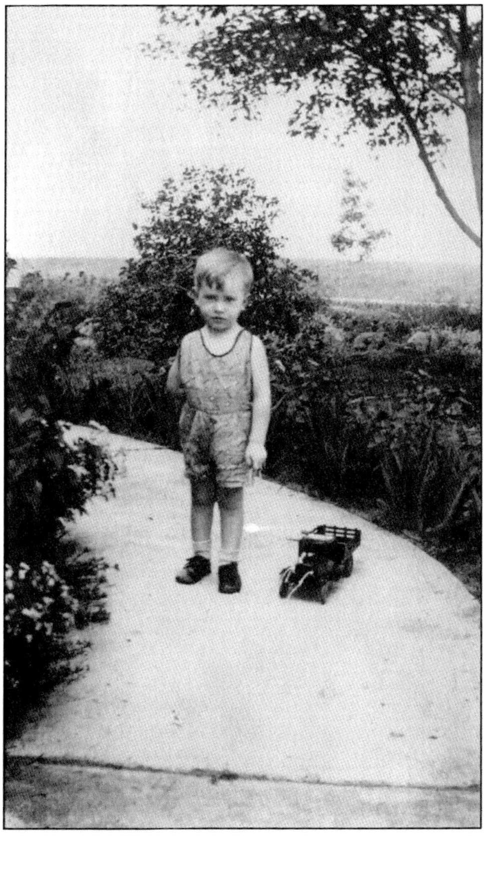

Donald Hulbert, the son of Charles and Bertha Wiegert Hulbert, was born July 25, 1933. He loved playing with his cousins and attending school at District No. 9 school on Marsh Road. In March 1941, Donald fell on some icy steps and died from his injuries, leaving his widowed mother devastated. He was laid to rest beside his father at Pittsford Cemetery. (Courtesy of Gail Hulbert Esker and Marilyn Hulbert Nielsen.)

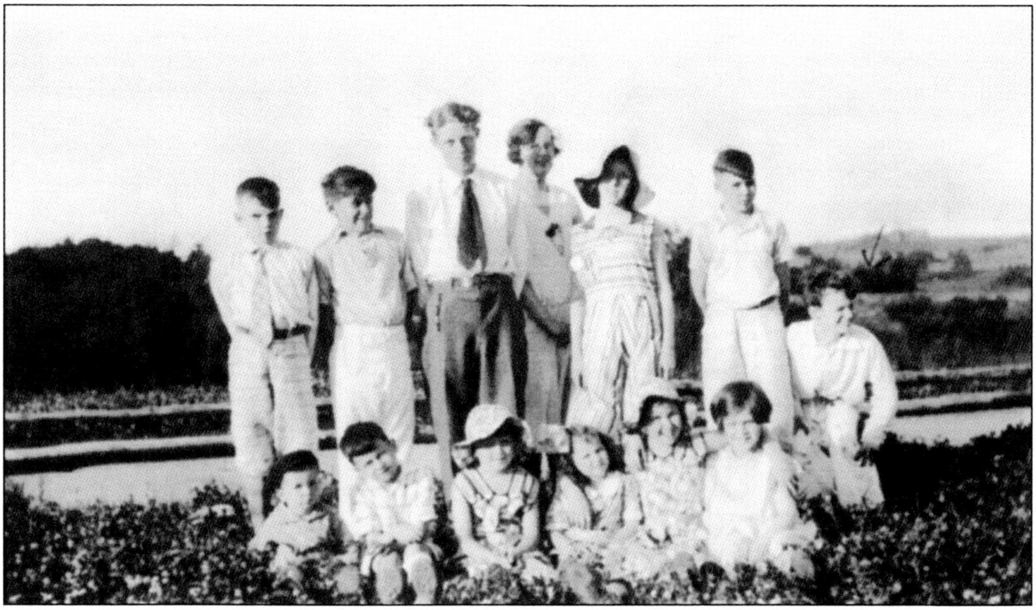

Students from the Clover Street District No. 5 school gathered together for a portrait in the early 1930s. Pictured from left to right are (sitting) George Hopkins, John Hopkins, Carol Tinker, Mary Hopkins, Priscilla ?, and Helen Ernst; (standing) Charles Conine, Tyler Tinker, Walter Willard, Florence Ernst, Winnie Conine, Charles Graves, and Edward Roskey. (Courtesy of Carol Tinker.)

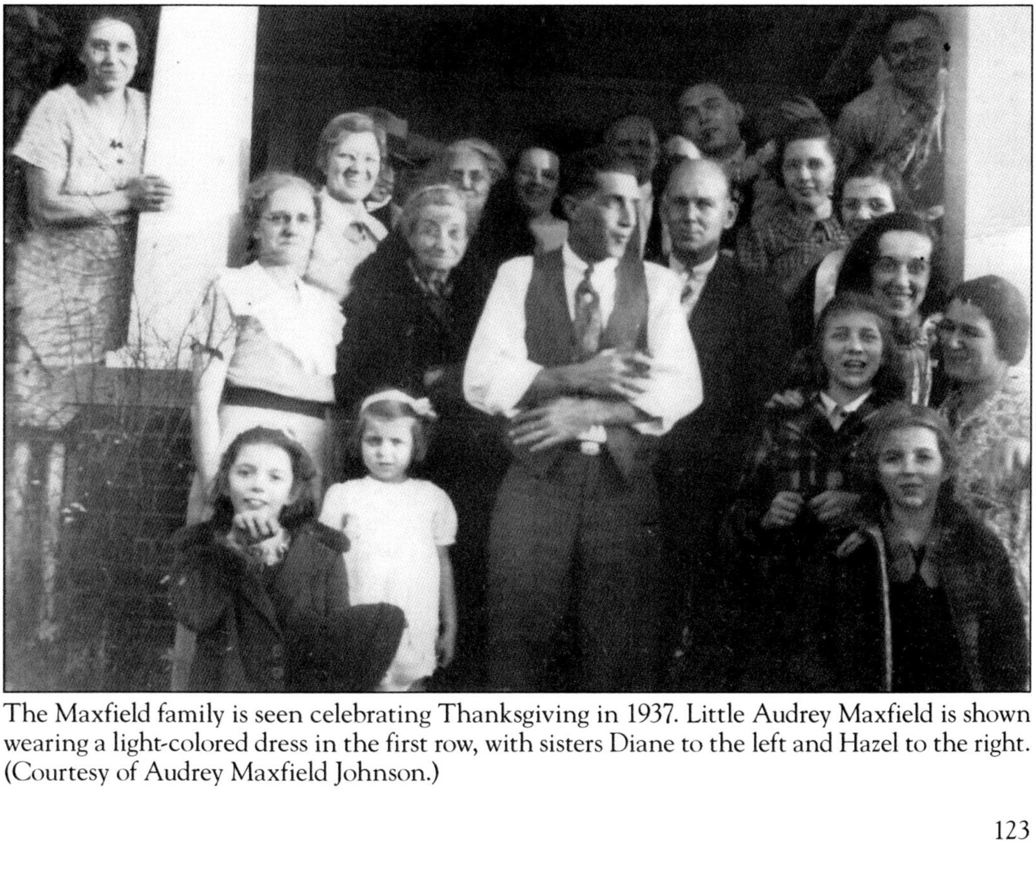

The Maxfield family is seen celebrating Thanksgiving in 1937. Little Audrey Maxfield is shown wearing a light-colored dress in the first row, with sisters Diane to the left and Hazel to the right. (Courtesy of Audrey Maxfield Johnson.)

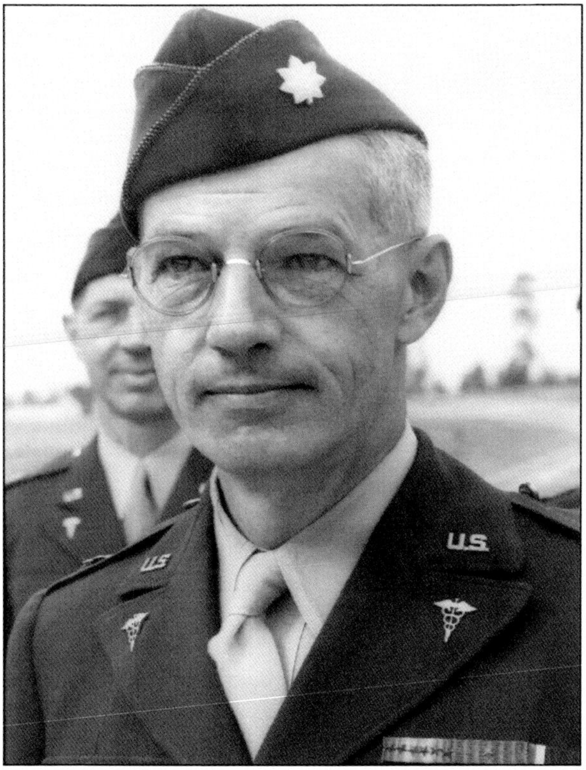

Lloyd F. Allen, the youngest of Alexander and Anna Suydam Allen's four children, was born in Gorham, New York, in 1890. After graduating from medical school, Lloyd married Hazel Hulburd in 1917, and they had three children. During World War I, Lloyd served as a doctor with the 19th General Hospital and was awarded the Croix de Guerre with Silver Star for displaying "rare courage, coolness and devotion to the wounded." In 1920, he became a charter member of American Legion Rayson-Miller Post No. 899 in Pittsford. Lloyd continued his military career with service during World War II, ultimately attaining the rank of colonel. Dr. Allen died in 1985, aged 94. His World War II uniform, hat, and decorations are part of the collection at the Rochester Medical Museum and Archives. (Both, courtesy of the Rochester Medical Museum and Archives, Rochester, New York.)

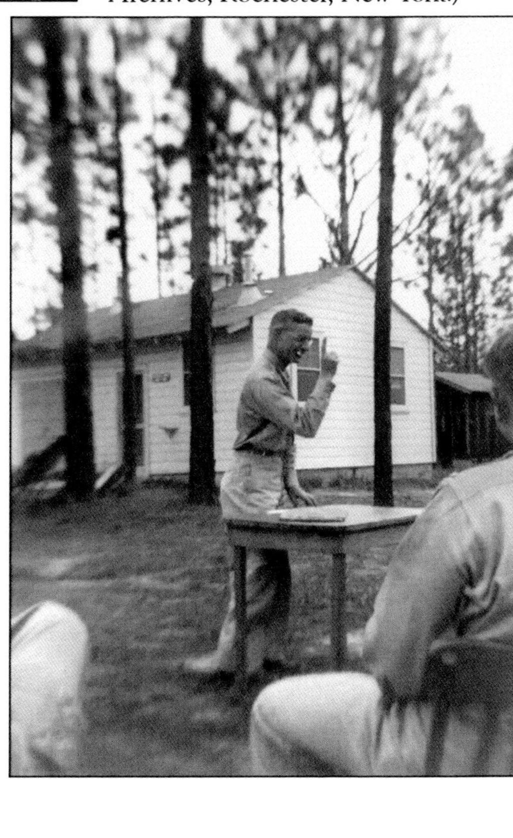

Earl W. Place greets his much-taller youngest son, John, at the family homestead, located at 149 West Jefferson Road at the corner of Sunset Boulevard. John, known as Jack, was the youngest of Earl and Florence Minniss Place's three sons. He enlisted in the US Army on August 13, 1942. This photograph was taken in 1943. (Courtesy of Bob Place.)

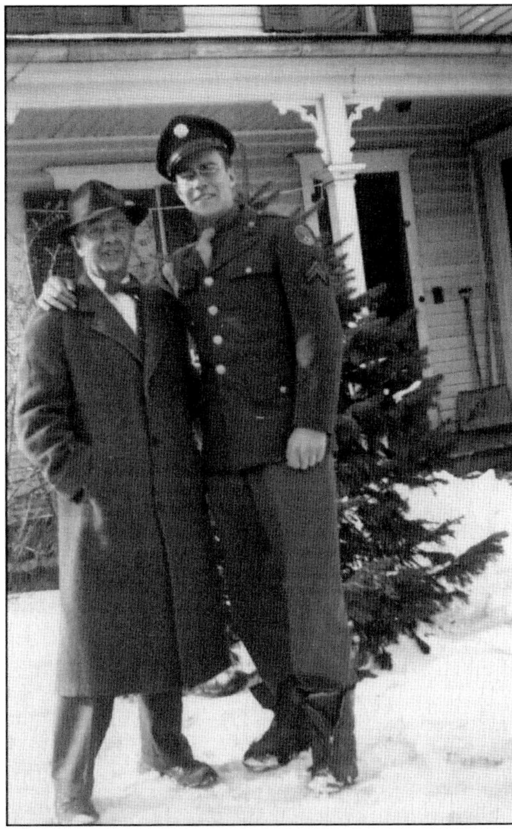

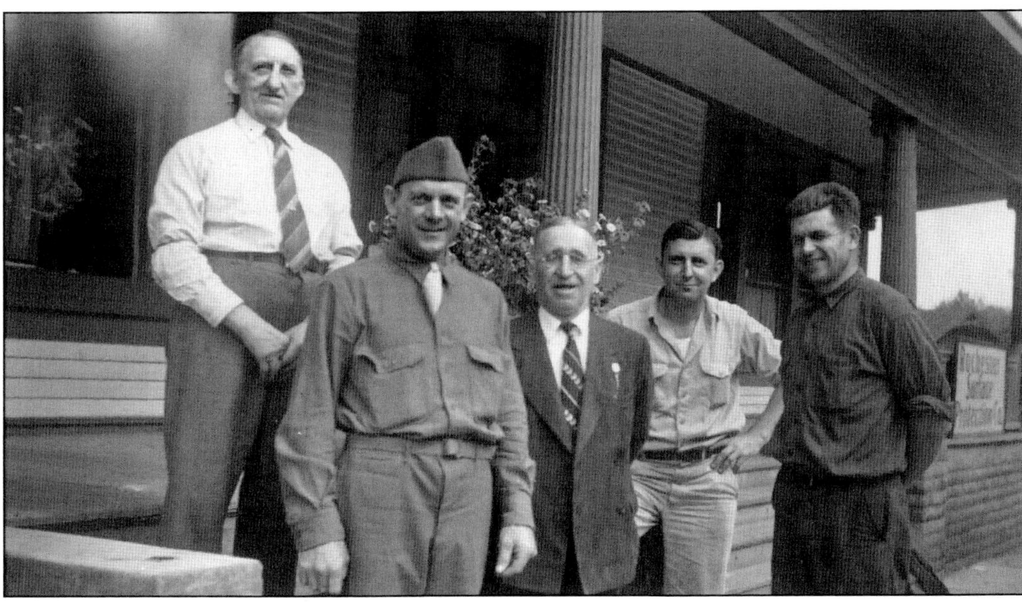

Pictured from left to right, Edward Stephany, Franklin P. Lusk, unidentified, John Rand, and Charles W. Lusk are gathered in front of the Stephany Hotel on North Main Street in the early 1940s. The occasion may have been Franklin's enlistment in the military in May 1942. The sign on the front right of the porch says, "Rochester Surface Protection Co." (Courtesy of Bill Lusk.)

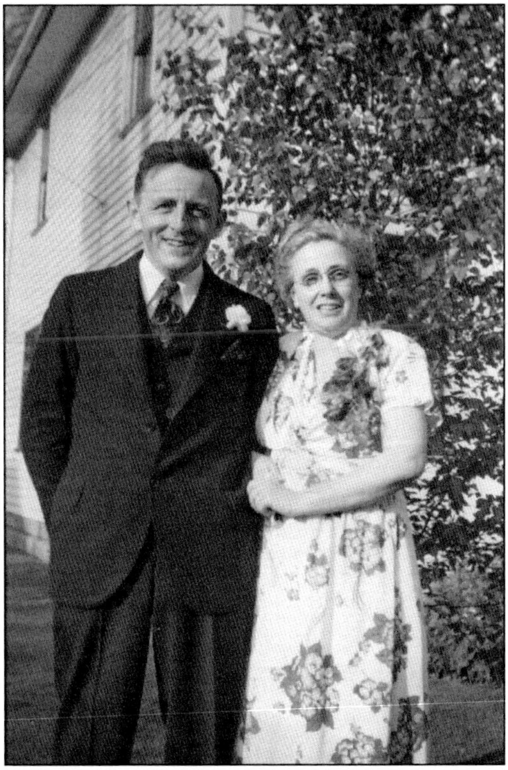

James and Irene Burdett celebrated their 25th wedding anniversary on May 20, 1946. They had three children, James Jr., Robert, and Richard. James owned and operated the Burdett Food Market for many years with his sons. Irene was active in the Northfield Chapter Order of the Eastern Star. (Courtesy of the Burdett family.)

Truman and Marguerite Brizee are shown with their six children, Lynda, Peter, Bill, Jon, Anne, and Jill. A seventh child, Tina, was born later. For 17 years, Truman was involved in the early stages of television broadcasting. The family is pictured watching an early Stromberg-Carlson television set. Truman Brizee died two years after Ivan Conklin took this photograph. The Brizees were descendants of early Monroe County settlers. (Courtesy of T. Peter Brizee.)

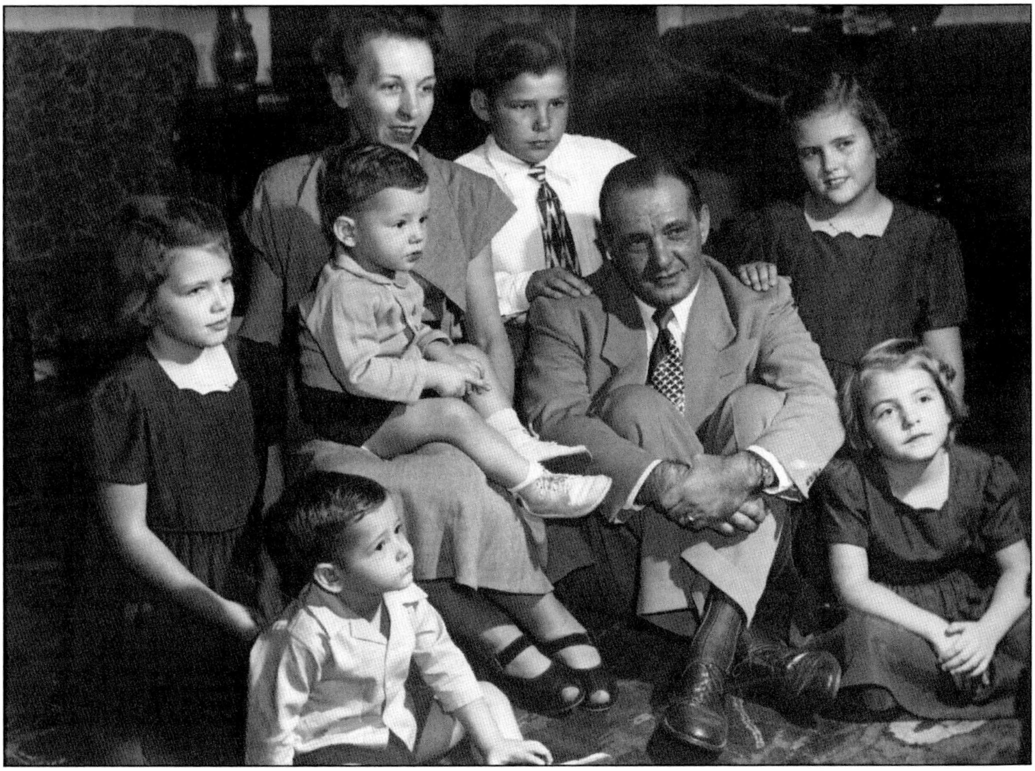

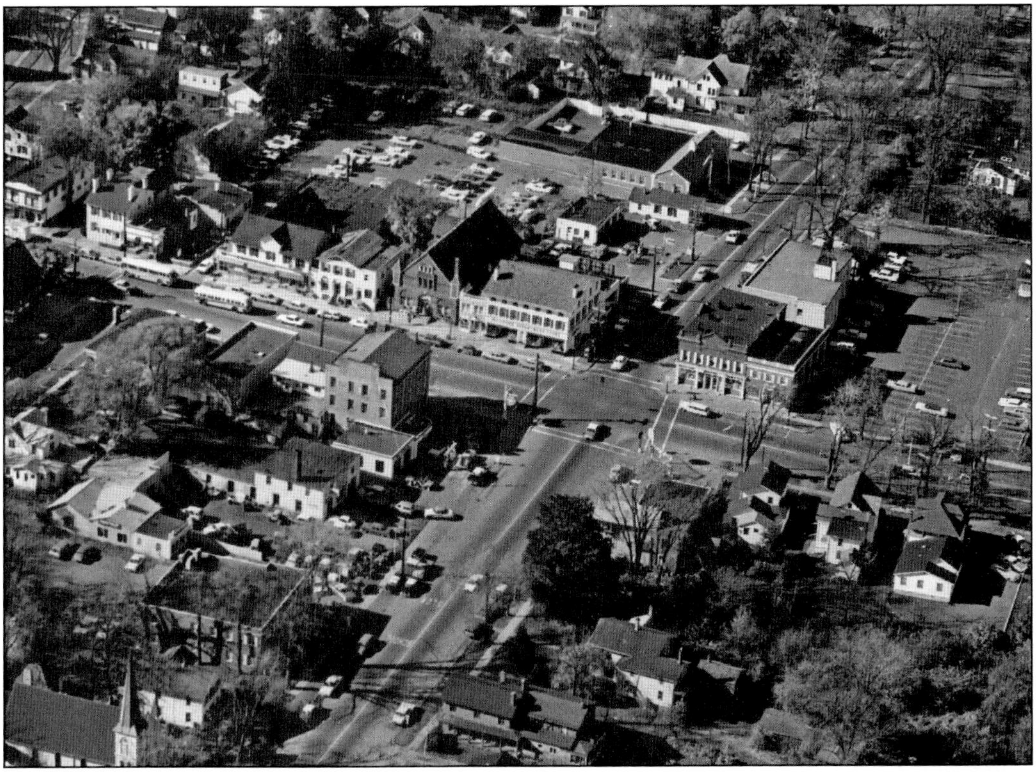

Photographer Henry DeWolf took this aerial survey of Pittsford village. It is undated, but the fact that the St. Louis Catholic Church is still standing on State Street at the time of the photograph means it was taken before 1968, when the church was demolished. The Pittsford Department Store was in the Parker Building, and Wiltsie & Crump is clearly visible at center right. (Courtesy of Anne Hilliard.)

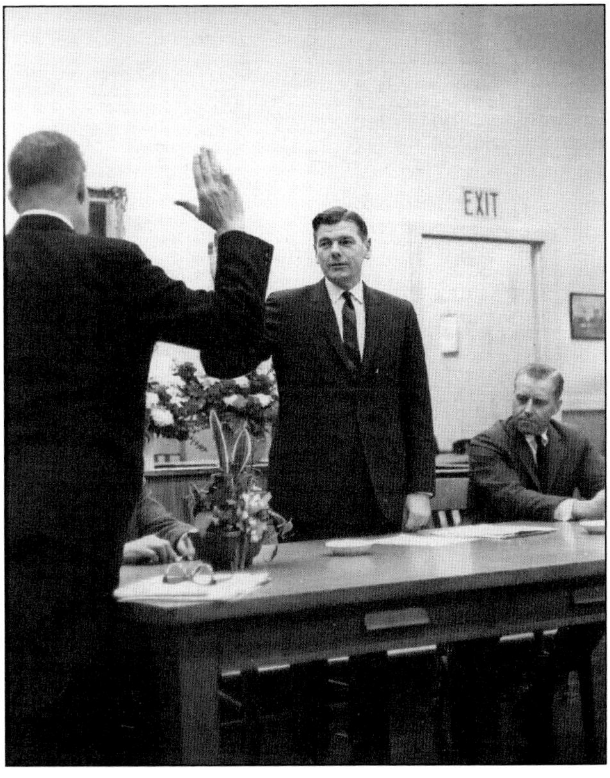

It seems appropriate to end this book with a photograph of Paul M. Spiegel. He is shown here in February 1966, being sworn in as town supervisor, a position he held for 20 years. Paul has been an avid supporter of the Pittsford community his entire life. His enthusiasm for Pittsford's past is inspiring, and residents are fortunate to have him as a steward of the town's history. (Courtesy of the Pittsford Town Historian.)

Consistent with our mission to preserve history on a local level, this book was printed in South Carolina on American-made paper and manufactured entirely in the United States. Products carrying the accredited Forest Stewardship Council (FSC) label are printed on 100 percent FSC-certified paper.

MADE IN THE USA